£14·99

# The Battle
# of the
# Nurses

03

## The Author

Susan McGann was born and educated in Dublin where she graduated from University College Dublin with an Honours Degree in History and Archaeology (1974) and a Diploma in Archival Studies (1975). From 1975 she worked in local authority archives in Glasgow until 1986 when she was appointed the first Archivist to the Royal College of Nursing, London. Her interest in nursing history began while working on the records of the Scottish Women's Hospitals in Glasgow.

**Cover illustration:**
International Council of Nurses, Geneva, 1927

# The Battle of the Nurses

*A study of eight women who influenced the development of professional nursing, 1880–1930*

## Susan McGann

Scutari Press – London

© Scutari Press 1992

Scutari Press is a division of Scutari Projects Ltd,
the publishing company of the Royal College of Nursing.

First published 1992.
Reprinted 1993.

*British Library Cataloguing in Publication Data*

McGann, Susan
  Battle of the Nurses: Study of Eight
  Women Who Influenced the Development of
  Professional Nursing, 1880–1930
  I. Title
  610.730922

  ISBN 1-871364-62-0

Printed in Great Britain by Page Bros, Norwich.

P06554

# Contents

*To Peter and Lucy.*

# Acknowledgements

I have received much help and kindness in working on this book and must thank my fellow archivists Geoffrey Yeo at St Bartholomew's Hospital, Claire Daunton and Jonathan Evans at the Royal London Hospital, Margaret Poulter at the British Red Cross Society, Mrs Joan Corfield Hall at the General Hospital, Birmingham, Derek Dow, former archivist for Greater Glasgow Health Board, and Mrs Joan Auld, University of Dundee.

In Dublin, I am indebted to Rosanne Cunningham, formerly of An Bord Altranais, for all her assistance in tracing records. And thanks are due to the late Miss Mary F. Crowley, Dean of the Faculty of Nursing, Royal College of Surgeons of Ireland, Robert Mills, Librarian, Royal College of Physicians of Ireland, and Miss Bridie Walsh.

In Glasgow, the interest and advice of Professor John Lenihan was gratefully received. For their assistance Mrs Gillespie, Librarian, Glasgow Eastern College of Nursing and Midwifery, and Alex Rodger, Librarian, Royal College of Physicians and Surgeons of Glasgow, many thanks.

I would like to thank Margaret Broadley, Sheila Collins, and Winifred Hector for sharing their memories with me. Alison Bramley, former Librarian at the Royal College of Nursing, provided the enthusiasm needed to start me on this book, and Tony Shepherd, the present Librarian, continued that support. Finally, I wish to thank Neasa MacErlean for her interest and encouragement throughout the progress of the work.

 # Introduction

NURSING HISTORY has been overshadowed by Florence Nightingale, and the attention which she receives overlooks the
important role nursing has played in the history of women's achievement. As the archivist of the Royal College of Nursing, I have studied
the background to the founding of the College in 1916 and it seems
to me that in the fifty years from 1880–1930, nursing was particularly
rich in the number of strong women who emerged as leaders. For
this book I have selected eight matrons from those years who influenced the development of nursing. They were all pioneers in nursing
education and management but they also emerged as key figures in
the nursing politics of their time.

The years 1880–1930 saw the development among nurses of the
movement for professional organisation and status. The movement
began among a handful of matrons in London in the 1880s and its
first public statement was the establishment of the British Nurses'
Association in 1887. The aims of the Association were to unite all
trained nurses in membership of a recognised profession; to provide
for their registration, as evidence of their having received systematic
training; and to promote their mutual help and protection. The founders of the Association believed that the best way to achieve professional status for nurses was to establish a statutory register of
trained nurses. Although the movement started in Britain and spread
from there, first to the other English speaking countries and then
worldwide, British nurses were among the last to achieve professional registration.

From the start, the nurses' campaign for professional organisation
and registration provoked such opposition that contemporaries spoke
of it as a battle. Sarah Tooley, writing in 1906, compared the situation
to the battle of Waterloo:

> In dealing with the question of the State registration of nurses at this
> juncture, one feels as an historian might have done, who, standing on the
> plain of Waterloo, began to describe the battle before the French cavalry

1

had made their fatal advance to the treacherous fosse, or the approach of Blucher had been heralded. The nursing world is divided into hostile armies, the battle rages, and who shall say what may turn the fortune of war? Distinguished generals lead either side, and the rank and file have ranged themselves in opposing camps. Each professes to have the welfare of the nurse and the good of the public at heart, but holds conflicting views as to whether compulsory registration of nurses by the State will bring about those desirable results.

*The History of Nursing in The British Empire*, p. 383

The American nurse historian Lavinia Dock in her History of Nursing, published in 1912, wrote

Thenceforth the hospital world of England was divided into two camps. The progressives had as their goal the organisation of nurses through a central governing body appointed by the State . . . the reactionaries would not admit the necessity for fixing a minimum standard of training and were strongly averse to organisation amongst nurses . . . For twenty-three years the battle was waged, and is not yet ended.

*A History of Nursing, Vol III*, pp. 33–34

## The Campaigners

The matrons who led the campaign for registration were for the most part educated and middle class. They were the generation of women who entered nursing in the 1860s and 1870s, influenced by Florence Nightingale and looking for a career. They found nursing unorganised and, with the enthusiasm of pioneers, they took up the cause. They raised the standard of training, improved the working conditions and pay, and determined to establish nursing as a profession. By 1887 there was a sufficient number of them to form the first professional organisation of nurses, the British Nurses' Association. The founder of the Association and the leader of the campaign was Ethel Fenwick, also known as Mrs Bedford Fenwick, Bedford being the Christian name of her husband.

## The Opposition

Opposition to the campaign for state registration came from three areas. Firstly, it came from hospital authorities who regarded the growth of professional ideas among nurses as unwelcome. All hospitals, both poor law and voluntary, relied on the work of poorly paid probationers to carry out the majority of the nursing work. The voluntary hospitals also relied on the income they made from their private nursing staff, these trained nurses earned good fees for the hospitals from private patients but were paid salaries only slightly more than the staff nurses, and a good bit less than the fees charged by the hospital. Any movement among nurses to organise themselves, threatened this double exploitation.

The medical profession was divided in its response to the campaign. The majority of doctors welcomed the improvement in the standard of nursing as a result of better training systems. However, they were used to nurses who had been trained to serve and obey the doctor and many of them feared that a nurse with professional ambitions would challenge their authority and, sooner or later, compete with them for patients. Their insecurity was not helped by the knowledge that many of these educated nurses were from the same social background as themselves.

Not the least opposition came from the nursing establishment itself. Florence Nightingale was against registration for nurses, and regarded it as a retrograde step. Her contention was that the emphasis of a nurse's training would shift from practical nursing skills to theory and examinations, and the essential qualities of a good nurse would become secondary. Many matrons shared Miss Nightingale's view and particularly her friend, Eva Lückes, who was the matron of the London Hospital. With the assistance of the Chairman of the London Hospital, Sidney Holland, who organised the voluntary hospitals into the Central Hospital Council for London, they countered every move of the nurses' campaign for state registration.

## The Campaign

The first round in the battle occurred in 1892, when the now Royal British Nurses' Association applied for a royal charter of incorporation which would give the association power to maintain a register of trained nurses. A Privy Council inquiry was held and, despite the support of the British Medical Association, the opposition to the application was such that the charter when granted did not include the power to maintain a register of trained nurses.

The second round was fought over control of the Royal British Nurses' Association. The new constitution of the Association, under the charter, stated that all members of the General Council had to stand for election every three years. This resulted in the removal of Mrs Fenwick, and some of the other founder members, from the council. Under the original constitution, as founder members they had permanent seats on the General Council as Vice Presidents, and Mrs Fenwick had been the permanent President. With the removal of the founders the opponents of registration gained control of the General Council.

The following year, 1894, Mrs Fenwick and Isla Stewart, the matron of St Bartholomew's Hospital, founded the Matrons' Council of Great Britain and Ireland and channelled their energies into this organisation. In 1902, they decided to promote a Private Member's Bill for state registration and founded the Society for the State Registration of Trained Nurses to take on the political side of their work. The Bill was introduced into the House of Commons in 1904. Another Bill for the registration of nurses was introduced by the Royal British Nurses' Association and, as a result of the intense lobbying on behalf of the two Bills and from the Central Hospital Council for London against the Bills, a select committee of the House of Commons was appointed to consider the question.

The report of the Select Committee, published in 1905, was a victory for the pro-registration party. The committee even accepted their argument that three years was the most practical training period for a nurse. However, the opponents of registration had more influence than a select committee report. Despite continuous pressure on the part of the pro-registration lobby over the next few years, no legislation followed. By 1909 there were three different Private Members' Bills before parliament for the registration of nurses and the promoters decided that the existence of rival schemes of registration was an obstacle to the progress of any legislation.

A meeting of representatives of the different societies promoting the Bills was held and it was agreed to form a Central Committee for the State Registration of Nurses, which would draft a Bill embodying a scheme of registration for the whole of the United Kingdom. This Committee consisted of 20 members, five from each of the four organisations represented, the Society for the Registration of Trained Nurses, the Royal British Nurses Association, the Association for Registration of Nurses in Scotland, and the Irish Nurses' Association.

In Scotland the campaign for registration had split into two parties, the Scottish Nurses' Association and the Association for the Registration of Nurses in Scotland. The latter had promoted a Bill for separate registration of nurses in Scotland. The former had been founded by Rebecca Strong, Matron of the Glasgow Royal Infirmary, who shared Mrs Fenwick's dream of an independent profession of nurses and who opposed separate registration for Scotland. In Ireland the founder of the movement for the professional organisation of nurses was Margaret Huxley, Matron of Sir Patrick Dun's Hospital in Dublin. She had trained at St Bartholomew's Hospital when Mrs Fenwick was the matron there, and was also a loyal supporter of Mrs Fenwick's political opinions.

The Central Committee's Bill was introduced into parliament in 1910, and reintroduced every year after that until the start of the First World War, but without government support it had little chance of success. With the outbreak of World War I, the government suspended the facility for Private Members' Bills and the campaigners concentrated their energies on nursing the sick and wounded. Many of them felt that there was an unwritten truce to refrain from campaigning during the war. As a result of this, the next round in the 'battle' took them by surprise. This was the establishment of the College of Nursing in 1916 and many of the old campaigners regarded it as a stab in the back.

The College of Nursing was the idea of Sarah Swift and Arthur Stanley, the Matron-in-Chief and the Chairman of the British Red Cross Society. They had not been involved in the registration battle before the war. Miss Swift's work during the war made her realise that nurses could not wait any longer for parliament to give them registration but must organise themselves. She proposed the establishment of a College of Nursing with membership restricted to trained nurses, which would give nurses a professional organisation and would be responsible for regulating the standards of the profession.

The success of the College in attracting the rank and file of nurses was due to the effect of the war on the profession. By April 1916, 18 months into the war, the majority of matrons and nurses had realised that the unorganised state of nursing was in no one's interest. The disruption caused by the war brought together nurses from every kind of hospital and training school, and brought home to them the problems caused by the lack of a uniform qualification and standard of training. On top of this, trained nurses found they were working with voluntary workers who, though untrained, were referred to as nurses.

When the war ended and the campaign for state registration was resumed, the balance of power had shifted. The opposition from within the profession had disappeared, Florence Nightingale had died in 1910 and the College of Nursing had a membership of 13,000, growing by over 4,000 a year. Following the war, public sympathy was behind the nurses and women now had the vote. The Government, recognising which way the wind was blowing, introduced legislation for the registration of nurses, which became law in December 1919.

## The Aftermath of the Battle

The battle for registration was over after 32 years of lobbying, delegations, rallies, meetings and propaganda. The profession, however, inherited many legacies from the long years of the campaign. The first was the College of Nursing. If registration had been achieved before the war, there would not have been a need, or at least the same need, to set up the College of Nursing. A second important legacy was the provisions of the 1919 *Nurses' Registration Acts*. Because the Minister of Health was very well aware of the opposition to professional independence for nurses, he did not give them that independence. From the start of the campaign for registration, the registrationists had spoken of the establishment of a central nursing council which would be responsible for regulating the profession. The profession had wanted one Council for the whole Kingdom, they got three separate ones for England and Wales, Scotland, and Ireland. Registrationists had wanted a one-portal system of registration so that all nurses would receive a general training before specialising. They got one system for general trained nurses and four supplementary systems for male nurses, mental health nurses, sick children's nurses, and fever nurses. All nurses had expected the Council to give them professional independence, but the General Nursing Councils which were set up under the 1919 *Acts*, were subject to the veto of the Minister of Health and of both Houses of Parliament.

The third great legacy of the battle was the division within the profession, which remained after the passing of the Registration Acts, and the eclipse of the minority group. Mrs Fenwick was never reconciled with the College of Nursing and its supporters. In the first General Nursing Council for England and Wales, appointed by the Minister, she was unable to agree with the majority decisions and caused much dissension and animosity which damaged the professional dignity of the General Nursing Council. When the first election to the General Nursing Council took place, at the end of 1922, it was fought on party lines. The College of Nursing, the Association of Hospital Matrons and the Poor Law Matrons' Association drew up an agreed list of candidates and secured a majority of the seats. Mrs Fenwick was not elected and her supporters formed a minority on the Council.

Mrs Fenwick saw the outcome of the election as evidence of the continuing interference of hospital authorities in the affairs of nurses. She contended that matrons who gave allegiance to the College were not free agents but employees of hospital authorities and, therefore, would not be able to protect the professional interests of nurses when they conflicted with those of their employers. Because she was not a member of either the General Nursing Council for England and Wales or of the College of Nursing, she was able to criticise these bodies when they compromised on issues which she regarded as a matter of professional principle. Until her death in 1947, she remained a divisive influence, extremely articulate but cut off from power.

Mrs Fenwick's views underestimated the many shades of opinion held by the matrons and nurses who joined the College of Nursing. Ellen Musson was one of her supporters who 'defected' to the College of Nursing. She had trained at St Bartholomew's Hospital under Isla Stewart and had been one of the most active members of the campaign for registration up to 1916. Miss Musson decided that the College offered the profession an alternative route to registration at a time when a new initiative was needed. She became one of the founders of the College and contributed significantly to its success. She also became the first nurse-Chairman of the General Nursing Council for England and Wales and played a major role in the International Council of Nurses, serving as Honorary Treasurer for 22 years.

## A Note on the Archives

Nursing biography suffers from the loss of most of its archives. In the case of the eight women studied here, there were no personal papers of any description for Sarah Swift, Isla Stewart, Margaret Huxley and Ellen Musson. A handful of letters and cuttings survive for Sidney Browne and Rebecca Strong. The best documented is Eva Lückes, with a collection of her personal correspondence and notebooks surviving among the records of the Royal London Hospital. In addition, the records of the nursing department of the London Hospital are extensive for the 39 years that she was matron.

The case of Mrs Fenwick is tragic. She was an exceptional woman and, unlike the other seven, she did want a place in history. She is known to have left a personal archive but, since her death, neglect and misplaced loyalty have contributed to its destruction. Today, only a small collection of papers is thought to survive among the records of the Royal British Nurses' Association and these are not available for research.

I have concentrated here on the careers, not the lives, of these women and my information has been drawn from hospital records and contemporary nursing journals. Each chapter is written as a separate study, so that it can be read on its own. This has meant a certain amount of duplication where the same events have been participated in by the eight women. A minimum of references are used as the book is intended for the general reader, but archival sources consulted are listed at the end of each chapter. I have not included a bibliography as there are many excellent ones available in recent books on the history of nursing.

I am aware of the limitations of a biographical approach to history but consider that for nursing history between 1880 and 1930 it is useful. Without the imagination, energy, determination and intellect of these eight women, the development of nursing would have been different.

 1

# Eva Charlotte Lūckes
## *A Great Maker of Matrons*
(1854–1919)

*Matron of the London Hospital for 39 years, pioneer of the
preliminary training school, author of two nursing text books,
friend of Florence Nightingale, and opponent of state
registration for nurses, RRC, CBE, Lady of Grace of the
Order of St John of Jerusalem.*

EVA LŪCKES was appointed matron of the London Hospital in July
1880, at the age of 26. The London Hospital was the largest
hospital in the country at the time, and Miss Lūckes had just four
years experience as a nurse. She had been inspired by the example
of Florence Nightingale to take up nursing and like Miss Nightingale,
she came from a comfortable, upper middle class background. The
family name was Swedish and her father, Henry Richard Lūckes,
was a successful banker.

She was born on 8 July 1854, the eldest of three girls, and spent a
happy childhood at the family's country house in Newnham,
Gloucestershire. She was educated at Malvern, where she was a
boarder, and at Cheltenham College and completed her education in
Dresden. She returned to her family home and helped her mother,
taking an interest in the local school and visiting the sick of the
parish. At about this time her father suffered a financial setback and
Eva decided to take up nursing. She started at the Middlesex Hospital
as a paying probationer in September 1876, and said later that her
greatest grief was when she had to leave her mother to take up
nursing. She found the work strenuous and gave up after three
months. Following a rest she started again at the Westminster Hospital and completed her training in August 1878. Her first appointment
was as a Night Sister at the London Hospital. She stayed three
months in this post and was then appointed Lady Superintendent
of the Manchester General Hospital for Sick Children, Pendlebury,

a hospital of about 100 beds. After several months at Pendlebury, Miss Lūckes clashed with the medical committee of the hospital and resigned her position. Like many matrons at the time, she tried to raise the standard of nursing in the hospital and her reforms were regarded by the medical staff and hospital authorities as a threat. For a short period she worked at the Hospital for Sick Children Great Ormond Street, and then in July 1880, applied for the matronship of the London Hospital. Miss Lūckes was the youngest of the five candidates and lacked experience at another large hospital but she impressed the committee and was appointed.

## Matron of The London Hospital

The London Hospital, situated in Whitechapel, was the only general hospital serving the east end of London, an area notorious for its poverty. The hospital had 600 beds and a nursing staff of 128. The previous matron, Miss Swift, had been in the post for 18 years and had been asked by the house Committee to improve the standard of nursing but without much success. The committee offered Miss Swift a pension of £100 per annum and turned to Miss Lūckes to reform the nursing. Miss Lūckes described the position in the hospital years later

> In 1880, when I came to the London Hospital, the total number of the nursing staff was 128, and there were no ward-maids. Scrubbers cleaned the grates and washed the floors, but the remainder of the housework, such as rubbing the tables, was a part of the nurses' duties. Dinner was the only meal served in the nurses' home and even this was not provided on Sundays. For that day they were served with raw chops and potatoes, which they cooked for themselves in the wards . . . The whole of the nursing staff, with the exception of the sisters, went to dinner at the same time, when they were waited upon by the scrubbers . . . The tired night nurses, who had been on duty for twelve hours, terminating at 9.20 a.m., and whose dinner was not served till noon, were all required to go back to their respective wards to take charge for the dinner-hour.
>
> *The Times* 1890

The House Committee was aware that the nursing in the hospital was in need of reform and a sub-committee had been appointed in November, 1879, to inquire into the present system of nursing. The sub-committee collected information about the nursing arrangements at the other large hospitals in London and made recommendations on how to improve the standard of nursing. The first step was the appointment of a trained matron

To place the nursing system here upon a level with the accepted and recognised nursing it is desirable that the head of the nursing establishment should be herself a trained nurse . . . if possible, more highly qualified, technically, than any of the sisters under her charge, but at any rate thoroughly capable of noting defects in ward work and of deciding for herself upon the progress of probationers and herself able to give technical instruction to those needing it . . . [she should] be in a position to provide the hospital with a full complement of nursing material, carefully supervised with a view to the encouragement of the good and skilful and to the speedy and sure weeding out of the worthless or unsuitable.

It is not for the sub-committee to indicate, in detail, what sort of person should be selected for the post in question, because the desired qualifications for the female head of a large household, many of them gentlewomen of some education are readily recognised . . . – one gifted with tact, temper, firmness, and much discretion, equally ready to act in emergencies and to seek advice when really needing it – and further not unfitted for the wholesome disicpline of a public institution by previous social standing – a condition too liable to attach to ladies who believe they have a 'Mission'.

London Hospital Archives, LH/A/9/61

Miss Lückes took up her appointment on October 4, and the next day reported to the House Committee that the nursing staff was inadequate in quantity and quality. The committee agreed to increase the number of nurses from 128 to 150. In November, she addressed the poor standard of the nursing, naming the sisters on the staff whom she considered were not up to the mark.

The only way that we can effectively raise the standard here is by securing the most efficient sisters possible when vacancies occur, and it is only fair to the probationers that we undertake to train, to give them the advantage of working under those who thoroughly understand every detail of nursing and ward work.

LH/A/5/39, 30 Nov 1880, p. 81

The Nursing Sub-committee and Miss Lückes drew up a new system of training which was introduced at the end of 1880. Previously, the probationers' training consisted of three years work in the wards without any instruction or supervision. The new scheme consisted of two years' practical and theoretical training with the time spent in the wards carefully allocated to give each probationer a wide variety of experience. The theoretical instruction consisted of three courses of lectures. The first course, commencing each autumn, was given by Miss Lückes on general nursing. The second and third courses were given by members of the medical staff on elementary anatomy and surgical nursing and elementary physiology and medical nursing. Lectures were given once a week in the evening, and nurses

*Fig 1. Miss Lückes when appointed Matron at the age of twenty-six*

on night duty were expected to attend before going on duty. An examination was held after each course and at the end of the first year the probationers took their annual, or final, examination. Miss Lückes considered that the first year of training was for learning the duties of a nurse, the second year was for acquiring experience and testing the nurse's qualifications. Second year probationers were give increased responsibility, nursing special cases, covering for staff nurses' holidays and sick leave, and taking staff duty under super- vision. At the end of the second year, the probationers received their certificates and were eligible to become staff nurses.

This system of training proved very efficient and the standard of nursing in the hospital was gradually improved. Miss Lückes introduced two lectures a year for the sisters to maintain a high standard. The reputation of the training school grew and by 1890 the number of applications to become probationers had reached 1500, and by 1900 it had risen to 2000. The number accepted was approximately 200 a year. Many of the applicants were unsuitable, being too old or too young, candidates had to be between the ages of 25 and 36, or they failed the medical examination.

Shortly after Miss Lückes' appointment she introduced ward-maids to relieve the nurses of the heavier domestic part of their work. In 1886 when the first nurses' home was opened, with a separate kitchen and dining-room for the nurses, she took the opportunity to take over responsibility for the nurses' food. The new nurses' home meant that for the first time at the London, separate bedrooms were provided for 102 nurses, with an adequate number of bathrooms and sitting-rooms. Previously all the nurses had slept in over-crowded dormitories, scattered throughout the hospital buildings and when Miss Lückes arrived there was one bath for the entire nursing staff of 130.

In one of her first reports to the House Committee, Miss Lückes pointed out that the principal obstacle to the success of the training school was the inadequate accommodation provided for the nurses. To attract the right type of woman for training, it was necessary to provide a degree of comfort and privacy. The initial response of the committee illustrates the prejudice that she was fighting

> While thinking it an excellent thing to supply separate sleeping accommodation to the nurses, the change involved would be of so enormous a character and would lead to so much expense that the Sub-committee must admit that they do not see their way to it. [The committee suggested that light screens could be erected between the beds and they were prepared to make one or two improvements, such as] . . . arrangements may be made for hanging dresses at a small expense. The water-bottles, looking-glasses and moleskin table covers should also be supplied.
>
> LH/A/5/40, 27 Jun 1882, p. 8

Miss Lückes prevailed and the first nurses' home was built. A new wing with 50 bedrooms was opened in 1895, and two years later a second nurses' home with 75 bedrooms was completed. It was not until the third home had been built, providing an additional 250 bedrooms for nurses and 26 bed-sitting rooms for sisters, that all the nursing staff had separate bedrooms. This nurses' home was opened in 1905 and was named after Miss Lückes as a tribute to her 25 years' anniversary as matron.

The key to Miss Lückes' plan for an efficient nursing department was the number of nursing staff. On her appointment she had requested an immediate increase in the nursing staff to 150, and in

*Fig 2. Nurses' sitting room, Lückes' Home, London Hospital*

July, 1882, she reported the need for a further increase. The committee agreed to the increase and to many similar requests over the next eight years. By 1890, the nursing staff had reached 201, consisting of 23 sisters, 34 staff nurses, 45 second year probationers, 73 first year probationers, 17 paying probationers, and 9 probationers from outside institutions. Of this total, only 57 were fully trained, the remainder had less than two years' experience. This practice of relying on probationers for the bulk of the nursing became very controversial.

In 1886 Miss Lückes started a private nursing institution attached to the hospital. The upper and middle classes still regarded hospitals as charitable institutions for the poor and the demand for 'trained' nurses to nurse the well-off in their homes grew in response to the reputation of the trained nurse. Hospital medical staff were relieved to be able to recommend nurses to their private patients who were properly trained and reliable, and the demand for the London Hospital's private nurses always exceeded the supply. Between 1890 and

1914, the number of nurses on the staff of the institution was increased by approximately 20 every year, but the number of applications rose at an even greater rate. In 1894, the number of nurses was 45, and the institution received 742 requests for nurses. In 1900, there were 127 nurses and 2,115 requests for private nurses. By 1914, the nursing staff numbered 284 and requests 3,495. The institution was refusing an average of 60 cases a week.

Miss Lückes took a personal pride in the reputation of the Private Nursing Institution and selected the nurses which she thought were personally suited to each case. When the probationers completed their training they were still under contract for a further year and became staff nurses or joined the private nursing staff. Nurses away from the hospital on a private case were expected to write to Miss Lückes each week reporting on the case. She believed that this kept the nurses in touch with the hospital so that they did not feel isolated, and they were able to discuss aspects of the case or the domestic arrangements. In a letter to Lord Knutsford, in 1915, she wrote

> I gather considerable knowledge of the individual characters of the nurses by the 'tone' of their letters. Human nature must have an outlet, and when a nurse has an anxious case or is strained by having to deal with difficult people, it is a great help to her to feel that she may write freely to me without betraying confidences . . . being kept in close touch with the hospital stimulates the nurses' loyalty to it, and makes her eager to bring back good reports and do it credit.
>
> London Hospital Archives, personal correspondence of Miss Lückes

She reminded the nurses that they were the London's 'ambassadors', representing her and the hospital in their standards and behaviour. Between cases the private staff worked on the wards of the hospital, and this Miss Lückes regarded as an important part of the success of the Private Nursing Institution. Unlike, the majority of private nurses who lost touch with hospital practices, the London private nurses were kept up to date by regular ward work. The reputation of the institution was publicly acknowledged when Sir Frederick Treves selected two of the nurses to nurse King Edward through his illness in 1902.

## Select Committee of the House of Lords, 1890–1891

Miss Lückes' management of the nursing department was not without its critics. Some hospital staff considered that she had become too powerful. Outside the hospital, the nursing press was critical of the practice of giving second year probationers the responsibility of staff nurses and in particular of sending them out as private nurses, since the hospital advertised that all the private nursing staff were 'thoroughly trained'. The problem arose because Miss Lückes insisted that a nurse was trained after her first year as a probationer, when she had received her instruction in the wards, attended the lectures, and taken her examination. The certificate was not awarded until the nurse had completed her second year as a probationer, but Miss Lückes held that uncertificated did not mean untrained.

A Select Committee of the House of Lords was appointed in 1890, to inquire into the management of the metropolitan hospitals. Among the witnesses called to give evidence were several former nurses and probationers who had trained at the London Hospital and who were unhappy about the treatment they had received from Miss Lückes. The charges against the hospital were: that the nurses were over-worked, they were on duty from 7 am to 9.20 pm, a total of 84 hours a week, with half an hour for dinner and perhaps half an hour for tea on the ward; that they did not get adequate holidays and were expected to work 50 weeks a year; that the nurses' food was bad and insufficient; that the wards were understaffed and the majority of the nursing was done by probationers who were expected to take the responsibility of trained nurses.

The newspapers carried reports of the proceedings with shock headlines, such as 'Does the London Hospital sweat its nurses?' in the *Pall Mall Gazette*, (5 Sept 1890). Three of the witnesses had been dismissed by Miss Lückes but they were not all malcontents. A former chaplain at the hospital, the Rev. Henry Tristram Valentine, gave evidence and supported the charges made by the nurses. He was concerned about the matron's power to dismiss probationers without the right of appeal, and that there were too many short-term probationers passing through the wards, these were paying probationers who were taken on for only three months' training. Miss Lückes regarded these as a useful source of revenue to the hospital but the Rev. Valentine thought that the patients and the permanent staff suffered from constantly having to work with inexperienced women.

Miss Lückes was called before the Select Committee to defend her management of the nursing department. Every aspect of the nurses' conditions was examined in detail and on each point Miss Lückes referred back to the position on her arrival in 1880, and the improve-ments she had made since then. When she was asked if she con-sidered an ordinary woman was overworked by 14 hours' work, she replied, 'I think nurses are not ordinary women, or they never would come and choose work that causes so much tax to their energies, physically and mentally, and their feelings altogether'.

The Lords questioned Miss Lückes about her practice of giving a qualified certificate to nurses whom she considered were not up to the mark. The hospital had two forms of certificate, one for nurses who had passed their examination and one for those who did not. The latter would state that the nurse had completed two years' training in the wards and that her work and conduct had been good, excellent, or some other remark. Equally, a nurse who had passed the examination but whose conduct was poor, would receive a certificate to that effect. A first class certificate was one which stated that the nurse's work had been excellent and her conduct exemplary.

Regarding the dismissal of probationers, the Select Committee were left in no doubt that Miss Lückes considered it necessary to have the power of terminating a probationer's engagement. While she always sent a report of the case to the House Committee, the committee had never disagreed with her opinion. In reply to the charge that the bulk of the nursing was performed by probationers, Miss Lückes explained that because a nurse was still a probationer did not mean that she was incompetent or untrained. When the Chairman said 'but they are uncertificated' she replied, 'They are not certificated nurses, but they are trained nurses; they will have attended their course of lectures and so on'. She denied that any nurse would be given responsibility for which she was unprepared. She freely acknowledged that probationers were expected to take staff duty, but always under proper supervision. She relied on her sisters to assess the capabilities of the probationers in their wards and from the records kept by the sisters, Miss Lückes felt that she knew each probationer sufficiently well to judge their competence.

Equally, when questioned about the use of probationers as private nurses, Miss Lückes replied that while technically they were probationers, she had never sent out any nurse who was not thoroughly trained. The Earl of Kimberley asked her, 'Do you think it consistent with plain English to offer a "thoroughly trained nurse", and then to send a nurse who is termed in your own language a probationer?' Miss Lückes replied, 'The estimation of the public is that a trained nurse is one who has had a year of hospital experience . . . At the majority of hospitals the certificate is given at the end of one year . . . I should consider it a great breach of confidence to send an incompetent nurse to any doctor or member of the public who applied to me for a nurse.' (Select Committee Evidence, par. 6613)

At the beginning and at the end of her cross-examination she was asked how often she visited the wards. She replied that now she went when something was needed, about every three weeks. To the question 'Has it ever occurred to you that it would be a good thing for the head nursing official of a hospital to go round the hospital every day?' she replied, 'I do not think much would be gained by it in our hospital, because our sisters occupy such a different position from any others I know.' (Select Committee Evidence, par. 6803)

The Select Committee made its report in 1892, and found the charges were not substantiated by the evidence. The majority of the allegations were considered to be exaggerated, while the facts were not denied, they were counted as exceptionally unfavourable instances, giving a wrong general impression. The Committee considered that the difficulties could have been avoided if the governing Board of the hospital had not allowed its authority to fall into the hands of salaried officials. The uncontrolled power of the matron to dismiss probationers was condemned. One newspaper reported the case in the following words, ' . . . the Governors neglected to govern the House Committee, the House Committee neglected to govern the House Governor, the House Governor neglected to govern the Matron, and the Matron governed the lot', (reported in *The Nursing Record*, 29 Sept 1892, p. 800–801). Throughout the inquiry the governors of the hospital supported Miss Lückes. In a letter to *The Times* on 28 July 1890, they wrote

> We believe our nursing is second to none in London, or indeed anywhere; in illustration, we are sending out from our ranks, in reply to a requisition from a colonial Government, an entire nursing staff for their hospital . . . a surprise visit would show how bright and happy our nurses are in their life and work, and how loyally devoted to and proud they are of their Matron, although she must of necessity rule with a firm hand if the high efficiency and moral tone are to be maintained.

The House Committee recorded its support in the minutes

> We desire to express our entire and unabated confidence in the Matron, and our sympathy with her in the trouble and anxiety to which she has been subjected owing to attacks recently made upon her.
>
> LH/A/5/44, 29 July 1890, p. 295

In November, 1890, the Medical Council of the hospital passed a resolution of support in the matron, and in December she was presented with a gold bracelet by over 100 ex-London nurses, including 20 matrons.

Miss Lückes' evidence to the Select Committee gives an insight into her system of management. By that time, she had four Assistant Matrons responsible for different areas of the matron's duties. The ward sisters were responsible for the nurses and probationers on their wards or in their departments and each made a daily report to the matron on the probationers' work. These details were entered in the Register of Probationers, kept in the Matron's Office. This register recorded the age on arrival of each probationer, her previous experience or occupation, an account of her work each day in the hospital, her holidays and sickness. In addition, each probationer kept a little black memorandum book in which they recorded their time in each ward and department, and which was signed by the sister in charge. On the last day of the month these books were handed into the Matron's Office, where they were checked, the information entered in the register, and the book stamped. Miss Lückes also entered an assessment of the nurse's character in the register based on the sisters' reports. An example of her assessment was

Bertha — — — — was deemed promising by the first sister under whom she worked but others soon found her less satisfactory. She was vague, self-absorbed and failed to realise the responsibiity of a nurse's work.

LH/N/1/18

A frequent comment was, 'She would probably make an excellent district nurse or manage a cottage hospital very well – but is not adapted for mixing with many fellow-workers'. On receiving her certificate, the nurse's details were entered in the Register, ' . . . failed examination but her character and practical work made her a desirable staff nurse and I was glad to appoint her to a ward'. Alternatively, for a nurse who passed her examination but was not up to Miss Lückes' standard, ' . . . received a very qualified certificate as she was wholly unfitted for nursing work'. Upon appointment to the permanent staff or as a private nurse, the record and assessment continued. For those nurses who left the hospital, there was a supplementary register and if the nurse kept the Matron informed of her appointments, her record was kept up to date.

## The Preliminary Training School

Miss Lückes introduced a six week preliminary training for all probationers in 1895, a system she had wanted to introduce for some time. It was postponed until the number of nurses was sufficient to allow her to release probationers from ward duty in their first weeks.

Each 'set' of 20 probationers spent their first seven weeks in the preliminary training school (PTS), away from the busy wards, where they received practical nursing instruction such as bed-making and bandaging, attended lectures on elementary anatomy, physiology and hygiene, and a weekly demonstration and practice class in sick room cookery. In the seventh week they were examined in these subjects.

The advantages of the PTS were immediately appreciated. When the probationers arrived on the wards they were able to perform routine tasks which might otherwise have taken months to pick up. Miss Lückes valued the mental atmosphere of the preliminary training school, the new probationers were introduced to the discipline of hospital life while still in a home surrounding, and the six weeks gave the hospital and the probationer time to decide whether she was suitable for a nursing career. The conditions for entry remained the same, candidates had to be between 25 and 35 years, later changed to 23 and 33 years, and they had to pass a medical test for physical fitness. During their seven weeks in the PTS, the probationers were referred to as pupil-probationers.

When the PTS opened it was in an old house in Bow Road, a short distance from the hospital. The house and freehold were a gift from Lord Tredegar and the school was called Tredegar House. Within four years the adjoining house was taken over and the size of the sets increased to 28 probationers. By 1910, the two old houses which formed the original school were worn out and a new Tredegar House was built, the new building being opened by Queen Alexandra in July, 1912. The number of probationers per set was increased to 30, which Miss Lückes considered the maximum size without losing the homelike atmosphere.

The success of the training school brought with it the problem of how to keep the trained nurses on the staff after they had finished their two year contract and received their certificate. By 1905, 1200 nurses had trained at the school since 1880, and gradually over the years more than half had left. On Miss Lückes' advice, the hospital governors introduced a four year contract for all probationers in 1899. On completion of two years' training, a nurse had to work a further two years on the staff of the hospital before she could take employment elsewhere.

*Fig 3. London Hospital Nurses' Training School, Tredegar House, Bow Road*

## Sidney Holland

In December 1896, Sidney Holland was elected Chairman of the London Hospital. He had first met Miss Lückes earlier that year when he had sought her advice about his application for a post in another hospital. Mr Holland was well known in hospital circles at the time through his work as Chairman of the Poplar Hospital but, by his own account, he wished to discuss his position with Miss Lückes as she was regarded as the greatest authority in the hospital world. He later described his talk with Miss Lückes as the most inspiring interview in his life.

> She advised me strongly to stand for the post, and in a way I can never forget, pointed out the possibilities if one would devote one's life to Hospital work and not make it just one of many occupations, and that not the most absorbing. She told me of her own aims and ambitions and ideals for Nurses and of her difficulties, and ended up by saying. 'I suppose you would not come here. I would serve you loyally and would give you all the help I can'.
>
> Eva C. E. Lückes (1919), p. 7

Mr Holland said that when he first knew the London Hospital he was more impressed with the dreariness of its long miserable passages, dark wards and poor furniture, than he was by its qualities. At the time of his appointment the hospital was seriously underfunded and lacking modern equipment. One of his talents was fundraising on behalf of the poor and this had earned him the title 'Prince of Beggars'. He now turned this talent to the benefit of the London and with Miss Lückes began a programme of development for the hospital. Just as Miss Lückes shared his sympathy for the poor, he shared her concern for the welfare of the nurses. In 1897, he produced a 'charter' for nurses setting down the working conditions which they hoped to achieve for the nurses. These were, two hours off-duty in daylight every day, not more than ten hours a day in the wards, a half day off weekly, one day off a month and four weeks annual holiday. At the time, the nurses worked 84 hours a week, 50 weeks a year. Through Mr Holland's successful fund-raising the hospital was in a position to steadily increase the number of nurses and to reduce the hours they worked. In 1893, the nursing staff totalled 275, including the private nursing staff, in 1900 it was 441, and by 1910 it had reached 715. The hours of work outlined in the charter were achieved by 1907.

The salaries of the nurses did not improve to the same extent. When Miss Lückes became matron in 1880, a probationer received £12 in her first year and £20 in the second. In 1916, this was increased to £17 in the first year and £24 in the second. Staff nurses, in 1890, were paid £22–£25 per annum, night nurses £24–£27, sisters £30–£40, and the nurses on the private staff £30–£45. In 1901, an additional £5 was paid after six years' service and another after twelve years.

By 1916 trained nurses received an increase of £5 to their maximum level. Since 1889, the hospital had recognised the need for nurses' pensions and had encouraged the nurses to join the (Royal) National Pension Fund for Nurses by paying half their annual premium. However, many of the nurses withdrew from the pension fund when they left the service of the hospital and in 1901, the governors introduced their own pension scheme, a full salary pension being paid after 18 years' service, or at the age of 45.

Mr Holland considered that the London Hospital treated as many in-patients every year as any two of the other large London hospitals combined. The number of in-patients grew annually, from 9,703 in 1894, to 18,933 in 1915, and to accommodate this growth the hospital began a rebuilding programme. New departments, operating theatres and wards were built, and all the existing wards were renovated. A large out-patients' department was opened in 1902, the Hebrew wards with special kitchens for Jewish patients in 1905, a massage department in 1907 and a dental department in 1911. One of the most famous new departments was the Light Department which treated patients suffering from the skin disease called Lupus. The treatment was by Finsen light, called after the Danish man who pioneered it. Princess Alexandra, Princess of Wales and president of the hospital, presented the equipment to the hospital and provided for two nurses to go to Denmark for training. The department opened in 1899 and for several years it was the only one of its kind in the country and trained nurses from other institutions in the use of the equipment.

In 1900, Miss Lückes provided midwifery training for the trained nurses. She arranged for five nurses at a time to work with a midwife in the district for three months. The nurses attended lectures at the General Lying-In Hospital and took the London Obstetrical Society's diploma. With the passing of the *Registration of Midwives Act* in 1902, the demand for trained midwives and maternity nurses increased and, in 1905, the Marie Celeste maternity wards were opened in the hospital. The midwifery department had been one of Miss Lückes' cherished dreams and it opened on the day she completed 25 years' service at the hospital. The training was reserved for past and present 'Londoners'. Twelve pupils were taken every three months for training in the wards and in the district. In 1906 the training was recognised by the Central Midwives Board and in that year 172 babies were born in the hospital and 1461 in the district.

With the establishment of the district midwifery service, nurses went into the homes of the people for the first time and it was not until then that the extent of the poverty in the area was fully realised.

The hospital authorities organised a fund to provide milk for the mothers attended by the district midwives and to provide baby clothes for those in need. Part of the inspiration for Miss Lückes' work was that it was done for the poor. She particularly cared for the children of the poor and in her course of lectures to the probationers she devoted one lecture to the nursing of children. Her lectures were published in book form, in 1884, and the chapter on children began

> The nursing of children requires special care, special training, and special study. It needs infinitely more knowledge, more skill, more observation, and more patience to become a really good children's Nurse than it does to attain an average amount of efficiency in nursing adult patients.
>
> It is essential for Nurses to recognise that when they enter a children's ward, they find themselves in a new world, of which the inhabitants are 'little people', with a different language, different manners, different feelings, and different thoughts . . .
>
> Nurses are entrusted with the task of guarding the lives of the little ones from the beginning. Nurses, who are constantly coming in contact with the pitiable specimens of humanity which find their way into the wards of a hospital, cannot fail to see for themselves the disease and suffering and misery which may result from ignorant or neglectful treatment in childhood. They scarcely need to be told of the ruined lives of those men and women who have been the unhappy victims of such neglect.
>
> General Nursing, 9th edition, Chapter XXV

## State Registration

By 1900, a three year training scheme for nurses was becoming the general practice. This was the period recommended by the British Nurses' Association and it had been accepted by the Select Committee of the House of Lords in their report in 1890. The British Nurses' Association was founded in 1887 by Mrs Bedford Fenwick (see chapter two). Its aims were 'to unite all British nurses in membership of a recognised profession and to provide for their registration as evidence of their having received systematic training, and to associate them for their mutual help and protection and for the advancement of their professional work.'

Mrs Fenwick had married Dr Bedford Fenwick of the London Hospital in 1887. Before her marriage, she had been Miss Ethel Manson, and from 1881, matron of St Bartholomew's Hospital. At the time of Miss Lückes' appointment as matron of The London, Miss Manson was sister of Charlotte Ward at the hospital. She wrote later of her feelings when Miss Lückes reduced the period of training from three to two years and, what in her opinion were, the dire consequences. On her marriage, Mrs Fenwick took up the cause of state registration for nurses. Through the British Nurses' Association (after 1893 The Royal British Nurses' Association) and her journal *The Nursing Record* (after 1902 *The British Journal of Nursing*), she led the campaign for registration. The campaign took 30 years to achieve its goal, the passing of the *Nurses' Registration Act* in 1919, the year Miss Lückes died.

During those 30 years Miss Lückes and Mrs Fenwick became sworn enemies. It was the clash of two strong personalities and may have been sparked off by the marriage of the Fenwicks, as some people consider that Miss Lückes was interested in Dr Fenwick. Both women had a vision of the future for the nursing profession and were prepared to fight for it. Mrs Fenwick's vision was of a well organised profession, controlled by nurses and independent of hospital authorities. To Miss Lückes, nursing was a vocation taken up for the sake of the work itself, not for gain and not for self. To defend this view she became one of the strongest opponents of state registration. She did not like publicity, preferring to remain in the background, but through Sidney Holland and the governors of the London Hospital she fought as hard as Mrs Fenwick.

Two years after the formation of the British Nurses' Association, Miss Lückes wrote 'What will trained nurses gain by joining the British Nurses' Association?', a pamphlet, published by the London Hospital, putting the case against the registration of nurses

> The scheme of registration is, in our judgement, calculated to lower rather than to raise the present standard of Nursing by concentrating the attention of Nurses on the theoretical examination, the passing of which is ultimately to get their names placed on a public Register.

It was this emphasis on the passing of an examination in theoretical knowledge as the standard by which a trained nurse would be defined, which Miss Lückes could not accept. She believed that only the training school and its matron were in a position to know if a nurse was a good nurse and therefore competent to issue a certificate to the nurse. If the certification of nurses were removed from the training schools and vested in an independent body, such as a general nursing council, certificates would become meaningless. The examination could only be of the nurse's theoretical knowledge and this gave no value to the nurse's personal characteristics which were the difference between a good nurse and an indifferent nurse.

Miss Lückes regarded the system proposed by the pro-registration lobby as a retrograde step for nursing. She did not accept the argument that state registration would provide the public and doctors with a safeguard from incompetent nurses. By her standards a registered nurse could still be a bad nurse. If the public or doctors wanted a guarantee of a nurse's capabilities under the present system, they had only to refer to her training school for a reference. She felt strongly that registration would 'stereotype mediocrity', by setting a minimum standard it would soon become the maximum and the losers would be the best nurses who already had a higher standard.

The campaign for state registration was supported by the various trained nurses' associations and by the nursing press. Miss Lückes used her Annual Letter to old Londoners, which she started in 1894 as a way of keeping in touch with former Londoners, to put the case against registration. The letter grew into an annual 30 page pamphlet, reviewing the work of the hospital in the preceding year and including statistics about the work of each department, note of any developments in the nurses' training or conditions, and staff changes and new appointments, including foreign appointments taken up by Londoners. Miss Lückes believed that her letter reinforced the standards of their old training school. In 1897 she wrote

> If the union between the 'London' and its old workers is as complete as we all like to believe, the vitalizing influences which promote our own growth, should not be without their effect on all those who regard themselves as active members of the same body . . . All reports of your successes are gladly welcomed, and we like even to have the opportunity of sympathizing with you in failure. There are always a good proportion of old workers in the hospital to rejoice in the welfare and the well-doing of the old workers who have left.
>
> Annual Letter, 1897

In 1902, Dr and Mrs Bedford Fenwick founded the Society for the State Registration of Nurses and the following year drafted the first Bill for state registration. The Bill was introduced to parliament in 1904 and met strong opposition both within parliament and without. Sidney Holland published a manifesto against state registration and organised the city teaching hospitals to fight the Bill. At the same time, the Royal British Nurses' Association (RBNA) promoted a separate Bill for state registration and the outcome of all this activity was the appointment of a Select Committee of the House of Commons on the registration of nurses.

Mr Holland and Miss Lückes were among the 33 people to give evidence to the Committee. Miss Lückes was the only nursing representative to speak against registration. The *British Journal of Nursing*, edited by Mrs Fenwick, accused her of supporting the employers of nurses and opposing the elevation of nursing into a recognised profession, organised for the benefit of nurses. Miss Lückes replied in her Annual Letter

> [The letters I receive] from so many have acted lately as unintentional, but most effective, antidotes to the newspaper attacks made upon my attitude towards the work and workers in my opposition to the state registration of nurses, and the motives which are falsely attributed to me for it.
>
> I have no time nor inclination for public controversy, though I fully recognise the plain duty of making our views known . . . we are all agreed that the subject is one of vital importance to nurses and to the public, and I hope every nurse will feel it her duty to be ready with 'the calm exposition of the true' whenever the occasion demands it.
>
> Annual Letter, 1904

The opponents of state registration had one very strong ally, Florence Nightingale. The two ladies had become friends at the start of the campaign for the registration of nurses when they had both opposed the rise of the RBNA. Miss Nightingale, like Miss Lückes, believed that the qualities of a good nurse could not be measured by a theoretical examination, but depended more on the spirit in which the nursing care was administered. Her support was a great reassurance to Miss Lückes and she often referred to it in her Annual Letter. In 1905 she wrote

> . . . when I was privileged to have a charming talk with Miss Nightingale four or five weeks ago, she deprecated any proposal for the registration of nurses as strongly as ever, and firmly adheres to her view that any such measure must inevitably prove detrimental in the long run to the development of that side of a nurse's work which we all care for most, and which Miss Nightingale herself has done so much more than any one else to preserve intact from mere professionalism . . .
>
> Annual Letter, 1905

In 1908 she wrote

> How much the steady development of trained nursing . . . would have been hindered, if Miss Nightingale and others had not spoken out with no uncertain tone twenty years ago, when the state registration of nurses was urged upon us with the same violence which characterises its advocates at the present time . . .
>
> When Miss Nightingale began her work, one of her chief difficulties was to make the necessity for a technical knowledge of nursing better understood . . . But nothing was further from Miss Nightingale's wish or teaching than the suggestion that technical qualifications should be

regarded as substitutes for those personal characteristics which make nursing, not only a useful service, but a gentle ministration towards those who
are sick and suffering . . .

                                                        Annual Letter, 1908

The report of the Select Committee was published in 1905 and came
down in favour of state registration and stated that the bulk of
evidence pointed to three years as the most suitable training period.
Despite this success, the campaign was far from over. The trained
nurses' associations continued to lobby parliament and to promote
Private Members' Bills for registration. Sidney Holland proposed a
Bill in 1906, to establish an Official Directory of Nurses, a voluntary
register which would provide the public, and doctors, with a method
of checking a nurse's qualifications before employment. Miss Lückes
supported this proposal as it did not interfere with the independence
of the training schools. Although the Bill was defeated in the House
of Lords in 1908, she continued to recommend a voluntary register
in her Annual Letters.

> . . . this [Official Directory] is a very different matter to attempting to
> introduce a uniform standard of theoretical attainment to be tested by
> central theoretical examinations, outside a nurse's own training school,
> and by an ill-advised attempt to attach undue, not due, importance to
> technical knowledge, whilst ignoring the primary importance of personal
> character in estimating the value of a trained nurse.
>
>                                                   Annual Letter, 1914

In 1914, the London Hospital published a pamphlet, 'State Registration of Nurses', which reproduced a speech by Sidney Holland
(now Lord Knutsford) to the Cottage Nursing Association, and an
article by Miss Lückes which had appeared in the magazine *19th
Century and After*. Miss Lückes wrote that the current difficulties
facing nursing arose because of the rapid increase in the demand for
trained nurses, and, due to the inadequate supply of the best nurses,
the public and doctors frequently had to employ second and third
rate nurses. She repeated her case that the nurse who did well in
examinations might be unsuitable for the care of the sick, and argued
that a uniform standard of training was not necessary, as different
branches of nursing required different degrees of technical knowledge. To insist upon a uniform standard would tend to eliminate a
certain social class which it was desirable to retain among the ranks
of trained nurses. She continued,

> It is very important that nurses should not aim to become amateur doctors,
> and it would be increasingly difficult to prevent them from doing so if

they are taught that the chief thing necessary to become a nurse is the successful passing of technical examinations . . .

The pseudo-scientific young person, who is more concerned with showing off her 'little knowledge' to the doctor, and more interested in the 'case' than the 'patient', has become a terror in the sickroom . . . Registration will tend to multiply this type indefinitely.

## The First World War

The outbreak of war in August 1914 brought an increase in the work of the London Hospital. The hospital had promised 250 beds to the army and, on 2nd September, received 300 wounded soldiers. By October the soldiers had been replaced by sick and wounded Belgians. The hospital authorities had also agreed to provide 60 nurses to the admiralty and 50 to the army in the event of war, and these nurses were supplied within the first months of the war. Miss Lückes appealed to the sisters not to join the nursing services as they were needed more than ever in the hospital. The location of the hospital, in the densely populated east end of London, meant that it treated more air-raid victims than any other hospital.

In all the London Hospital supplied 229 nurses to the nursing services during the war and this figure did not include the large number of London trained nurses who volunteered from all over the country. There was a strong link between the London and the services. Miss Lückes had been involved in the establishment of the Queen Alexandra's Royal Naval Nursing Service and received the Royal Red Cross, First Class, in 1914, for her work in this connection. Mr Holland had been a member of the governing board of Queen Alexandra's Imperial Military Nursing Service since its establishment, and the Matron-in-Chief and the two Principal Matrons of the Service were 'Londoners'.

With the outbreak of war, the number of applications from women wanting to train as nurses more than doubled. In the first seven months of 1914, the hospital received 1006 applications, from August to December it received 2857. Miss Lückes did not make any relaxation in the rules for admission of probationers but she did increase the number of paying probationers. She also agreed to take 10 Royal Army Medical Corps orderlies at a time for one month's training.

## The College of Nursing

Through their war work in military and auxiliary hospitals, trained nurses from all over the country came into contact with each other and, for the first time since the campaign for registration began, a significant number of them realised that the present unorganised state of the profession was not in the interests of nurses or of the public. Standards of training from one hospital to another varied so much that a trained nurse could mean anything and was no guarantee of any standard. The need for a central body to organise and regulate the standard of training led to the establishment of the College of Nursing in the spring of 1916. The support which nurses gave the College played a large part in persuading the government to pass the *Nurses' Registration Act* at the end of 1919.

Miss Lückes was opposed to the College of Nursing for the same reasons that she was opposed to state registration. The aim of the College was to estabish a uniform standard of training and examination for all nurses, and it recommended a three year training period, the two points on which Miss Lückes was not prepared to alter her opinion. In July 1916, in a letter to Sir Henry Burdett, a prominent figure in the world of hospital management, she made clear that she was not prepared to change the training system at the London Hospital, although she realised it was now out of line with the opinions of the profession and the public

> I would give up anything if it were only a personal view. But our London Hospital training is so efficient and we turn out such excellent nurses that I'll be hung if I will give up what is proved successful simply because other people with less good organisation and with less care cannot do likewise.
>     . . . our nurses are in world wide demand. If the Royal family from the King downwards want a nurse they send to us. We are nursing a great number of the public schools. We have Matrons all over England. Every week we are asked to 'send us a matron'. The War Office are on their knees to us to send nurses. The Matron-in-Chief of the army is a London Hospital nurse. The Principal matron at the front is a London Hospital nurse, and so on . . . and now we are asked to change this? Why? Because forsooth other hospitals are not so successful.
>     London Hospital Archives, Personal Correspondence of E. C. Lückes

She felt as strongly about the College of Nursing and published 'Reasons against the London Hospital becoming affiliated with the College of Nursing' in January 1917. In reviewing this pamphlet in the *British Journal of Nursing*, Mrs Fenwick wrote 'Let it suffice that there is only one Training School . . . With Louis XV Miss Lückes may take heart of grace. *'Après Moi le deluge'*. (*British Journal of Nursing*, 20 Jan 1917, p. 47).

Two months later, March 1917, Lord Knutsford and Miss Lückes published a Memorandum on the position of the London Hospital concerning the College of Nursing. They regretted that they found themselves in strong opposition to the College of Nursing but they disagreed with the principles which the College advocated. With disappointment, they referred to the defection of many of the other London teaching hospitals, which had previously supported the London, particularly St Bartholomew's Hospital, the matron of which was a 'Londoner' and yet had become a member of the Council of the College of Nursing.

Shortly before her death, in reply to an old Londoner who had written to ask her opinion about joining the College, Miss Lückes wrote

> The College of Nursing has done and is doing more than any other Association of nurses to drag down nursing into a trade . . . you must not hope to find in this connection anything in support of 'London' traditions of nursing.
>
> Personal Correspondence of E. C. Lückes, Feb 1919
> London Hospital Archives

Miss Lückes' health was deteriorating – in 1916 she was forced to give up work completely for five months. She suffered badly from arthritis and in her last years was unable to walk and used a bath chair. She also had diabetes and cataracts. She took four weeks holiday each year in September and since 1911 she had gone to Bexhill-on-Sea, but she always took one of her Assistant Matrons with her so that she could continue her office work. She died in office on 16 February 1919, at the age of 64. She was buried at Golders Green and a memorial service was held at the hospital church on 22 February. The service was attended by over 1000 people, including over 500 sisters and nurses, medical and surgical staff, members of the House Committee, and her old ally Sidney Holland (now Lord Knutsford) represented Queen Alexandra.

## Conclusion

The obituaries of Miss Lückes were unanimous in acknowledging her contribution to nursing. *The Daily Telegraph* described her as 'The greatest personality in the profession of nursing since Florence Nightingale'. Under the headline 'The Passing of the Mother', *The*

*Nursing Mirror* described her as, 'a great maker of matrons'. *The Nursing Times* wrote of her personality, 'gentle and sympathetic in manner, in spite of her very strong will, with an old-world courtesy and deliberation, she was a type of the early pioneer'. In a pamphlet about her, written shortly after her death, Lord Knutsford, who had worked with her for 23 years, said that her life was simply 'The London Hospital'.

Her contribution to the development of nursing at the London Hospital was immense. She raised the nursing from its mid-nineteenth century level to a place among the leading teaching hospitals. She developed a system of training nurses in two years which gave them a wide range of experience and theoretical instruction. The training scheme was innovative, combining theoretical instruction by lectures and systematic practical instruction in the wards. She began the practice of matrons' lectures on general nursing and pioneered the preliminary training school system. The PTS model was copied by Guy's Hospital in 1902 and St Thomas' in 1910, and subsequently became the standard practice in all training schools.

Miss Lūckes often wrote about the importance of a nurse's practical nursing skills, not because she underestimated the need for a nurse to have a good theoretical foundation but to counteract the emphasis placed by the pro-registration lobby on theoretical knowledge. To ensure that probationers had sufficient opportunity to study she introduced a tutorial class after each lecture and two study periods a week. She also recommended the appointment of an external examiner. The training scheme was very efficient in terms of the hospital's needs, producing approximately 200 nurses a year and the standard of training ensured that there was no shortage of applicants. No assessment of her contribution to nursing could overlook the number of nurses which passed through her training school between 1880 and 1919.

Miss Lūckes' character was ideally suited to the job of matron of a large hospital at the end of the 19th century. She was a born administrator, combining clear thinking with a good memory and a capacity for hard work. She rose every morning at six and never finished before midnight. She planned the details of the nursing department and the training school thoroughly and her system of record keeping was meticulous. Combining administrative ability with an authoritative personality, she commanded the confidence of the hospital governors and the loyalty of the nursing staff. Like many matrons of the period, she was described as a disciplinarian, but many who knew her also spoke of her genuine love for the nurses in her care.

In addition to the paper work involved in running a hospital with a daily average of 800 patients, and a nursing staff of over 700, Miss Lückes kept up a huge correspondence. All private staff away from the hospital on cases and all old Londoners no longer on the staff, received a personal reply to their letters. Her reputation as matron of the largest hospital in the country, and as the author of two text books, brought additional correspondence. Both of her books, 'General Nursing', based on her lectures to the probationers at the London Hospital, first published in 1884, and 'Hospital Sisters and their Duties', 1886, became standard text books, reprinting in nine editions and four editions respectively. Every year between 1894 and 1916, she also produced her 20 to 30 page Annual Letter.

When Eva Lückes developed her two year training system in the 1880s, the majority of hospitals that had any training, had a one year system. By the end of the century, leading hospitals had adopted a three year programme but Miss Lückes saw no reason to change her system to conform to, what she called, the three year fetish. She considered that the variety of work at the London made two years there equivalent to three years elsewhere. By 1916 her position was one of splendid isolation and the London's certificate was no longer of the same status as those of the other major training schools, but her strength of character forced her to go against the tide and to take the hospital governors and Lord Knutsford with her. Within a year of her death the hospital adopted a three year training system and, in 1921, Lord Knutsford accepted a seat on the Council of the College of Nursing.

Equally reactionary on the question of state registration, she acknowledged in her evidence to the Select Committee in 1905, that a majority of hospitals gave their probationers a very mediocre training. Yet, she would not accept that the solution was to establish a minimum standard by a statutory examination and certificate. Nurses could not be compared to doctors and midwives, in these professions the possession of theoretical knowledge was vital and registration by examination was an appropriate system. Miss Lückes regarded nursing as an Art, similar to music or painting, no matter how much technical knowledge a woman learnt, if she did not have an instinct for nursing, she would still be an indifferent nurse.

Her own career had begun when nursing was still in a fluid state and pioneer matrons were able to develop different methods in the search for the ideal nurse. She believed that the Bills for state registration were premature, that nursing was still in a developing stage, and that it was too early to stereotype one system. Miss Lückes drew her ideals on nursing from Florence Nightingale and, like Miss

Nightingale, her standards were high. She was unwilling to accept anything less. This approach to nursing was already losing ground in her life time and her death, in February 1919, was timely in that it weakened the opposition at the very moment when there was a swing in favour of state registration.

## Sources

### London Hospital Archives

LH/N/1 Registers of Nurse Probationers
LH/N/4 Registers of Sisters and Nurses
LH/N/5 Registers of the Private Nursing Institution
LH/N/6 Official Ward Books
LH/A/5/39–44 House Committee Minutes, 1878–1891
LH/A/9/61 Sub-committee on nursing, minutes, 1879–1880
LH/A/17/47–50 Reports on Nursing Department, 1880–1900
LH/A/26/3 Scrapbook, 1890 controversy
Matron's Annual Letter, 1894–1916
Personal correspondence and notebooks of Eva Lückes

### Royal College of Nursing Archives

*General Nursing*, Lückes, Eva, London, 9th edn. 1914
*Hospital Sisters and their Duties*, Lückes, Eva, London, 2nd edn. 1888
House of Lords Select Committee on Metropolitan Hospitals, Minutes of evidence, 1890
House of Commons Select Committee on Registration of Nurses, Minutes of evidence and report, 1904–1905
RCN 4 Papers relating to State Registration
*Nursing Record/British Journal of Nursing*, 1888–1919
*Nursing Timees*, 1905–1919
*The Hospital*, 1916–1919
*Nursing Mirror*, 1919
*Eva C. E. Lückes*, by Sidney Holland, Viscount Knutsford, [1919] (Historical Pamphlets Collection, 3B)
*Eva C. E. Lückes*, Matron, The London Hospital 1880–1919, compiled by Margaret McEwan, The London Hospital League for Nurses, 1958 (Historical Pamphlets Collection, 3B)

# 2

# Mrs Bedford Fenwick
## *A Restless Genius*
(1857–1947)

*Matron of St Bartholomew's Hospital, 1881–1887, founder of the Royal British Nurses' Association, 1887, originator of the movement for the state registration of nurses, 1888, founder and first President of the International Council of Nurses, 1899, founder and first President of the National Council of Nurses of Great Britain, 1904, editor of The Nursing Record/ British Journal of Nursing, 1893–1946.*

ETHEL GORDON MANSON was born at Spynie House near Elgin, Morayshire, Scotland, on 26 January 1857. She was the third child, and second daughter, of David Davidson Manson, a farmer, and Harriette Palmer, of Thurnscoe, Yorkshire. Her father died before she was a year old and her mother took her young family back to her native Yorkshire. When Ethel was three years old her mother married the Tory Member of Parliament for South Nottinghamshire, George Storer, and Ethel grew up at his country house, Thoroton Hall, in the Vale of Belvoir.

Miss Manson started her training as a nurse, on 1st April 1878, at the age of 21, at the Children's Hospital, Nottingham. It was a small hospital with just two wards of twelve cots each, one for boys and one for girls. Although she enjoyed the work she later described the matron, Miss Minks, as 'the strictest disciplinarian and the most able administrator' she had ever met. She continued her training at the Royal Infirmary, Manchester, from September 1878 to September 1879, again as a paying probationer. She soon showed an aptitude for management and was given charge of a woman's surgical unit for eight weeks and, during the absence of the matron, was given responsibility for the Barnes Convalescent Hospital nearby. Her testimonials from the medical and lay staff of the Infirmary, refer to her energy, her tact in dealing with the staff and her kindness to the patients.

At the end of her year's training Miss Manson received a letter from the matron of the London Hospital, Miss Swift, offering her the post of sister of the women's medical ward. She had been recommended by Miss Minks, the matron of the Children's Hospital, Nottingham. Miss Manson accepted and arrived at Whitechapel, London, in the middle of September. The ward had 52 beds and was staffed by four nurses during the day and two at night, with one scrubber. As the sister, she was never off-duty and lived in two rooms, a bedroom and a sitting-room, adjoining the ward. The work was physically demanding with two daily ward rounds by five house physicians and five visiting physicians but she got on well with the medical staff and enjoyed the work.

Eleven months later, Miss Manson applied unsuccessfully for the post of matron at the Richmond Hospital, and some months later she applied for the matronship of St Bartholomew's Hospital. Despite her age, only 24, she was appointed to the job and became matron of one of the largest and most famous voluntary hospitals in the country. The references she received from the staff of the London Hospital testify to her managerial abilities and the intelligent discharge of her duties.

Miss Manson commenced her duties as matron of St Bartholomew's Hospital in the spring of 1881. Starting with the training of the nurses, she set out to improve the standard of the nursing. The hospital had begun to train nurses in 1877, at first over a period of one year, then, in 1879 it was extended to two years. Miss Manson increased the training to three years and organised a system of practical work and theoretical instruction. The majority of the nursing staff had received no formal training, so as the newly trained probationers qualified, they were encouraged to become staff nurses, gradually building up a staff of trained nurses.

In 1884, Miss Manson started taking paying probationers in groups of 12 to 15. These were educated young ladies who came for a minimum of three months, though many stayed for two or three terms. Miss Manson regarded their presence among the staff as a good influence. In 1885 she started a private nursing department, called St Bartholomew's Hospital Trained Nurses' Institute. She admitted that she had high standards and expected a lot from her staff

I own that where duty was concerned I was a somewhat exacting taskmistress. I was young and an enthusiast; sixteen hours' work made up a normal day. Ease, unpunctuality, omissions, short measure of work – these were unpardonable crimes.

*British Journal of Nursing*, 4 Jul 1903, p. 10

The same high standards applied to the conditions of her nursing staff and she was not satisfied until she had effected an improvement in the food and increased the off-duty hours and holidays. Miss Manson had a professional interest in the health of the nurses and her weekly reports, cataloguing the incidence of illness and infections among the staff, provide a record of the risks involved in nursing at the time.

During her years as matron two issues emerged which convinced her of the need for nurses to have professional independence. The first was the lack of protection afforded to both trained nurses and to the public from women who called themselves nurses but who had no training. She proposed to the hospital authorities that the ward assistants be contracted for three years to prevent them leaving after one year and taking posts as nurses in other hospitals. The second issue was the exploitation of private nurses by their employers. While matron of St Bartholomew's, she ensured that the extra fee charged by the hospital's private nursing institute, for nursing maternity and massage cases, was paid to the nurse herself and not to the institution. Miss Manson had identified the cause to which she was to dedicate her life's work, the professional standing of nurses. In 1887, she resigned the position of matron, married Dr Bedford Fenwick, a well-known physician, and started the campaign for the registration of trained nurses.

## Campaign for the Registration of Nurses 1887–1899

Within months of her marriage, Mrs Fenwick commenced her most important work, the professional organisation of nurses. On 21 November, she held a meeting of matrons at her home, 20 Upper Wimpole Street, to discuss the future organisation of the nursing profession and it was decided to form an association of nurses. At a second meeting, on 10 December, attended by 30 matrons, it was decided that it would be called the British Nurses' Association (BNA). The aim was to raise the standard of the profession as a whole by uniting all trained nurses in membership of an association which would support and protect their interests and provide for their registration. In her speech to the assembled matrons, Mrs Fenwick referred to the importance of registration for the profession

In my opinion Registration, to be of any value at all, must be undertaken by a legally recognised body, largely composed of the heads of the Nursing Profession themselves, with the full concurrence of medical men. We must recognise the fact that Registration is only the lever to that high, irreproachable position to which all nurses should aspire, and if unanimous can easily attain. The time has come when this great movement is to be publicly discussed, and I call upon you ladies present, representing as you do by virtue of your office the leaders of the great army of nurses, to rise up and protect them and guard their interests with that determination and zeal which springs alone from knowledge.

*British Journal of Nursing*, 15 May 1920, p. 288

The Hospitals' Association had discussed the question of nurses' registration in 1886 and had proposed a scheme for nurses with one year's training. This decision had been taken against the recommendation of the nurse members of the association who had shown their disapproval by resigning. Mrs Fenwick condemned the scheme as derogatory to nurses and of no value to the public who would be misled into believing that a nurse with one year's training was competent. Several of the matrons, who had resigned from the Hospitals' Association, were among the founders of the BNA. The founders considered that the best way to protect the trained nurse from the competition of untrained women, was to establish a register of trained nurses, similar to the register of doctors. They decided that the minimum qualification for registration should be three years training in a hospital. Mrs Fenwick was determined to set the standard of the 'trained nurse' as high as that of the best nurses. She considered that nursing was a worthwhile career for educated women and she wanted to make sure that it had a professional standing which would attract intelligent women.

The British Nurses' Association was formally launched at a public meeting in February 1888. Princess Helena, Queen Victoria's daughter and the wife of Prince Christian of Schleswig Holstein, who had identified herself with the cause of nursing, accepted the presidency. Mrs Fenwick was appointed the Honorary Secretary and Dr Bedford Fenwick the Honorary Treasurer. Over 400 nurses and medical men joined the association within the first few weeks and within a year the membership had reached 1000. This was the first organisation of nurses and from its inception it provoked opposition from two quarters, the medical profession and hospital managers. The opponents of the association had a powerful spokesman in the person of Henry Burdett. A well known authority on hospital administration and finance, Mr Burdett (later Sir) had founded the Hospitals' Association in 1884, and was the editor of its journal, *The Hospital*. Mr Burdett openly criticised the motives of the founders of the BNA in his journal and advised his readers, mainly hospital managers, to ensure that none of their nursing staff were members. In April 1888, he started a nursing section in *The Hospital*, called *The Nursing Mirror*, which followed the editorial line of the main journal. This was in response to a new radical journal for nurses, *The Nursing Record*, which was 'written by nurses for nurses', and which supported the BNA and the registration cause. It attacked the opponents of registration, especially the matron of the London Hospital, Eva Lückes, who had written a pamphlet questioning the need for an association of nurses and the value of registration (see chapter one). Dr and Mrs Bedford Fenwick took over *The Nursing Record* in 1893, Mrs Fenwick becoming the honorary editor. Previously they had contributed articles to the journal, Dr Fenwick writing on medical nursing and Mrs Fenwick on the education and organisation of nurses. In her first editorial she announced that the goal of *The Nursing Record* was to accomplish state registration for nurses. As the campaign to achieve registration lengthened into decades, and the opposing sides became more entrenched, Mrs Fenwick's pen never spared her opponents.

In 1892, the Royal British Nurses' Association (RBNA), which had been granted the prefix 'royal' the previous year, applied for a royal charter of incorporation. The application was strongly opposed by all the opponents of registration, fearing that such extra powers would make the RBNA too powerful and its influence on nurses throughout the country might be a threat to the medical authorities and the smooth running of the hospitals. In the pages of *The Nursing Record* and *The Hospital*, Mr Burdett and Mrs Fenwick accused each other of unworthy motives. To Mrs Fenwick, Mr Burdett represented the vested interests of the employers of nurses and male arrogance. To Mr Burdett, the RBNA represented the cutting edge of organised labour and women's rights. A Privy Council inquiry was held which decided in favour of granting the charter. Mrs Fenwick and her supporters were jubilant. It was the first occasion that a royal charter was granted to an association of professional women and Mrs Fenwick regarded it as recognition of the association as a professional body. She told her readers that it was only a matter of time before state registration would be achieved.

It was a pyrrhic victory – the powers granted by the charter were not as extensive as those which the association had sought and the bye-laws had been subtly altered. The power to maintain a register of nurses had been applied for, whereas only the power to maintain a list of nurses was granted, this was a small improvement on the voluntary register which the association had started in 1891. The changes in the bye-laws were exploited by the opponents of registration. By 1895, they had secured a majority on the council of the RBNA and by voting for a change in the regulations, which removed the right of founder members to a seat on the council, removed Mrs Fenwick from the council. At a joint meeting between the British Medical Association and representatives of nurses to discuss registration, the RBNA delegates voted for a resolution which stated that state registration was 'inexpedient in principle, injurious to the best interests of nurses and of doubtful public benefit'. In 1897, Mr Burdett became secretary of the association and, in 1899, the voluntary register of nurses was replaced by the membership roll of the association.


## Professional and International Contacts 1892–1912

Shortly after her marriage, Mrs Fenwick opened the Gordon House Home Hospital, a private nursing home, near her home in Upper Wimpole Street, London. Here she put into practice her theory that 'sick people could have the scientific nursing of the best hospitals combined with the refinements and luxuries of a well-ordered home'. As her commitment to the professional organisation of nurses increased, she found that she did not have the time to manage the home herself and appointed a matron.

In 1892, Mrs Fenwick had been appointed a member of the Women's Committee of the British Royal Commission for the 1893 World's Fair in Chicago. She was also appointed president of the British nursing section and was responsible for organising the exhibition of nursing effects and for this she received two medals of distinction. She crossed the Atlantic in October 1892 to make arrangements for the exhibition and again in April 1893 to attend the Congress of Representative Women held in Chicago during the Fair. En route, she visited the major nurse training hospitals in the north eastern states, including the Johns Hopkins Hospital in Baltimore, where she met Lavinia Dock, assistant director of the nursing department.

Lavinia Dock and Ethel Fenwick were kindred spirits, sharing a dream of a nursing profession, well organised and independent. They both believed, in Mrs Fenwick's words, that 'the nurses' question was the women's question'. Miss Dock wrote

> . . . to attain such an end [professional organisation] where women are concerned arouses prehistoric prejudices and touches a multitude of vested

interests. Hence the stringent opposition with which every effort of nursing reform has been and is being met . . . the industrial spinster does not
count, she is a voteless, voiceless item of humanity.
*American Journal of Nursing,* 1901 p. 865

In London in 1896, Mrs Fenwick organised a major nursing exhibition
and conference to promote 'scientific nursing', the aim being to provide nurses with the opportunity to see the latest appliances and
inventions for nursing the sick. She hoped that the conference, by
eliciting the opinions of nurses on various subjects, including state
registration, would raise the professional awareness of nurses, and
demonstrate to the public the determination of nurses. Her own
contribution to the conference was a paper on 'the nursing of our
soldiers', a subject in which she took a great interest. The whole
venture was a success and in her journal she suggested that the
forthcoming congress of the International Council of Women, to be
held in London in 1899, would be an opportunity to hold an international conference of nurses.

The following year, 1897, she was appointed Honorary Secretary
of the National Fund of Greek Wounded, a fund started by *The Daily
Chronicle* to send nurses and supplies to Greece during the Graeco-
Turkish war. The first 20 nurses were selected by Mrs Fenwick and
went out to Greece in April. In May, Mrs Fenwick travelled to Athens
and took over the superintendence of the nursing in the military
hospitals. Her work was admired, and especially by Queen Olga and
Crown Princess Sophie who often visited the Ecole Militaire Hospital,
and she was awarded the Distinguished Order and the Diploma of
the Greek Red Cross.

Mrs Fenwick's involvement in the International Council of Women
(ICW) began when she met Mrs May Wright Sewall, the founder of
the ICW, in Chicago in 1893. On her return to Britain, she helped to
promote the work of the ICW in Britain and was appointed a member
of the committee to arrange the programme for the 1899 Congress
in London. She proposed that nursing should form a department of
the professional section and was then appointed chairman of that
section and treasurer of the congress fund. Distinguished nurses
from America, Denmark, Holland and the Cape Colony attended the
Congress, and the nursing section was the first international gathering of nurses.

The overseas nurses were invited to attend the annual meeting of
the Matrons' Council, which was held the day after the congress.
The Matrons' Council was an association of matrons, founded by
Mrs Fenwick and her friend Isla Stewart (see chapter three), who

had succeeded her as matron of St Bartholomew's Hospital in 1887, which aimed to bring about a uniform system of education for nurses in British hospitals. The members of the Matrons' Council and the foreign nurses welcomed Ethel Fenwick's proposal that an international council of nurses should be established, and a provisional committee was appointed to draft and circulate a constitution. One year later the International Council of Nurses (ICN) was founded to promote international cooperation between nurses of all countries and to provide them with opportunities to meet and discuss professional issues. Mrs Fenwick was elected president and Miss Dock the honorary secretary. For the first twelve years the offices of the ICN were at the office of the Registered Nurses' Society, in Oxford Street, London. The Registered Nurses' Society was a non-profit making society, set up by Mrs Fenwick for private nurses who were members of the RBNA. The structure of the ICN was based on that of the International Council of Women, membership being restricted to one national association from each country. The national associations would consist of representatives of the various self-governing nurses' organisations in each country. The ICN held its first meeting in September, 1901, in Buffalo, New York, to coincide with the Pan-American exposition being held there. Ethel Fenwick attended the meeting and delivered a presidential address and a paper on the professional organisation of nurses. Also she addressed a meeting of nearly 2,000 nurses, organised as part of the exposition, on the need for the higher education of nurses.

In June 1902, the Matrons' Council in Britain launched the Society for the State Registration of Nurses, with Mrs Fenwick as the secretary and the treasurer. Within a year the society had 900 members and put forward the first Bill for the registration of nurses. The Bill, drafted by Dr and Mrs Fenwick and Isla Stewart, was introduced into the House of Commons as a Private Member's Bill in February 1904. At the same time, a second Bill on behalf of the RBNA for the registration of nurses was promoted in the Commons. The RBNA was still under the control of Mrs Fenwick's opponents, and, although they were now supporting registration, she did not trust them and labelled their Bill the 'employers' Bill'. Both Bills sought to establish a central nursing council to be responsible for the system of registration, but they differed in the proposed composition of the council. The Bill drafted by the Fenwicks gave a majority of seats on the council to nurses whereas the Bill promoted by the RBNA gave hospital and medical authorities the controlling vote. The two parties lobbied Members of Parliament to gain support for their respective Bills. After months of campaigning, the House of Commons

*Fig 4. Congress of the International Council of Nurses, Buffalo, 1901: Officers and foreign delegates; seated (2nd left) Isla Stewart, (3rd from left) Mrs Bedford Fenwick*

appointed a Select Committee to consider the expediency of providing for the registration of nurses.

Meantime, at the next ICN meeting, in 1904 in Berlin, Mrs Fenwick retired as president, and was elected an honorary vice-president with a seat on the grand council. By this date, the first three national councils had been set up, Great Britain and Ireland, USA and Germany. Mrs Fenwick had been elected president of the National Council of Trained Nurses of Great Britain and Ireland, which represented 15 affiliated nurses' organisations. At the Berlin congress, the ICN adopted the *British Journal of Nursing* as its official journal. This was the former *Nursing Record* which Mrs Fenwick had renamed in 1902 and through which she aimed to link English-speaking nurses all over the world. She was influenced by the *American Journal of Nursing*, with which her friend Lavinia Dock was associated, and said the aims of the two journals were identical.

The Select Committee on Registration reported in favour of registration in 1905. It had taken evidence from 33 witnesses, including Dr and Mrs Bedford Fenwick, Sir Henry Burdett, Sydney Holland, Eva Lückes and Isla Stewart. Mrs Fenwick and the pro-registration party were convinced that statutory recognition of their profession could no longer be postponed. However, they overestimated the influence of a select committee report. The two registration Bills were re-introduced in the House of Commons, in 1906 and 1907, by private members, without government support. Each time they were blocked by their opponents.

In 1907, Mrs Fenwick and Isla Stewart went to Paris to make arrangements for the ICN Congress to be held there that year. They met Mlle. Chaptal, later president of the National Association of Trained Nurses of France and of the ICN, and through her secured the interest of the Director General of the Assistance Publique, who opened the congress and gave every assistance to the proceedings.

A third Bill for the registration of nurses was promoted in February 1908, this time in the House of Lords, by the Central Hospital Council for London, representing the London general hospitals. The Bill proposed the establishment of an official directory of nurses, to be maintained by an official registrar. No provision for the self-governing of nurses and no minimum standard of training was made. Mrs Fenwick called it 'the Nurses' Enslavement Bill' and urged all nurses to protest against this piece of reactionary legislation. It was lost on the second reading in the Lords. This was interpreted as a sign of support by the registration lobby, and they withdrew their Bill from the Commons and introduced it instead in the Lords. The Bill was passed in the Lords but, without government support, failed to get a reading in the Commons.

In 1909 the ICN met in London and Mrs Fenwick as president of the national association of the host country, welcomed the foreign delegates. In her address, she spoke of the international aspect of nursing, a profession with no national borders. Among the delegates on the platform at the opening session, held in the Great Hall of Church House, Westminster, was Annie Goodrich, President of the American Nurses' Association. She asked Ethel Fenwick to accept honorary membership of their association, the only foreign nurse to receive this honour. The proceedings of the congress were interrupted by Sidney Holland, the chairman of the London Hospital and staunch ally of its Matron, Eva Lückes. He told the gathering that the convenors of the congress did not represent English nursing or English hospitals, and presented a manifesto against registration signed by 67 matrons, all of whom were members of the Central Hospital Council for London.

In June 1909, after a delegation to the prime minister had failed to secure any guarantee of government support for registration, representatives of the trained nurses' organisations held a meeting to discuss the possibility of a joint Bill. They agreed to form the Central Committee for the State Registration of Nurses, with Ethel Fenwick as one of the joint honorary secretaries, and to draw up a joint

*Fig 5. International Council of Nurses, London, 1909: Mrs Bedford Fenwick with her sister*

Bill. The Bill incorporated the three principles which Mrs Fenwick regarded as beyond compromise, a minimum standard of three years' training as the qualification for registration, a uniform curriculum and examination for all nurses, and the appointment of a central nursing council to govern the profession. After 21 years of campaigning in Britain, this committee, representing eight different nurses' organisations, had produced a joint Bill for registration. Outside of Britain, state registration of nurses had already become law in New Zealand, the Cape Colony and Natal, and in ten of the United States.

The joint Bill was introduced in the House of Commons as a Private Member's Bill each year between 1910 and 1913. On each occasion it failed to get a hearing through lack of government support. The government's attitude was interpreted by Mrs Fenwick and her supporters as evidence of women's lack of political power – the government could ignore the wishes of nurses as long as women did not have the vote. The government's argument was that they could not afford to ignore the opponents of registration.

The number of nurses represented by the Central Committee was estimated at 10,000, while the total number of nurses in the country at the time was approximately 70,000. Aware of this discrepancy, Mrs Fenwick repeatedly scolded nurses in her journal for not taking an interest in their profession and its future. In her evidence to the select committee in 1905, she admitted that the *British Journal of Nursing* was read by a small, intellectual minority of nurses.

The fourth ICN Congress was held in Cologne in 1912, and Mrs Fenwick proposed that the ICN inaugurate an educational memorial in the name of Florence Nightingale, who had died in 1910. The proposal was unanimously accepted but due to the First World War, which was soon to overtake events, it was over 20 years before the necessary arrangements were made. Mrs Fenwick was appointed chairman of the memorial committee in Britain and finally in 1934, the Florence Nightingale International Foundation was inaugurated. It was a matter of regret to Mrs Fenwick that Florence Nightingale had opposed the registration of nurses and supported Eva Lückes. She regarded Miss Nightingale as the pioneer of trained nurses and believed her opposition to their organisation was due to the length of time between Miss Nightingale's experience of hospital nursing and the development of the registration movement.

In February 1914, the Central Committee introduced a revised Bill in the House of Commons which received a majority of 228 on its first reading but was refused a second reading by the government. A deputation to the Home Secretary in July failed to change the government's attitude, and before the Central Committee had time to lobby support, the war broke out. At that point the government passed a rule disallowing Private Members' Bills for the duration of the war.

## War Work

At the start of the war, the government delegated the responsibility for organising the voluntary nursing services to the British Red Cross Society (BRCS). The National Council of Trained Nurses, of which Mrs Fenwick was president, passed a resolution at its annual meeting in December 1914, placing on record its 'unqualified disapproval' of the organisation of the nursing of sick and wounded soldiers in military and auxiliary hospitals at home and abroad. The resolution called on the Secretary of State for War to prevent the expenditure of public subscriptions on 'inefficient nursing and the subjection of the sick and wounded to the dangerous interference of untrained and unskilled women' (*British Journal of Nursing*, Supplement, 30 Jan 1915). This was an attack on the members of the Voluntary Aid Detachments (VADs), and the amateur hospitals run by aristocratic ladies in their country houses, voluntary work which had been encouraged by the BRCS.

Trained nurses were disappointed that, after years of campaigning for statutory recognition of professional status, they still had to contend with government departments which regarded nursing as philanthropic work. When it became apparent, as early as the spring of 1915, that there was a serious shortage of nurses, Mrs Fenwick did not hesitate to point out that had the registration of nurses been introduced the problem would not have occurred.

> Had the expert opinion of nurses themselves, expressed over and over again for the last quarter of a century, been heeded by the Government, the shortage would never have assumed the present serious dimensions . . . They have pleaded for the passing of a Nurses' Registration Act . . . Such a Register would at the present moment be invaluable, both as evidence of the qualifications of nurses seeking appointments, and as affording a means of communicating with trained nurses throughout the Kingdom.
>
> *British Journal of Nursing*, editorial, 27 March 1915

During the war Mrs Fenwick worked for the British Committee of the French Red Cross, which sent over 250 trained nurses to France to help the French nursing services. She was appointed honorary superintendent and treasurer of the French Flag Nursing Corps, under the French War Office, which involved selecting nurses for work in certain districts and visiting them periodically throughout France. For her contribution she was awarded the Médaille de la Reconnaissance Française and, after the war, she was appointed by the Committee to select nurses for work in the devasted areas of France. At home she was a member of the grand council and executive committee of the Territorial Force Nursing Service for the City and County of London, and a member of the ladies' committee of the Order of St John of Jerusalem. She believed in the righteousness of the British cause and came out in favour of interning all Germans in Britain.

The war served as a catalyst once again to encourage nurses to do something about the unorganised state of nursing. At the end of 1915, the Matron-in-Chief of the British Red Cross Society, Sarah Swift (see chapter seven), approached the Chairman of the BRCS, Arthur Stanley, a well known 'neutral' on the issue of state registration. Together they proposed the establishment of a College of Nursing which would promote a standard training for nurses. They invited the support of the matrons and hospital managers of the country's nurse-training schools, and after an encouraging response, the College of Nursing was launched as a limited company, in April 1916.

The pro-registration lobby was divided in their response to the College of Nursing, and Mrs Fenwick was suspicious of the involvement of hospital managers. Both she and her supporters thought the aims of the College were a distraction from the real cause of state registration. But not all the registrationists were as uncompromising. Two prominent supporters of state registration, Ellen Musson (see chapter eight), Matron of the General Hospital, Birmingham, and Rachel Cox-Davies, Matron of the Royal Free Hospital, London, decided to support the College of Nursing. They hoped to bring the College behind the registration cause rather than leave it open to the influence of its opponents.

The College of Nursing gained wide support among matrons who encouraged their staff to join. By 1918, the College had a membership of 8000 and, in response to the wishes of its members, it drew up a Bill for the registration of nurses. Negotiations were held with the Central Committee for the State Registration of Nurses in an effort to produce a joint Bill, but after many months, agreement proved impossible and both parties published separate Bills. Mrs Fenwick denounced the College Bill as an 'employers' Bill', because it failed to give nurses the degree of self-government which she regarded as essential for professional independence. The profession and the nursing press were divided in their support for the two Bills and both parties lobbied members of parliament to introduce their Bill. Early in 1919, Major Barnett agreed to introduce the Bill of the Central Committee.

The Bill survived its first reading in the Commons and, in the interests of the profession, the College of Nursing decided to support it on the second reading. At the committee stage, however, the College promoted several amendments which it considered essential to make the Bill acceptable. There were so many amendments to the Bill that eventually the College withdrew its support and promoted its own Bill in the House of Lords. The College Bill survived its first reading in the Lords in May and was waiting for a second reading when the Minister of Health, Dr Addison, asked both parties to withdraw their Bills on the promise that the government would introduce a Bill for the registration of nurses as soon as possible. When Parliament reassembled in the autumn, the government's Bill for the registration of nurses was introduced, passed and became law on 23 December 1919. Mrs Fenwick watched, what she described as the last act in the drama, from the public gallery.

## The General Nursing Council

*The Nurses Registration Act*, 1919, provided for the establishment of a General Nursing Council (GNC) to be responsible for the maintenance of the register of nurses. The Council was to be elected by the nurses on the register but in the meantime, while registration was proceeding, a provisional council responsible for the details of that procedure, was appointed by the Minister. Mrs Fenwick was appointed a member of the provisional Council and chairman of the registration committee. She regarded the *Nurses Registration Act* as a great step forward, comparable to the enfranchisement of women, and the fact that nurses were given a two-thirds majority on the council, she claimed as a personal achievement. However, when the whole council had been appointed, Mrs Fenwick and her supporters were in the minority among the other nurse members, outnumbered by the supporters of the College of Nursing.

The proceedings of the first General Nursing Council were dominated by the old animosities of the registration campaign. It was inevitable that the two factions would have trouble in reaching mutually acceptable decisions. As chairman of the registration committee, Mrs Fenwick regarded herself as personally responsible for the veracity of the qualifications of every nurse whose name was admitted to the register. The process of registration was so slow that in December 1921, two-thirds of the council, including the chairman, resigned in protest. The Minister of Health intervened and asked Ethel Fenwick to resign from the registration committee. She refused. After several weeks, the Minister appointed a new chairman of the council and reinstated the councillors who had resigned, and the council passed a resolution with immediate effect, that committees would be appointed on an annual basis. A new registration committee was appointed and Mrs Fenwick was excluded. She fought back through the pages of her journal, reproaching nurses for having allowed their professional independence to be compromised by the College of Nursing.

> Had the majority of nurses taken an intelligent interest in their own affairs, acquainted themselves with the privileges granted to them by parliament . . . acted for themselves, instead of allowing themselves to be manipulated by a company of lay men, there would have been a very different tale to tell.
>
> *British Journal of Nursing*, editorial, Dec 1922

The first election of councillors to the GNC took place at the end of 1922 and, due to an administrative error, had to be held again in February, 1923. By that time there were about 12,000 nurses on the register eligible to vote. The College of Nursing put up its own candidates with Mrs Fenwick and her supporters standing as independents to represent 'the free nurses' organisations'.

Ethel Fenwick lost her seat, and in a series of articles in the *British Journal of Nursing*, under the title 'How the College Caucus Captured the Council', she gave her view of the election. Although excluded from the GNC, she continued to follow its proceedings closely and to report all decisions made which affected the development of the profession. She criticised much of the Council's work, but especially the failure to make the training syllabus compulsory and the lack of progress on the examination syllabus. Through the Registered Nurses' Parliamentary Council, which was the old Central Committee for the State Registration of Nurses renamed, she lobbied Members of Parliament for intervention and, following questions in the Commons, a Select Committee was appointed in 1925 to consider aspects of the GNC's rules.

The committee sat for less than six weeks and called 15 witnesses, among them Mrs Fenwick. In its report, the committee did not accept Mrs Fenwick's point that the 1919 Nurses Act had intended that the training syllabus should be compulsory. However, it did agree that the rule stipulating that 6 of the 11 representatives of the nurses on the general part of the register should be matrons, was contrary to the spirit of the Act, and all 11 seats should be open to general trained nurses.

When the next election for the GNC took place in 1927, Mrs Fenwick did not stand realising that she did not have enough support to beat the College of Nursing candidates, 'the majority of nurses in this kingdom are too ignorant of the true condition of nursing politics, and too subject to economic control, and to financial patronage, to give a free vote for candidates' (*British Journal of Nursing*, Nov 1927, p. 258).

In 1926, Mrs Fenwick founded the British College of Nurses, which was to be an educational body with membership and fellowship by examination. She intended the college to provide nurses who desired professional self-government, and therefore did not wish to join the College of Nursing, with the opportunity of professional development. The foundation was made possible by an anonymous benefactor who donated £100,000. The first fellowships and diplomas were presented, with full graduation ceremony, on 27 April 1927, and were awarded to nurses who had contributed to the advancement of professional nursing, including Mrs Fenwick herself.

Her last campaign in defence of the professional standard of nursing was fought over the issue of a second grade of nurse. The 1905 Select Committee on Registration had foreseen that one likely consequence of a three year training period for nurses would be a shortage of candidates entering the profession. The committee had advised that it might be necessary to consider a separate register of a lower standard. Mrs Fenwick had always believed that the supply of educated, intelligent girls was sufficient and that it was a case of attracting them into the profession. After the war, the increase in the choice of careers open to women contributed to a shortage of nurses in the 1920s and 1930s, which was so acute that the smaller voluntary hospitals and infirmaries advertised for and employed assistant nurses. These were women who did not wish to undertake a three year training, or girls who had been rejected by the training schools.

The number of assistant nurses had become so large by 1936, that their unofficial status could no longer be ignored and the College of Nursing recommended their enrollment, on a separate roll to be set up by the GNC. The British Medical Association came out in support of recognition in 1937, and in the same year the government committee, under the chairmanship of Lord Athlone, made similar recommendations to those of the College.

The RBNA, the British College of Nurses and the *British Journal of Nursing* protested against this threat to the trained nurse. Ethel Fenwick who had spent the best part of her life fighting to establish the professional status of nursing, based on the qualification of three years' training, defended that standard to the last. In a newspaper interview the 'fiery old lady' said

> We shall fight this proposal to the death. It is 62 years since I entered a hospital for training . . . During the fight for the Registration Bill I practically lived in the lobbies of the Houses of Parliament. We won, and it cost us between £20,000 and £30,000. But this proposal to give professional

status to unqualified nurses would destroy everything we worked for, and
we won't have it.

*The Evening Standard*, 18 Mar 1939

She organised a public meeting in Caxton Hall, Westminster, to
protest at the proposal, and published a pamphlet, 'A Demand for
Justice for the State Registered Nurse'. But in May the GNC accepted
the necessity of recognising a second grade of nurse. The inevitable
outcome of the issue was, if anything, accelerated by the outbreak
of the Second World War. The Civil Nursing Reserve, which was
responsible for the recruitment of nurses during the war, accepted
assistant nurses from the start. In 1943, the Minister of Health introduced a nurses' Bill to enable the GNC to set up a roll of assistant
nurses. Mrs Fenwick wrote to the prime minister, Winston Churchill,
to protest, and in an editorial under the heading 'The Rise and
Decline of the Profession of Nursing in England and Wales', she
compared the proposed legislation to the registration of quack doctors, and considered the prospect that nursing as a profession for
educated women may cease to exist. At the age of 86, she returned
to the lobbies of the House of Commons, her last hope of support.
However, the Nurses Act became law on 22 April 1943.

## Travelling and Writing 1920–1939

The first congress of the ICN after the First World War was held in
Helsinki, in 1925. Mrs Fenwick had intended to go to the congress
but changed her plans to stay in London and give evidence to the
House of Commons Select Committee on the GNC. As the founder,
Mrs Fenwick was always an honoured and welcome guest enjoying
both the social and professional functions. For the Helsinki Congress
she had prepared a paper 'The Trained Nurse's Part in Peace', which
was read in her absence by a colleague.

In 1927, Mrs Fenwick attended an interim conference of the ICN in
Geneva, and the following year she went to Rome for an international
reunion of nurses, part of the International Union against Tubercu-
losis. While in Rome she was presented to Mussolini, the head of
the Italian government, and she had an audience with the Pope. She
also visited the villa where Florence Nightingale was born in Florence. On her return to England she was taken ill and was confined
to bed for six months, which prevented her from attending the ICN
meeting in Montreal in 1929.

The next ICN congress was held jointly in Paris and Brussels in

1933, and Mrs Fenwick was there to enjoy the ceremonies, meetings and receptions. Four years later in 1937, the Congress was held in London, and Mrs Fenwick at the age of 80, was chairman of the organising committee. She produced the guide to London for the foreign delegates, and the Congress was attended by over 3,000 nurses from 44 countries. At the ceremony to receive three new national councils into membership, Mrs Fenwick spoke of her joy as the founder at seeing the 'rich flowering of the seed planted in 1899'. This was to be her last international congress, the Second World War intervened and it was ten years before the ICN and its members were able to meet again.

During the 1920 and 1930s, Mrs Fenwick continued to edit and write articles for the *British Journal of Nursing*. In 1924, due to falling readership, the journal changed from a weekly to a monthly publication. Mrs Fenwick assumed that her readers were intelligent and professional and she did not alter the style of the journal to increase sales. The journal reported the activities of nurses, social and professional, and the proceedings of the various nurses' organisations, whether in sympathy with Mrs Fenwick or not. It had also reported the ups and downs of the suffrage campaign, Mrs Fenwick regarding the vote as the right of professional women. She constantly urged nurses to take an interest in the issue and to keep themselves informed of the facts. She was a keen royalist and all royal events and anniversaries were given extensive coverage. She believed that the patronage by the royal ladies of the various nurses' organisations and causes added to the standing of the profession.

For many years Mrs Fenwick lived in a small eighteenth century house in Barton Street, Westminster. The house was filled with her priceless collection of Chinese and English porcelain, mahogany furniture and miniature animals. During the Second World War she moved into accommodation at the headquarters of the RBNA in Queen's Gate, Kensington. In June, 1946, she fell and fractured her femur, and was given a private room in St Bartholomew's Hospital, where she was nursed with all the care due to a former matron. Her fracture never healed, and in November she was transferred to the home of a friend, the wife of the vicar of Colney Hatch, London. Her death in March, 1947, was described in her journal in the following words

> For some time she appeared to rally, and once more she interested herself in Nursing affairs . . . Her 90th birthday came round on January 26th, and she received many little tokens, and cables from friends abroad . . . But her rally was only short-lived and gradually she became weaker . . . she

became unconscious on March 10th, and never recovered. She died on the evening of March 13th, at 10.30 p.m., and at long last that courageous and indomitable spirit found rest.

*British Journal of Nursing* April 1947, p. 42

Widespread floods, following the severe winter, prevented Ethel Manson Fenwick's body being taken north to her family burial ground. Her remains were cremated at Golders Green on 18 March where 28 years previously her opponent in the 'battle of the nurses', Eva Lückes, had been buried. The next day a memorial service was held at St Bartholomew's Hospital. Her greatest tributes came from the international nursing world. She was an honorary member of the national nurse associations of America, Germany, Finland and India. Two months after her death, in May 1947, the ICN met in Atlantic City where it had been intended to present their founder with a citation, in recognition of her 'unique and life-long contribution to the advancement of the nursing profession throughout the world'. In her absence, the citation was read out to the assembly and a memorial service was held.

## Conclusion

At the age of 21, when she went to work in the Children's Hospital, Nottingham, Ethel Manson was described as full of spirit, with a will of steel. She had decided to train as a nurse and although still too young to be accepted for training at the bigger hospitals she was not prepared to wait. Her suitability to nursing and to taking responsibility were apparent even to her first matron, who recommended her for the job at the London Hospital. In less than two years she had a reputation as a practical administrator and disciplinarian and though only 24 years old, she had the confidence to apply for the post of Matron of St Bartholomew's Hospital. Her six years at St Bartholomew's was a period of hard work and fulfilment, she introduced reforms in the nursing and won the respect of the older, established sisters and the medical staff, one of whom, Harrison Cripps, FRCS, described her as a 'restless genius'.

She had said that she intended to have a family and so, characteristically, at the age of 30 she gave up active nursing to marry. With extraordinary foresight, she saw the need for nurses to organise to protect their professional interests and she led them towards professional registration for almost 30 years. Her ideas on the status of nurses were strongly influenced by her contact with American

nurses, particularly Lavinia Dock, Adelaide Nutting and Annie
Goodrich. Miss Dock was an ardent feminist and the other two were
leading nurse educationalists. As early as 1895, Mrs Fenwick was
writing that the English system of nurse training was unsatisfactory
due to probationers' training being secondary to the manpower needs
of the hospital. Impressed by the advances made in America, where
some hospitals had adopted the non-payment of probationers and
treated them as pupils, she advocated the 'collegiate' system, with
pupils paying for the cost of training, partly in money and partly in
labour.

Her constant demand for a uniform curriculum and training in
Britain was a recognition that the key to the professional status of
nursing was in the education of nurses, making it a suitable profession for intelligent women. She wrote

> The era of the 'ministering angel' and the silly sentimentality inseparable
> from that aspect of the work, and which did so much harm, has, we hope,
> as completely passed as the days and degradation for ever associated with
> Sairey Gamp. The era of the trained nurse as a woman desirous to do the
> best possible professional work in her power has dawned . . .
>
> *The Nursing Record*, editorial, 21 Sept 1901

She was better at leading than representing, and her adherence to
her principles made her a poor politician. Up to 1910, and the death
of her friend Isla Stewart, she was prepared to talk and to reach
agreements with the other parties in the campaign for registration.
The loss of her friend and her tactful influence, meant that Mrs
Fenwick became more autocratic and eventually, isolated. When the
College of Nursing was founded, many efforts were made to bring
her in but she was unable to accept its constitution and threw away
one of her last opportunities to represent British nurses. Although
she founded at least half a dozen associations and representative
bodies, few of them survived after the death of her personal friends.

The Nurses' Act of 1919 was accepted by her as the long-awaited
legislation on state registration and she was prepared to work within
the terms of the Act as she saw them. Her ideas on the role of the
GNC were not shared by the majority of the Council members and,
instead of compromising, she cut herself off from the representative
body which she had worked for so long to establish. *The Nursing
Times* (8 Apr 1922) commented at the time

> The nursing profession has suffered much from those whose public spir-
> itedness has a strong flavour of personal antagonism to other leaders in
> the same good cause.

Mrs Fenwick was always an optimist and despite the fact that, in her opinion, nurses constantly demonstrated their lack of foresight and political awareness, she never lost interest in their professional development.

Her influence as editor of, and frequent contributor to the *British Journal of Nursing* for over 50 years, was as important as her professional activities. Through the journal, which was distributed in all English-speaking countries, she contributed to the development of professional nursing organisations in many countries. She enjoyed writing and editing her journal, and continued the work for 53 years, almost until her death. She wrote as she spoke, with directness and conviction. Her journal was often a *cri de cœur*, warning nurses that their professional independence was threatened, or that the future development of nursing demanded a particular course of action. She was elected president of the Society of Women Journalists from 1910–1911, and represented the society in Westminster Abbey at the coronation of King George V. Her journal survived her by nine years, it ceased publication in 1956, in what would have been the 100th year of her life.

Her husband, Dr Bedford Fenwick, physician to the Hospital for Women, Soho Square, until his retirement, died in October 1939. They had lived apart for many years but he had remained a supporter of all her campaigns on behalf of the nursing profession. They had one child, a son, who became a county court judge and through him, they had two grandsons.

Her greatest achievement was the creation of the International Council of Nurses. She developed the idea of a world-wide organisation of nurses from her experience of the meetings of the International Council of Women. At these meetings she absorbed the optimism of the new century and the belief that women could regenerate the world. These feelings matched her own inclinations and, with her abilities as an orator and as a journalist, she inspired a generation of nurses to realise their part in international peace and progress.

### Sources

**St Bartholomew's Hospital Archives**
MO1/1–3 Matron's Report Books 1880–1887
MO53/1 Register of Probationers 1877–1895
Papers relating to Ethel Manson

**Royal College of Nursing Archives**
House of Lords Select Committee on Metropolitan Hospitals, minutes of
  evidence, 1890–1892
House of Commons Select Committee on Registration of Nurses, minutes
  of evidence and report, 1904–1905
House of Commons Select Committee on the General Nursing Council,
  report 1925
RCN 4 Papers relating to State Registration
*Nursing Record/British Journal of Nursing*, 1888–1947
*Nurses' Journal*, 1891–1898, 1905–1908
*American Journal of Nursing*, 1901
*Nursing Times*, 1907, 1922, 1925
*The Hospital*, 1916–1917
Breay, Margaret, and Fenwick, E. G., *History of the International Council of
  Nurses*, 1899–1925, Geneva 1931
Hector, Winifred, *The Work of Mrs Bedford Fenwick and the Rise of Professional
  Nursing*, London 1973

 3

# Isla Stewart
## *The Incarnation of Common Sense*
### (1856–1910)

*Matron of St Bartholomew's Hospital, 1887–1910, founder
member of the Royal British Nurses Association, 1887,
founder and first president of the Matrons Council, 1894–1910,
founder and President of the first League of Nurses,
1899–1908, President of the Society for the State Registration
of Trained Nurses, 1907–1910, member of the nursing board
Queen Alexandra's Imperial Military Nursing Service,
1906–1910, Principal Matron, Territorial Force Nursing
Service, 1908–1910, author of nursing text book and leading
educationalist.*

ISLA STEWART was born on 25 August, 1856 in Slodahill, Dumfries-shire, Scotland, one of the daughters of John Hope Johnstone Stewart, a soldier and a journalist as well as a fellow of the Scottish Society of Antiquaries. Although her sisters were sent to school aboard, Isla was educated at home by a governess, and later regretted that she had not had the experience of school life which she believed developed a wider outlook on life. However, she had happy memories of her childhood summers on an island off the coast of Argyllshire and she remained close to her sister, Janet, throughout her life.

In 1879, at the age of 23, she became a special probationer at the Nightingale Training School for Nurses, attached to St Thomas' Hospital, in London. She was inspired to take up nursing by reading the 'Life of Agnes Jones'. The training at St Thomas' in 1879 consisted of one year working in the wards, with the ward sister and staff nurse responsible for training the two or three probationers assigned to their ward. Probationers also received lectures in medical and surgical nursing and basic chemistry and at the end of the year, were examined on these subjects and on their practical work. The Nightingale probationers lived under the rule of the Home Sister and the Matron. In 1879 the matron was Mrs Wardroper. She had been matron of St Thomas' since 1854 and Superintendent of the Nightingale Training School since its foundation in 1860. Miss Stewart recalled how Mrs Wardroper struck terror into the hearts of probationers, 'she had a firm belief in the wickedness which lies at the heart of all probationers'. The Home Sister she remembered as 'narrow-minded and hard'.

After nine months as a probationer, Miss Stewart was appointed a sister of Alexandra Ward, a woman's surgical ward of 20 beds. Many years later, looking back, she remarked that she was ill-equipped for the post with only nine months experience. 'After I had been a Sister for a couple of years I realised how much I had learned as a Sister at the expense of the patients. I do not like to remember how much my inexperience must have cost them'.

The discipline practised at St Thomas' strongly influenced Miss Stewart and for the rest of her life she regarded discipline as an important part of a nurse's training. Her views were also formed by two other aspects of the Nightingale training, the emphasis on practical nursing experience over theoretical instruction, and the important role the moral values of the hospital and the nurses' home played in forming the character of the nurse.

In the spring of 1885, Sir Edmund Hay Currie, Vice Chairman of the Metropolitan Asylums Board (MAB), invited Miss Stewart to become Matron of the smallpox camp set up to cope with the epidemic of 1884–85, at Darenth, near Dartford, Kent. Patients were taken down the Thames to three hospital ships lying at Long-Reach, opposite Purfleet. When convalescent they were transferred to the Darenth camps which were in a field on the side of a chalky hill, a male camp on the high ground and a female camp on the low ground. Each camp contained about 22 tents erected on platforms, comprising staff tents, store huts, discharge and receiving rooms, linen stores, the steward's tent and one for the matron.

Miss Stewart described the situation when she arrived as 'chaos'. The camps had been thrown-up quickly to meet the emergency and there were 1,800 patients and a nursing staff of several hundred, male and female, all living in tents. In wet weather the chalk became slippery, the wood pavements were covered in a slimy stickiness, and the tent walls dripped. In particularly bad weather the tent floors were wet, 'nurses and patients looked wet and draggled, with water dropping off their noses' (*The Nursing Record*, 19 Apr 1888, p. 30).

When the camps closed in 1886, special record was made of Miss Stewart's services and the faithful discharge of her duties. Despite terrible conditions and the lack of trained nurses, she had reorganised the nursing to achieve a high standard. The nature of the disease combined with the isolated position of the camps and the fact that the work was temporary, did not attract trained nurses. Miss Stewart gained valuable experience from the work and for the rest of her life recalled that Sir Edmund's dictionary had not contained the word 'impossible', and 'he helped me to erase it from mine, for which I have every reason to thank him'.

After a few months rest at home, she began her new job as Matron of the Eastern Fever Hospital, Homerton, East London. This hospital was also run by the MAB and, although she remained only a year in this post, she considered her two years' employment with the MAB was the best possible school for matrons. At Homerton she worked hard to raise the status of the nursing staff, insisting on high standards and introducing trained nurses for the first time.

In 1887, at the age of 30, Miss Stewart applied for 'the biggest appointment in the nursing world', the matronship of St Bartholomew's Hospital. The post had become vacant by the resignation of Ethel Manson on her marriage to Dr Bedford Fenwick. Miss Stewart was appointed and took up the position in June 1887. In her two previous posts, at Darenth and Homerton, she had reorganised the nursing departments on modern lines, at St Bartholomew's she faced the challenge of a well-organised nursing department with a staff of 143, and a training school with a reputation that put it among the best in the world.

## Matron of St Bartholomew's Hospital

The training school had been reorganised by Miss Manson between 1880 and 1887. The period of training was three years and, besides practical work in the wards, the probationers received lectures on medical and surgical nursing from members of the medical staff of the hospital. Six years after her appointment, Miss Stewart revised the regulations of the training school as follows:

> The age of probationers on appointment must be between 23 and 35. They must produce evidence of good health, moral character, and general fitness of disposition and temperament for the duties of a sick nurse.
>
> They must engage to serve at the hospital for a term of four years, three years as probationers, and one year (after obtaining their certificate) as Staff Nurses.

The times for the commencement of the term of training are 1st February, 1st May, 1st August and 1st November, but no one can be appointed at those times unless she has previously been in the hospital on trial for at least a month.

The hospital shall make the following quarterly payments; £2 during the first year, £3 during the second year, £5 during the third year, and £7 10s (£30 p.a.) during the fourth year.

They must provide, at their own cost, all requisite uniform for wear during the time they are on trial for probationership. In the event of their being appointed probationers, after their period of trial, a certain supply of dresses, caps and aprons will be allowed them by the hospital during the remainder of their term of service. They will be required to wear this uniform at all times when they are in the hospital.

They will be lodged and boarded within the hospital. At the end of their first year, they will be required to pass an examination in the subjects covered in the year. If they pass the examination, and are otherwise efficient, they will be employed as Staff Probationers for the remainder of the three years. During the second and third year of training, they will receive lectures in medical and surgical nursing from members of the hospital staff. At the end of the third year, they will be examined on their knowledge of nursing.

They will be subject to dismissal at any time for misconduct, inefficiency or repeated neglect of duty. Failure to pass the examination at the end of the first year will be considered a sufficient cause for the termination of a probationer's contract.

At the end of the third year a certificate of competency as nurses will be awarded to those who, besides having discharged their ward duties efficiently, have passed both examinations and conducted themselves in all respects to the satisfaction of the hospital authorities.

At the end of a year after obtaining their certificate they will be free to quit the hospital. By arrangement they may remain in the service of the hospital as Staff Nurses after that time; and they will be paid £35 p.a. for the first year, and £40 p.a. subsequently.

Before being admitted on trial, applicants must undergo a medical examination and, as proof of general education and intelligence, pass an examination in elementary anatomy, physiology and science.

St Bartholomew's Hospital Records HA/3/20, 7 Dec 1893

Miss Stewart also recommended that in future probationers should not attend the lectures on medical and surgical nursing in their first six months and instead should attend classes in basic nursing practice. These classes would be given by the Matron and would include an introduction to medicines and terms in general use, the principles of invalid cookery, the preparation of patients for operations, the administration of enemata, in addition to the basic skills of washing patients in bed and bedmaking.

The new training scheme came into operation at the beginning of 1894 and remained basically unchanged for 12 years. During that time the medical council of the hospital made one recommendation, that probationers should not be put on night duty during their first six months. Miss Stewart disagreed, she thought that it was more acceptable for probationers' periods of night duty to be limited to three months twice in their first year, with intervals of three months day duty, than they should be on night duty for six months continuously. She recommended that the subject of bacteriology and its practical bearing on surgical nursing should be included in the training, in view of the increasing importance of asepsis in surgery. The hospital pathologist drew up a course of eight lectures which was included in the instruction of the third year probationers.

In October 1899 Miss Stewart published, with Dr H. E. Cuff, Medical Superintendent of the North Eastern Fever Hospital, Tottenham, the first volume of a nursing text book, *Practical Nursing*. The aim of the book was to provide a description of the practical part of a nurse's work, with a rationale for carrying out the treatment ordered. In the first chapter, 'Nursing As A Profession', Miss Stewart described the state of the profession's development and outlined the need for a minimum standard of education, a definite period of training and centralised examinations. She recommended the use of preliminary training schools as the most efficient way of selecting probationers and proposed the idea of a central training school or home, from which hospitals could choose their own probationers. A continuation volume was published in 1903 and described the practical nursing of individual diseases. The work was well received and was reprinted six times before the second edition was published in 1909. Miss Stewart had begun work on a third edition before her death, in 1910, but the work was completed by Miss Cutler, Assistant Matron of St Bartholomew's Hospital, and published in 1911.

By 1905 Miss Stewart felt that the training scheme needed updating to take account of the developments in medicine and surgery. A sub-committee was appointed to consider her revised syllabus, and in January 1906 the new scheme was introduced. The major differences were the introduction of a six week preliminary training course and a more detailed syllabus of lectures for each year. In the preliminary period candidates were instructed in elementary anatomy, basic nursing care and invalid cookery. They were examined in the various subjects at the end of the six weeks, and those who passed transferred to the nursing staff on three months' trial. After the trial period, if their health remained good, and their work satisfactory, their appointment as a probationer was confirmed.

In the first year of training, probationers attended 18 classes on practical nursing, given by the matron and the sisters, and 14 classes on elementary anatomy and physiology, given by a qualified person.

At the end of the year the probationers were examined, those who passed became staff probationers, those who failed were dismissed. During the second year, they attended 16 lectures on medical nursing and 16 lectures on surgical nursing.

In the third year, probationers attended nine lectures on elementary bacteriology, five classes of practical instruction in the nursing of gynaecological cases and three in the nursing of ophthalmic cases, and later classes on the work of the operating theatre nurse were introduced. At the end of the third year probationers were examined and a certificate of efficiency awarded to those who passed. Those who did not pass were allowed to remain in the service of the hospital for a further six months and were then re-examined.

On completion of three years' training the trained nurse had to remain on the hospital staff for a further year. This last year provided the nurse with the invaluable experience of being given responsibility and standing on her own. It was also of benefit to the hospital as it ensured that there were fully trained nurses in the wards. This was officially acknowledged in 1908, when the hospital authorities decided that in future the nurses' certificates would be awarded at the end of their fourth year of service. A nurse who had completed her four year contract was eligible to join the Private Nursing Department of the hospital. The working conditions of the private nurses were very attractive and in 1909 were further improved when the hospital authorities allowed the nurse to take her own fee and to pay the hospital 7½ per cent, instead of the hospital taking the fee and paying the nurse a salary. Between cases the nurses could lodge and board at the hospital for a small weekly sum.

During the 23 years of Miss Stewart's matronship of St Bartholomew's the working conditions of the nurses steadily improved. The nursing staff increased from 143 in 1887, to 250 in 1910, allowing Miss Stewart to reduce the hours worked by the nurses and to increase their annual holidays from two to three weeks. In 1890, when six nurses were added to the staff, it was possible for the first time to have two nurses in each ward at night. Two years later, the nursing staff was increased to 172, and additional ward assistants were taken on to allow two to each ward. The hours of duty were from 7 am to 8 pm, with off-duty organised on a four-weekly cycle.

In 1891 the Treasurers and Almoners Committee of the hospital decided that there should be a minimum of 36 certificated nurses on the staff in addition to the probationers but it proved impossible to retain this number after they had completed their four year contract. An increase in the nurses' salary was authorised, £30 per annum in

*Fig 6. Isla Stewart, Matron of St Bartholomew's Hospital with her staff nurses, 1907*

their fourth year, £35 in the fifth year, and £40 in the sixth and subsequent years of service. An extra week's annual holiday between the first of January and the first of May was added for the senior nursing staff in 1894.

By 1896 the nursing staff numbered 205, made up of 71 first year probationers, 107 staff nurses and staff probationers (second and third year), and 27 paying probationers. In 1905 another 30 nurses were added and, in 1907, a further 14 were necessary to staff the new out-patients department and special departments. By 1909, the total was 250 nurses and the hours worked on average were nine hours a day with one whole day and one half day off on alternate weeks.

The last change which Miss Stewart made to the organisation of the nursing department reflected the increase in the amount of administrative work associated with the matronship of a large hospital. This was the appointment of a Matron's Office Sister. Formerly these duties had been performed by the three night superintendents. Under the new structure, the two night superintendents and the Matron's Office Sister had equal standing. Despite all the improvements which Miss Stewart achieved, she did not live to see the building of a nurses' home. She regretted that the nurses lacked proper classrooms for their lectures, and she felt that their living quarters were not up to the standard provided at other leading London hospitals. In 1903 the rebuilding programme included plans for a nurses' home and though Miss Stewart and the nurses' league raised money towards the building fund, the foundation stone was not laid until 1921.

## The Wider World of Nursing Politics

Throughout her matronship of St Bartholomew's, Miss Stewart played a prominent role in national and international nursing politics. She and her close friend Ethel Fenwick (see chapter two) shared the belief that a system of state registration for nurses was needed. Her own priority was to raise the standard of nurse training and she believed that a minimum standard would only be achieved with statutory backing.

Miss Stewart was one of the seven matrons present at Mrs Fenwick's house in November 1887 when the decision to establish the British Nurses' Association (BNA) was made. During the first five years of its existence, she was one of the most active members but when the BNA moved away from the aims of its founders, she withdrew and eventually resigned in 1896.

From 1894, her energies were directed into the work of the Matrons' Council, which was formed as a result of a meeting she and Ethel Fenwick called of several like-minded matrons. The new association would provide its members with a venue for discussion and enable them to speak with one voice. After the initial meeting in May, 1894, they organsed a meeting of approximately 100 matrons in London in July, and it was resolved to form the Matrons' Council. The objectives were to hold conferences and meetings and to work for the introduction of a uniform system of education, examination, certification and state registration for nurses in British hospitals.

At the first meeting, held in the Medical Society's Rooms in Chandos Street, in November 1895, Isla Stewart gave a paper on 'A uniform curriculum of education for nurses'. The Matrons' Council had sent out a questionnaire on the subject containing 12 questions about nurse education and training. The questions covered such issues as the advantage of a uniform curriculum of training for all hospitals, the benefits of preliminary training, the content of the preliminary training, how many years' training were required, the theoretical subjects to be taught, how many examinations were necesary during the training period, the conduct of examinations, the form certificates should take, and whether nurses should pay for their training.

Miss Stewart summarised the replies, which included one from Miss Nightingale and gave her own opinion on each question. She was not in favour of a uniform curriculum, she thought that a minimum standard over a uniform period of training would allow each school to work up to the standard which suited it best. The benefits of a preliminary training scheme were indisputable and she thought the practice of the Matron selecting probationers after a short personal interview was inefficient and largely responsible for the high percentage of probationers who did not finish their training. On the question of the final examination, Miss Stewart said, 'We must all agree that the most essential qualities of a nurse are just those which cannot be proved by examinations, and can only be known to those who are able by constant observation to see that the candidate possesses them' (*The Nursing Record*, 16 Nov 1895 p. 349). She accepted that a central examining body was a necessary evil and observed, 'In all reforms something that was good in the old system is lost, and something that is not desirable is gained in the new'. She thought that nursing as a whole would be brought up to a higher level by the introduction of a standard examination and it would make the profession take the training and education of nurses more seriously.

At the summer meeting of the Matrons' Council, in June 1896, Miss Stewart read a paper on 'The Training School', in which she outlined what she considered to be the principal elements of a successful school. These were the method of selecting probationers, the quality of the teaching, and the content of the syllabus. On the subject of teachers, she emphasised the importance of properly qualified instructors and the need for sisters to have more than a year's experience after qualifying before taking on teaching commitments. Regarding the syllabus, she reiterated the scheme she put forward at the spring conference – mastery of the technical side of nursing in the first year by working on the wards, with some instruction on theory and practice, and in the second and third year the acquisition of experience along with lectures on the theory of medicine and related subjects.

The Matrons' Council held its first annual conference in June 1898, at which Miss Stewart was the chairman. It was attended by matrons from all over the country and included papers on a matron's duty to her profession, specialisation in nursing, the training of male nurses, the nursing of the middle classes and a practical standard of nursing. The following year, the annual conference was held in July to coincide with the meeting of the International Council of Women (ICW) in London.

The Matrons' Council had affiliated to the National Union of Women Workers, which acted as the National Council of Women in Britain. Ethel Fenwick was a member of the organising committee for the ICW congress and successfully pleaded, on behalf of the Matrons' Council, for the inclusion of a nursing section. The session occupied one day, with papers by visiting nurses from America, the Cape Colony and New Zealand. That evening the Matrons' Council hosted a banquet at the Criterion Restaurant for over 100 guests, presided over by Miss Stewart. All the foreign nurse delegates were invited and the guest of honour was Mrs May Wright Sewall, the President of the ICW.

The Matrons' Council held its annual conference the day after the nursing session of the ICW congress. The foreign nurse delegates were invited to attend and Miss Stewart gave a paper on 'Discipline in Training', emphasising the importance of a strict discipline during training to provide the nurse with the necessary self-restraint and reserve to carry her creditably through life. At this meeting Ethel Fenwick proposed her scheme for the formation of an International Council of Nurses (ICN) and her proposal was enthusiastically received. Miss Stewart's own enthusiasm and support were evident from the start and she called a meeting at her house to discuss what steps were necessary to establish the ICN (the story of the beginning of the ICN forms part of chapter two).

Miss Stewart was influenced by the American nurses' professional organisation and, in August 1899, she called a meeting at St Bartholomew's to discuss the formation of an association of the trained nurses of the hospital. Following the custom of schools and universities in America, the graduates of the different nurse training schools had formed themselves into post-graduate associations, known as alumnae associations. The first one was founded in 1889 and by 1897 almost every training school in the states had one. The purpose of the associations was professional, to provide trained nurses with an organisation for post-graduate education, benevolent aid, a headquarters and a club and also providing a network for the formation of a national federation of nurses.

A provisional committee was appointed and circulars were sent to the 400 past pupils announcing the formation of the League of St Bartholomew's Nurses. The objectives of the league were to encourage the members to strive for a high standard of work and conduct, the mutual help and pleasure of the members, and the establishment of a benevolent fund.

The inaugural meeting was held on 4 December, 1899, in the Great Hall of the hospital, the first time that this historic hall had been used by the nurses for professional purposes. By that date the membership of the league had reached over 225. Miss Stewart was elected president and, in her presidential address, reminded the members of the responsibility and power which they now possessed as the first society of certificated nurses attached to a training school in Britain. The opinion of the league could be used to influence matters affecting the nursing profession. She asked members to decide whether they were in favour of state registration for nurses, and if they decided that they were, then they should be prepared to work for it. A sub-committee, of which Miss Stewart was a member, was appointed to produce the League News which became a twice yearly publication, the first issue appearing in May 1900.

The Matrons' Council wrote, in February 1900, to the various government departments concerned with nursing the sick, about the necessity for reorganising these departments on modern and professional lines. The memorandum referred to the inevitable reorganisation of the army medical services in the aftermath of the Boer war and recommended that the government's nursing departments be placed under the control of a fully trained and experienced nursing officer. Criticism was made of the haphazard way 600 nurses had been shipped off to South Africa with no matron-in-chief and no central office at the Cape.

In April the following year, 1901, as President of the Council, Miss Stewart headed a deputation to the War Office. They presented a report to Lord Raglan, Under-Secretary of State for War, setting out the reforms required in the army nursing service. The principal reform was the formation of an army nursing department, under the War Office, with a trained superintendent of nursing in charge, who would be responsible for the members of the Nursing Service. Also recommended was the organisation of an Army Nursing Service Reserve as an integral part of the service, controlled by the War Office, which they hoped would eliminate the involvement of philanthropy and lay control in the army nursing services.

A Departmental Committee was appointed in July 1901, to consider the future organisation of the army medical services and when the report of the committee was published, three months later, it incorporated the principal recommendations made by the Matrons' Council. These were, the formation of a nursing department, the appointment of a Nursing Superintendent to head the department, the appointment of staff nurses, and the formation of an Army Nursing Service Reserve under professional control. The new nursing service, to be known as Queen Alexandra's Imperial Military Nursing Service, was set up in 1902. Four years later Miss Stewart was appointed a member of the Army Nursing Board, the advisory body to the new nursing service. Her appointment was regarded by the pro-registrationists as an achievement, and by the opponents of registration for nurses as a set-back.

On 29 August, 1901, Miss Stewart sailed from London to attend the first congress of the ICN in Buffalo, New York, where she was to give the opening address. While there she planned to visit major hospitals in the cities of Philadelphia, Baltimore, New York and eastern Canada. Her paper on 'Hospital Administration' outlined the administrative structure of the hospitals in Britain – voluntary, poor law, Local Government Board, and Metropolitan Asylums Board – comparing the size, cost and efficiency of their nursing departments. As president of the Matrons' Council, she attended the meeting of the American Society of Superintendents of Training Schools, held during the Congress, and took part in the discussion.

In April 1904, she called a meeting in London of delegates of the eight nurses' leagues and self-governing nurses' societies then in existence, to discuss the formation of a national council of nurses which could affiliate to the ICN. The meeting appointed a provisional committee to represent Britain and decided that when the committee represented 3000 nurses a National Council of Nurses would be established.

Miss Stewart attended the congress of the ICN, held in Berlin in June 1904, as a delegate of the Matrons' Council. The congress was timed to coincide with the International Council of Women's Congress in Berlin. The ICW congress lasted for a week, and was divided into four sections, one dealing with women's professions and industries, and including a session on the education of nurses. Miss Stewart was one of the speakers and she reviewed her 17 years as matron of St Bartholomew's and the changes which she had seen in candidates coming into the training school. She commented on the lack of discipline in the home, compared with her youth, which meant that girls entering the hospital as probationers were unaccustomed to discipline and rebelled against it. However, she did not say this change was for the worse

I have a sincere belief in the progress and gradual perfecting of human nature. I believe that, when time has helped to remove the disadvantages, this greater freedom will produce greater women, and even now the women who are fully trained are not in any way behind former generations either in technical skill, tenderness of treatment, or ethical standard, but they are certainly more difficult to train and teach in many ways.

*British Journal of Nursing*, 20 Aug 1904, p. 147

She outlined the training she considered necessary to produce a good nurse and emphasised the importance of having sisters in the wards who were interested in the education and progress of the nurses under them. Her conclusion was that a good training should produce a self-reliant, open-minded nurse, with sufficient technical knowledge to practice efficiently.

## Society for the State Registration of Nurses

At the quarterly meeting of the Matrons' Council in May 1902, the final report of its registration sub-committee was received, after which the work on registration was handed over to the Society for the State Registration of Trained Nurses. The first meeting of the new society was held following the business meeting of the Matrons' Council. The launch of the Society had been announced in *The Nursing Record* and within a week 209 applications for membership had been received. By the date of the first meeting there were 461 members.

The president-elect, Louisa Stevenson, a member of the Board of Management of the Royal Infirmary, Edinburgh, and of the Council of the Scottish Branch of Queen Victoria's Jubilee Institute, was unable to attend and in her absence Miss Stewart presided. The meeting adopted a constitution and elected officers, with Isla Stewart as Senior Vice President. In the afternoon, a public meeting in favour of state registration was held in Morley Hall with Miss Stewart presiding and delivering an address on the benefits of state registration.

In 1904 the Society introduced a Bill in the House of Commons, through the support of Dr Farquharson, MP for West Aberdeenshire. This was the first Bill for state registration and had been drafted by Dr and Mrs Bedford Fenwick and Isla Stewart. The Matrons' Council called for the appointment of a Select Committee of the House of Commons to inquire into the nursing question, as a preliminary to legislation. A Select Committee was appointed and Miss Stewart was called to give evidence. Her evidence to the committee restated her views, often expressed, on the necessity for the introduction of a standard of training which would specify the length of training, the content of training and the system of examination and certification. Asked if she approved of allowing nurses to obtain certificates for training in special branches of nursing, she replied that she favoured specialisation only as a post-graduate qualification, believing as she did that all nurses should receive the same basic training before specialising.

The Select Committee were concerned that registration would cause a shortage of nurses, but Miss Stewart declared that on the contrary, more women would be attracted into nursing by giving it professional status. The committee asked what effect she thought registration would have on cottage nurses. Miss Stewart replied that registration would not effect them as they were not nurses. Cottage nurses were usually midwives with a little knowledge of nursing, who were employed by nursing associations to nurse poor people in their homes and do housework where the mother was ill. The Select Committee heard evidence from 33 people, members of the medical and nursing professions and lay people and reported in favour of registration.

In the magazine _Nineteenth Century and After_, Miss Stewart defended the case for a minimum training of three years as the qualification of a trained nurse. The article was in reply to one by Eva Lückes, Matron of the London Hospital, who maintained that a nurse with two years' experience in the London Hospital was as competent as a nurse with three years' in any other hospital. Miss Lückes rejected the argument that nurses should have a standard training and examination, considering this placed too great an emphasis on examinations and the best nurses were often the ones who performed badly in examinations. Miss Stewart replied

> Technical skill alone will make a nurse, but when combined with sympathy, and the charm of gracious manners, it makes the great nurse . . . the untrained stupid woman, who cannot pass examinations, is not always kindly – indeed, she is much less likely to be so than her highly-trained, well-disciplined sister.
>
> _British Journal of Nursing_, 4 Jun 1904, p. 452

In 1905, a scheme to establish a 'Society for Promoting the Higher Education and Training of Nurses', was proposed by Sir Henry Burdett, Cosmo Bonsor, Treasurer of Guy's Hospital, and five other city financiers involved in hospital management. The Matrons's Council and the Society for the State Registration of Trained Nurses held an emergency meeting to protest against the scheme which they saw as a threat to their objectives. Isla Stewart spoke out strongly at the meeting that a voluntary system of registration would deny nurses statutory recognition and would place the supervision and government of the profession in the hands of a self-appointed council.

The promoters of the scheme applied to the Board of Trade for a licence to incorporate without using the word 'limited' and due to the protests, the Board of Trade decided to hold a hearing. Isla Stewart, representing the Matrons' Council and the League of St

Bartholomew's Hospital Nurses, stated the reasons for opposition. The scheme made no provision for direct representation of nurses on the governing body, and she added that the government of the nursing profession was not a philanthropic exercise. In defence of the scheme, the promoters said they would fade into the background once the society was established, and that the council of the society would consist of trained nurses and medical men. Rather than being opposed to state registration they were neutral, and if Parliament passed a Nurses' Registration Act, they would hand over their work to the state. Their hope was to set up the machinery which would eventually lead to state registration. Only two matrons openly supported the scheme, Miss Swift, matron of Guy's Hospital (see chapter seven) and Miss Wood, former Lady Superintendent of the Hospital for Sick Children, Great Ormond Street. It was opposed by all the existing nurses' associations, and in the event the Board of Trade refused the licence.

At a meeting of the Matrons' Council in November 1905, Miss Stewart gave a paper on 'The Twentieth Century Matron'. She reviewed the changes she had seen among matrons and probationers in 30 years of hospital work and compared the matrons of the present day with those of her youth. Speaking of her first matron, Mrs Wardroper at St Thomas's Hospital, she said

> The matrons of those days were hard, stern women who had few weaknesses, though they were open to the flattery of fear. They ruled well with an iron hand, and there was no pretence of a velvet glove.
>
> *British Journal of Nursing*, 11 Nov 1905, p. 392

The qualities of a good matron she considered were loyalty, justice, a sense of proportion, a moral standard, and professional responsibility. To expect loyalty from her staff a matron must be loyal to them and to her superiors. By exercising unfailing justice she would be rewarded with the confidence of her nurses, but not with popularity. A sense of proportion was the most difficult quality for a matron to develop as she was used to deference and 'apt to think herself a little god'. The balance was in the ability to see each person and each event, including herself, as they stand in relation to each other, and as they might appear through the wrong end of a telescope. This could only be acquired by going outside the hospital and mixing with people of different and larger interests. By always doing what is right, because it is right, a matron will be able to maintain a moral and ethical standard among her staff. And finally, a matron has the responsibility of imparting to her nurses an awareness of their duty to their fellow nurses and pride in the membership of their profession.

The National Council of Nurses organised a nursing exhibition and conference in St George's Hall, Berkeley Square, London, in November 1906. Miss Stewart chaired the first session which was on the care of the consumptive. On the second day, Miss Stewart gave a talk about nurses' leagues and their value as a professional organisation. By forming professional associations, nurses were able to cooperate for their mutual benefit. The League of St Bartholomew's Hospital Nurses had recently appointed a medical man to give postgraduate lectures to the members. By the federation of the different leagues, all over the country, a national council of nurses could be formed and, through affiliation with the ICN, the national councils of trained nurses all over the world became members of the same professional organisation.

With Mrs Fenwick, Miss Stewart attended the 1907 ICN meeting in Paris, held from 18–22 June. She presided at one session on professional organisations and at another gave a paper on 'The Training of the Nurse in the Wards, and the Position and Duties of the Matron'. She once again stressed the greater importance of the probationer's practical work in the wards over the theoretical part of her training, a lesson she had learnt during her own training at the Nightingale School. To produce the best nurses, she said, experienced sisters are needed who are fully trained and able to teach; probationers who are intelligent, have good health, a good education, and good manners; and a systematic training which teaches obedience, punctuality, careful observation and accurate reporting. The duties of the matron include the domestic arrangements of the hospital, office work, and responsibility for the training of probationers. Her first duty is the efficient running of the hospital, but her biggest responsibility is the training of the nurses.

Due to ill-health, Miss Stewart spent several months in Italy at the beginning of 1908. Upon her return she was greeted by tributes from colleagues to mark her twenty-first anniversary as matron. On 27 June, the day she had started at St Bartholomew's in 1887, she attended her last meeting as president of the League of St Bartholomew's Nurses. She had announced her intention to resign as she did not want the office of president of the league to become synonymous with the office of matron of the hospital and, as the first nurses' league in the country, she wished to set a good example. She received a standing ovation when she entered the room, and later she was appointed a Vice-President of the League. After the meeting, the members adjourned to the Great Hall for a celebration and while the

Blue Austrian Band played 'For She's A Jolly Good Fellow', she was presented with bouquets of flowers and gifts. To mark the occasion the Matrons' Council held a banquet for 200 guests in the Gaiety Restaurant. She was presented with an illuminated address in appreciation of her public work and telegrams and bouquets were received from all over the world. André Mesureur, Chef du Cabinet du Directeur de l'Assistance Publique, Paris, was a guest and presented her with a special medal in recognition of her work on behalf of professional nursing everywhere. Ethel Fenwick was chairman of the proceedings and made a speech in honour of her friend.

In response to the speeches and toasts, Miss Stewart, whose sister Janet was seated beside her, said that it was a very special evening for her, the evening of her life. She looked back happily over her life as a nurse, and commented that the charm of a nurse's life was its acute human interest, especially so for a matron. She dealt mainly with the young, and in the training of the probationers, in watching their development, the Matron received her chief pleasure. She noted the changes she had seen in nursing over the years but was optimistic about the future of the profession, and she looked forward to the time when the most important branch of nursing would develop, the prevention of disease.

The National Council of Nurses of Great Britain and Ireland invited the ICN to hold its 1909 meeting in London. It took place in July, in the Church House, Westminster, and was opened by Miss Stewart. The meeting of the ICN was followed by a four day public congress. The social functions associated with the congress included a reception at St Bartholomew's Hospital for over 400 nurses and a banquet for 180 guests in the Gaiety Restaurant. At the banquet, Mrs Fenwick, as the president of the national council of the host country, made a speech charting the growth of the movement for state registration since the founding of the ICN ten years previously. She paid tribute to the work of Miss Stewart on behalf of the cause, saying that she had shown more courage and kindness than any other matron in the country. Her contribution to professional nursing at an international level was acknowledged in another speech by André Mesureur. Since 1906 pupils from the Salpêtrière, Paris, had been coming to work for short periods at St Bartholomew's Hospital, to gain experience of English standards of nursing. He presented silver medals to Miss Stewart and Miss Cutler, her Assistant Matron, in appreciation of their work.

One of the speakers at the congress was Mrs Garrett Fawcett of the International Women's Suffrage Alliance. She spoke of the mutual interests of the ICN and the International Women's Suffrage Alliance,

Fig 7. *Congress of the International Council of Nurses, London, 1909, Caxton Hall; Miss Stewart in the chair, speaker Mr Haldane, Secretary of State for War*

both aimed at elevating the status of women, and the congress passed a resolution in favour of women's suffrage. The main speaker at the conference was the Secretary of State for War, R. B. Haldane, who spoke on the role of the nurse in the newly established Territorial Force Nursing Service (TFNS), the object of which was to create a nation under arms, not for aggression but for its own defence, and a corps of trained nurses was an integral part of this organisation. Miss Stewart chaired the session at which Mr Haldane addressed the Congress and had to contend with repeated interruptions by suffragettes and their removal from the hall.

Miss Stewart took part in the discussion following Mr Haldane's speech, speaking as a member of the Army Nursing Board and as a Principal Matron of the Territorial Force Nursing Service. She had been appointed Principal Matron of the No. 1 General Hospital of the TFNS for the City and County of London in 1908. The medical staff of this hospital were all from St Bartholomew's and Miss Stewart was asked if it would be possible for all the nursing staff to be St Bartholomew's nurses. The actual number of nurses which would be called up to staff the hospital was 92, but it was necessary to enroll a larger number to allow for eventualities. Since it was impossible to withdraw such a large number of nurses from the staff at one time, she called on the League for volunteers, and the response was immediate.

## Illness and Death

During the second half of 1909, Miss Stewart's health was failing. Her last public appearance was at a conference on 12 February, 1910, to discuss the Bill for state registration. Although much weakened by her illness, an impartial observer recalled that she dominated the meeting through her patience, dignity and self-control. She went to Chilworth, Surrey, with Ethel Fenwick for a rest at the beginning of March, 1910, and died a few days later, on 6 March.

Her body was brought back to St Bartholomew's and laid in the mortuary chapel where the sisters kept a vigil for two days and nights. Then in procession they accompanied her coffin to Euston Station, from which it was taken by train to Moffat, Dumfriesshire, where the funeral took place on 10 March in the small Episcopal Church. The Prince of Wales sent his condolences to the governors of St Bartholomew's, he said he had known Miss Stewart for several years and realised what a great power for good she was, not only in the administration but as a personal influence in the hospital. The Queen sent the badge of the TFNS to her sister Janet Stewart, which she would have presented to Miss Stewart the following week, with a letter of appreciation of her work for the service.

Memorial services were held at St Bartholomew's and at Chilworth. The parish church of the hospital, St Bartholomew's the Less, was too small to accommodate all those who wished to attend and the service was held in St Bartholomew the Great, West Smithfield. One side of the church was reserved for the hospital nursing staff and the service was attended by Lord Sandhurst, Treasurer of the Hospital, several of the governors, the medical and surgical staff, members of the civil staff, the late Lord Mayor of London, and almost all the leading figures of the nursing profession in Britain and representatives of the profession abroad.

In her will Miss Stewart left £1,400 to set up an educational grant for the benefit of St Bartholomew's nurses. The League and the societies with which she was connected decided that a suitable memorial would be an educational bursary for nurses undertaking postgraduate studies. The first recipient was Mary Rundle, a St Bartholomew's trained nurse, who chose to go to Teachers College, Columbia University, New York, in 1910, to study hospital economics and teaching methods under Adelaide Nutting. Miss Rundle later became the first secretary of the College of Nursing in 1916.

The hospital authorities showed little appreciation of Isla Stewart's work and reputation when they appointed as her successor the Assistant Matron of the London Hospital, Miss Annie McIntosh. Not only was the Matron of the London Hospital, Miss Lückes, the leading opponent of state registration but Miss McIntosh had also trained at the London where a two year training scheme was still in practice. The appointment aroused bitter feelings among all St Bartholomew's trained nurses and among Miss Stewart's friends and admirers throughout the world. They felt sorrow and indignation that Miss Stewart's life's work on behalf of professional nursing had been disregarded and they felt that the prestige of their training school had been damaged. The League held a meeting to discuss the issue and a resolution was carried unanimously, calling for a public inquiry into the appointment. Mrs Fenwick organised a public meeting and formed the 'Defence of Nursing Standards Committee'. The Committee sent a petition to the governors of the Hospital, pointing out that the new matron's qualifications did not qualify her to become a staff nurse at the hospital where, since 1881, the minimum standard for staff nurses had been three years' training.

When the General Court of Governors met in July, to approve the appointment of the new matron, a resolution referring the appointment back to the Election Committee for reconsideration was proposed. Lord Sandhurst, the Treasurer and President of the Court, successfully squashed the protest by threatening to resign if the resolution was carried. He defended the appointment and dismissed the criticisms as outside interference and the work of one or two troublemakers. Ethel Fenwick felt that the loyalty of the nurses had been betrayed and attributed the contentious appointment to the influence of Sir Henry Burdett, one of the governors of St Bartholomew's. She saw the affair, nevertheless, as the deathblow to the idea that nurses' training was a domestic and private matter of individual hospitals. In future, nurses would need a guarantee that the standard of nursing was not subject to the caprice of a committee.

## Conclusion

As a matron Miss Stewart was efficient and progressive, but it was as an educationalist that her contemporaries admired her. As Superintendent of St Bartholomew's Training School for 23 years, she developed the training scheme to meet the increasing demands of the medical staff, the hospital and the nursing profession. She never stood still from the moment she took over from Ethel Fenwick and welcomed the development of the role of the nurse into specialist areas. The reputation of the training school grew under her supervision, as did her own reputation as a leading nurse educationalist. She was a frequent speaker at conferences, including the congresses of the ICN, and through the printed proceedings of these meetings her ideas were spread abroad. The American Federation of Nurses made her an honorary member and the French government presented her with a special silver medal in recognition of her contribution to nurse training in France.

Her contribution to the development of professional awareness among nurses was as great as her work for the development of nurse training. She recognised the need for nurses to organise themselves into professional associations if they were to achieve professional advancement. To promote this end, she was a founding member of the Royal British Nurses' Association, the Matrons' Council, the League of St Bartholomew's Nurses, the Society for the State Registration of Nurses, the International Council of Nurses and the National Council of Nurses of Great Britain and Ireland, each organisation founded to meet a particular need of the profession between 1887 and 1904.

Her two interests, education and professional organisation, came together in the establishment of the first nurses' league, the League of St Bartholomew's Hospital Nurses. From the start she said to her nurses 'This is not to be for tea-parties alone, it is to be educational for you all, to help you to grasp and aim at the highest interests and ideals for your profession'. She encouraged nurses to take an interest in the world of nursing and always urged them to send delegates to the ICN congresses. She valued the reciprocal training arrangement between the Salpêtrière, Paris, and St Bartholomew's, and worked to establish similar arrangements within Britain.

Her contemporaries always referred to her strength of character, broadmindedness, and good humour. D'Arcy Power, for many years the surgical instructor of the probationary nurses at St Bartholomew's, regarded her as a valued friend and in a tribute to her in the hospital's journal he wrote, 'If I were asked to name the dominant feature in Miss Stewart's character I should say it was her extreme level-headedness, for she appeared to be the incarnation of common sense . . . as her reserve melted away and I came to be considered less as a member of the Staff and more as a friend, a fund of geniality and humour appeared, which the exigencies of her position usually compelled her to keep in the background'.

Her character combined courage, determination and a sense of justice; when she believed something was right, she pursued it. Her determination made her a strong leader and an inspiration to her followers. Her broadmindedness and liberal approach to life made her an excellent teacher. She enjoyed her work, particularly her role as superintendent of the training school, and regretted deeply that she had to give up her classes to probationers in the last year of her life. She was energetic with an impatient disposition, and regarded work as the panacea for all things. Her good humour and charity made her a good matron and counsellor. All of these qualities she displayed in her public work on behalf of state registration of nurses, and she was the only matron of the 12 leading London teaching hospitals to identify publicly with this cause in the early years. Her capacity for diplomacy was a restraining influence on her good friend Ethel Fenwick, who took a more aggressive approach to their opponents and, as the battle for registration became more bitter, Isla Stewart's untimely death was regretted by many.

The nurses who trained and worked with Miss Stewart valued her example and advice. Although she was an old-fashioned disciplinarian in the Nightingale tradition, they remembered her kindness and cheery laugh. In her obituary in the *League News*, Ellen Musson wrote

> Her nature was a buoyant and happy one and she liked other people to be happy and bright. She had little sympathy with those who made much of small ills, which she regarded as inevitable in every walk in life . . . She was a woman with a great heart and a great desire to help the weak and suffering, and was convinced that to make a good Nurse technical skill and trained intelligence must go hand in hand with the Charity that never faileth.

## Sources

**St Bartholomew's Hospital Archives**
MO1/4–5 Matron's Report Books 1887–1889
HA3/18–32 Treasurer and Almoners' Committee Minutes 1889–1910
St Bartholomew's Hospital Nurses' League News, Vol 3 1910

**Royal College of Nursing Archives**
Stewart, Isla, and Cuff, H. E., *Practical Nursing*, Edinburgh 1909
*Isla Stewart: her life, and her influence on the nursing profession*, by R. Cox-
    Davis, 1912 (Historic Pamphlets Collection 3B)
*Nursing Record/British Journal of Nursing*, 1888–1910

# 4

# Sidney Browne
## *A Great Matron-in-Chief*
(1850–1941)

*Army Nursing Service 1883–1902; Matron-in-Chief, Queen Alexandra's Imperial Military Nursing Service, 1902–1906; Matron-in-Chief, Territorial Force Nursing Service, 1910–1920; College of Nursing Council Member 1917–1927, Hon. Treasurer 1918–1927, President 1922–1925, Vice-President 1927–1941; Hon. D.N. Leeds University 1925; International Red Cross Gold Medal 1927; RRC, GBE.*

SIDNEY JANE BROWNE came from a medical family – both her father and brother were doctors. She was born in Kent on 5 January 1850, and her childhood and youth were spent in West Bromwich where she was educated privately. At the age of 28 she went to work as a nurse at the Guest Hospital, Dudley, and less than a year later, entered a formal three year training at the District Hospital, West Bromwich. She decided to become a nurse after attending a course of lectures given by Florence Lees, a Nightingale School nurse who was one of the pioneers of district nursing.

The West Bromwich District Hospital was a small hospital of about 50 beds, with a staff consisting of matron, six sisters and nurses, and five probationers. The training consisted of three years practical work, with lectures given by the house surgeon and the matron. At the end of their training the nurses took an examination and the successful candidates received a certificate. Miss Browne qualified in 1882, and was appointed a staff nurse at St Bartholomew's Hospital, London. The matron of St Bartholomew's at this time was Ethel Manson, the future Mrs Bedford Fenwick (see chapter two).

## Army Nursing Service 1883–1902

Within a year, Sidney Browne had departed to join the army nursing service. She joined as a sister on 1 July 1883, one of approximately 20 attached to the service at the time, and was posted to the Royal Victoria Hospital, Netley, near Southampton. New regulations in 1885, extended the female nursing service to all military hospitals of 100 beds or more, but it was not until 1888 that it became known as the Army Nursing Service. Although it was 20 years since the Crimean war and the work of Florence Nightingale, the position of the nursing sisters in the British army was still ambivalent. In peacetime they were responsible for nursing care in the larger military hospitals at home and overseas, but their small numbers, three or four in each hospital, meant that most nursing work was done by orderlies with the sisters acting as superintendents. The improvements which the sisters could effect were limited, as the orderlies and the patients were under the wardmaster's authority.

In March 1884, during the Egyptian war, Miss Browne was posted to Egypt on active service, and in 1885, she worked for six months on the hospital ship Ganges, nursing the sick and wounded in the Sudan campaign. The sisters' work in the face of great danger was recognised and Miss Browne was awarded the Khedive's Star and the Egyptian Medal and Bar. In August 1885, she was posted to the military hospital at Woolwich, where she remained for two years, receiving excellent reports from her superiors and regular recommendations for promotion. In May 1887, she was posted to Malta as Acting Superintendent Sister of the Cottonera Hospital. She spent five years in Malta before being posted to the Curragh, Ireland, again as Acting Superintendent Sister. After a further two years, she was appointed Superintendent Sister of the Royal Herbert Hospital, Woolwich, taking up the post in August, 1894. Her work continued to receive the highest praise and after five years at Woolwich, she was promoted to Superintendent of the Connaught Hospital, Aldershot. From July to October, 1899, she held this post; then the war in South Africa started and she was ordered on active service.

Miss Brown sailed from Southampton on 4 November 1899, to take up her new post as Superintending Sister of the base hospital at Wynberg, six miles from Cape Town. This was the 3rd General Hospital and consisted of 520 beds and a staff of eight sisters. Nursing sisters were confined to the base hospitals; the nursing at the front and in the clearing stations was done by the medical orderlies. By the end of the year, the medical establishment on service in South Africa was over 3000. Of this number 350 were medical officers and surgeons, 56 were nursing sisters and superintendents, and the remainder were medical orderlies. Reports from the war varied, the official reports said that the sick and wounded were being well cared for, but newspaper reports and the accounts of eye-witnesses, told of scurvy among the prisoners, dysentery and enteric fever in the camps and hospitals, and everywhere a shortage of nurses.

The War Office's handling of the war became a major controversy, particularly the recruitment of nurses. It insisted that nurses volunteering to go to South Africa must be selected from the Army Nursing Reserve. The Reserve had been formed in 1896 to supplement the regular army nursing service, in the event of war the Reserve nurses would replace at home the active service nurses when they were sent abroad. The number of sisters in the Reserve had been fixed at 100, but as the demand for nurses in South Africa grew, the number was increased, and they were asked to volunteer for active service.

In peacetime, the Reserve was the responsibility of a special committee of which Princess Christian was the President. In wartime, it came under the control of the War Office. The selection committee consisted of Princess Christian and several society ladies. The absence of a trained nurse on the committee provoked the nursing profession, and when the committee selected nurses with less than three years' training in preference to more highly trained nurses, the criticism became outspoken. *The Nursing Record* accused the committee of favouring nurses from certain hospitals in which it had an interest, and predicted that the lack of any defined system of selection and training for volunteers, many of whom had no practical experience of army nursing, would result in a wholly inadequate service. The selection of nurses for the Reserve was only part of the much larger problem of the attitude of the War Office to nursing. To meet the shortage of nurses at the front, additional orderlies were drafted from other sections of the army, and as the supply of medical orderlies was exhausted, the bulk of the nursing work was done by untrained orderlies.

At the beginning of 1900, Miss Browne was posted to the base hospital at Rondebosch, where she worked for six months, and then to Springfontein where she remained until 1902. The conditions in the base hospitals were described by some eye-witnesses as worse than the conditions in the field hospitals. The outbreak of typhoid and dysentry had stretched the army medical services beyond an acceptable standard of efficiency, and the average nurse-patient ratio was one sister to 40 patients during the day and one to 180 at night. The shortage of nurses was regarded as a scandal. Not only were there plenty of qualified nurses in the Colony willing to join the

*Fig 8. Sidney Browne (2nd from right) with the Army Nursing Service, South Africa, 1901*

army nursing service, but at home hundreds of trained nurses were eager to go to the war. The British Medical Association's correspondent at the Cape openly criticised the War Office's handling of the situation, and considered the system of employing male orderlies as back-up nurses was obsolete.

Under existing arrangements there was no responsible head of nursing at the Cape, and *The Nursing Record* called for the appointment of a Superintendent who would be responsible for all the nursing staff in South Africa, and would be able to appoint nurses from the pool of existing nurses in the Colony. In the opinion of the journal there were half a dozen Superintending Sisters already at the Cape who could undertake such duties. The advice was not taken by the War Office, although 200 additional trained nurses were taken on in South Africa.

By the summer of 1900 concern about the suffering and disease among the sick and wounded led to the appointment of a Royal Commission to investigate the hospitals in South Africa. The Commission arrived in the Colony in August and took evidence in Cape Town and Bloemfontein. The composition of the Commission was criticised by the nursing profession as it did not include a nurse or a woman, and its methods of investigation were criticised by the medical profession. *The Nursing Record* was certain that the whole demoralising condition of affairs in South African hospitals could be traced to the Army Medical Department which had purposely ignored the professional status of trained nurses.

The Commission's report was published in February 1901, and it was condemned as a 'white wash'. However, it was followed by the appointment, in July, of a Departmental Committee to consider a scheme for the future organisation of the army medical services. The Matrons' Council had previously submitted a memorandum to the War Office outlining a scheme for the establishment of an Army Nursing Department under the control of a nursing board. The Departmental Committee's recommendations included the establishment of a separate nursing department, controlled by an independent nursing board. The following January, the Secretary of State for War appointed a committee to draw up a definite scheme for the army nursing service, and the outcome of this initiative was the establishment of Queen Alexandra's Imperial Military Nursing Service (QAIMNS) and the appointment of Miss Browne as the first Matron-in-Chief of the service.

## Matron-in-Chief, QAIMNS, 1902–1906

Miss Browne was notified of her appointment in South Africa and returned to England in April 1902. For her service in South Africa she was awarded the Royal Red Cross. The new service, called after Queen Alexandra who accepted the office of President, consisted of the Matron-in-Chief, two Principal Matrons, matrons, sisters and staff nurses. A Nursing Board was appointed to be responsible for the service and its composition was one of the most innovative aspects of the new service. It included the matrons of three large civil hospitals with training schools, their presence on the board was to ensure that the organisation of the military hospitals was kept up to date.

The Matron-in-Chief was officially recognised and given offices within the War Office. She was a member of the Nursing Board and had a seat on the Army Medical Board whenever nursing matters were under discussion. She was directly responsible to the Director General of the Royal Army Medical Corps for the efficient organisation of the nursing service in all the military hospitals. Conditions of entry to the service were that candidates should be between the ages of 25 and 35, of British parentage and have a certificate of three years training in a recognised general hospital. Successful applicants had to be well-educated, of good character, and willing to serve a three year contract, subsequently changed to two. The Matron-in-Chief's salary was £250–£300 per annum, with a lodging allowance. The Principal Matrons received £150–£180 per annum, matrons, according to the size of the hospital, £70–£120 and £100–£150, sisters £37 10s–£50, nurses £30–£35, with allowances for board, washing and uniform.

In the first few months after its appointment the Nursing Board drew up regulations for the new service. It was decided that the uniform would be a grey dress with a scarlet cape. One of the most important new duties assigned to the service was the training in nursing and ward work of the orderlies for the Royal Army Medical Corps. Previously this had been the responsibility of the medical services. Miss Browne drew up a three year training scheme, which included lectures and demonstrations to be given by the nursing staff and the medical officers, class examinations and a certificate on completion of training.

The success of the new nursing service depended, to a large extent, on the personality and the abilities of its first Matron-in-Chief. Alfred Keogh, the Director General of the Army Medical Services, had worked with Sidney Browne in South Africa when he was Commanding Officer and she the Matron of the first General Hospital. His admiration for her work and character meant that he had no hesitation in selecting Miss Browne as the first Matron-in-Chief of the new service, and explains how the War Office came to appoint a woman who held advanced ideas about the nursing profession.

Miss Browne had been a member of the Royal British Nurses' Association since 1890, and a founder member of the Matrons' Council in 1894, both organisations which stood for the state registration of nurses. In her new post she worked for the establishment of the army nursing service on professional lines, and within months of her appointment, made a special appeal for all the members of the service to hold officer rank. In August 1902, she wrote to General Keogh, asking him to champion the cause of the nursing corps, and not to put the non-commissioned men on the same footing or over the nurses.

Queen Alexandra took a personal interest in the new nursing service and supported Miss Browne's efforts to give the service a high social standing. When new accommodation was being built for the nurses at the military hospital, Millbank, Westminster, the Queen rejected the plans on the grounds that the accommodation was not of a standard suitable for the rank of officer. She contributed a large sum of her own money to ensure that the new quarters were appropriate.

The structure of the service was designed to encourage qualified nurses to join as staff nurses and work their way up to matron. The responsibilities of both nurses and sisters were similar to those in large civil hospitals with administrative and educational duties. In addition, the service offered the attraction of foreign postings and active service in war time. In 1906, the Nursing Board introduced a new system for the promotion of sisters, in future they would be required to take an examination before promotion to the rank of matron. After five years' service all sisters could volunteer for the examination and a special two months course of instruction in the duties of a matron was started. This development was in line with professional nursing opinion at the time as the Matrons' Council had tried to start a similar course in 1899 for nurses who wished to prepare themselves for the position of matron.

Miss Browne was 55 years old in 1906, and in accordance with army regulations she retired. When she joined in 1883 the service had consisted of 20 nurses, in 1902 when she was appointed Matron-in-Chief it had risen to 87, and when she retired its strength was over 400. The achievements of Sidney Browne and the Nursing Board were not without their critics. The old guard of the Royal Army Medical Corps objected to the social status required for entry to QAIMNS and retained its preference for orderlies over nursing sisters. They regretted the end of the traditional system of training orderlies, and considered the new training, given by the sisters, was of too civilian a nature. Another criticism concerned the large increase in the size of the service, this was justified by the increased duties required of the sisters and also the fact that the ratio of nurses to patients was still lower than in most civil hospitals. These criticisms led to a question in parliament in 1906, when the Secretary of State for War, R. B. Haldane, readily defended the nursing service.

A general feeling prevailed that Miss Browne's retirement was unfortunately early for the new nursing service. Her long experience of army nursing, her administrative skills and her ability to get on with people, made her particularly qualified for the post. She was, moreover, in excellent health and walked two miles to work every day. During the four years that she was head of QAIMNS, Miss Browne became acquainted with Queen Alexandra and, a few days after she retired, she was invited to an interview with the Queen who presented her with the personal gift of a brooch in gratitude for her work. The Royal Army Medical Corps held a farewell dinner in her honour and the nurses of the QAIMNS celebrated her with a party.

Queen Alexandra showed her genuine personal regard for Sidney Browne on another occasion two years later when the King and Queen were invited, in July 1908, to open the new building of the Royal National Pension Fund for Nurses. After the opening ceremony which was attended by over 2000 nurses, the Queen sent for Miss Browne, who she had noticed in the front row, and both the King and Queen shook hands with her and spoke to her from the platform.

## State Registration of Nurses 1890–1910

After her retirement, Miss Browne was able to take a more active role in the campaign for the state registration of nurses. Her support for the campaign went back to 1890 when, while stationed in Malta, she joined the first professional organisation of nurses, the British Nurses' Association, which had been founded by Mrs Bedford Fenwick, her former matron when briefly she had worked at St Bartholomew's Hospital. Later, in 1894, Miss Browne became one of the founding members of the Matrons' Council and attended the meetings when she was in London. In March 1901, when she was stationed in Springfontein, she sent a subscription to the Buffalo Delegate Fund sponsored by the Matrons' Council which was to pay the travelling expenses of a delegate to the International Council of Nurses (ICN) congress in Buffalo, New York. In sending her subscription she wrote, 'I am sure that the educational value of the Congress will be very great'. Having become a member of the Society for the State Registration of Trained Nurses, founded in 1902, she was appointed a Vice President in February 1908.

As a former staff nurse of St Bartholomew's Hospital, she was a member of the nurses' League, one of the most political of the nurses' leagues. It had been founded and was led by the hospital's matron, Isla Stewart (see chapter three), who was one of the leaders of the registration campaign. Miss Browne had worked with Miss Stewart on the Army Nursing Board and they were regarded as the 'radical' opinion on the Board.

Miss Browne's views on the professional organisation of nursing and the need for registration, were shared by her elder brother, Dr Langley Browne. He gave evidence to the House of Commons Select Committee on the Registration of Nurses in 1905, representing with Sir Victor Horsley the British Medical Association (BMA). Dr Browne had been responsible for the resolution, passed by the BMA in 1904, approving the principle of registration for nurses. In his evidence to the Select Committee, he acknowledged his presidency of a large society of general practitioners in the Midlands who were unanimously in favour of registration for nurses. They believed the present state of affairs under which they had to work with incompetent nurses would continue until a system of state registration was introduced. In his opinion, medical opposition to nurse registration was almost entirely from London doctors where the situation was unique. He wanted to see a uniform training for nurses, and believed this could only be effective if it was enforced by the State.

When the National Council of Nurses of Great Britain and Ireland was formed in 1908, Miss Browne was appointed a member of the first executive committee. This was the organisation through which British and Irish nurses affiliated to the ICN, and both the National Council and the ICN were working to promote the professional status of nurses. A conference was held in the House of Commons in July 1909, to discuss the tactics of the campaign for state registration. The outcome was the formation of the Central Committee for State Registration, composed of five members from each of the four participating organisations, the Royal British Nurses' Association, the Society for the State Registration of Trained Nurses, the Irish Nurses' Association and the Association for the Registration of Nurses in Scotland. Sidney Browne was one of the delegates on the Committee, the object of which was to promote a joint Bill for registration.

## The Territorial Force Nursing Service 1908–1914

The War Office invited the matrons of all the large London hospitals to a meeting in February, 1908, to discuss the formation of a nursing reserve for the army. The idea for the formation of the Territorial Force Nursing Service belonged to Elisabeth Haldane, sister of R. B. Haldane, Secretary of State for War. The virtual breakdown of the army administration during the Boer war had made reform inevitable, and in particular a system of supplying a reserve of trained men was needed. Unlike the other great European powers which had introduced compulsory military service by this date, Haldane set up the Territorial Force which combined the good-will of the traditional militia and local volunteers with the modern concept of a nation-in-arms. Enrolment was voluntary and administered locally, but the service was under the control of the War Office. The role of the Territorial Force was to defend the country in the event of invasion.

Miss Haldane was a Vice President of the Society for the State Registration of Trained Nurses, and Chairman of the Scottish Registration Committee. She and Miss Browne became friends in 1906 when Miss Haldane was appointed to the Army Nursing Board. Miss Haldane, Miss Browne and Sir Alfred Keogh met at the Haldane's house in London in December 1907, where they drafted a scheme for the establishment of a reserve of nurses willing to serve in military general hospitals on the home front, in the event of war. The War Office accepted the scheme and called the meeting of the London matrons to discuss its formation.

In the event of war, medical services would be based on 23 General Hospitals, located in the major cities throughout the country, with four in London. Existing civilian buildings would be converted to hospitals on the outbreak of war, and would accommodate 520 beds each. To staff these 23 hospitals it was estimated that a nursing service of 3000 nurses was required, and it was Miss Haldane's plan to use volunteers from the nursing staff of the civilian hospitals. Each Territoral Hospital would require a staff of 91, drawn from a pool of 120 volunteers, and consisting of two matrons, 30 sisters and 88 staff nurses.

An Advisory Council was set up by the War Office in August, 1908, to draw up regulations for the new service, to be called the Territorial Force Nursing Service (TFNS). The Chairman of the Council was Sir Alfred Keogh and Miss Browne was appointed the Secretary. Queen Alexandra accepted the office of President and Miss Haldane was appointed Vice Chairman. Also on the Advisory Council were the matrons of six London hospitals and four society ladies.

The new service was open to all nurses between the ages of 23 and 50 with a certificate of three years' training. Conditions of service were the same as applied to QAIMNS with the difference that members of the TFNS would not be posted on active service abroad, their role being in military hospitals on the home front. They received no pay in peacetime, but once mobilised they would receive the same as the members of the regular service. The Advisory Council decided upon a uniform of blue-grey, similar to that of QAIMNS but instead of the red cape, the TFNS cape would be grey with a deep scarlet border. A Principal Matron, responsible for recruitment, was appointed in each of the 23 areas based on the hospitals. Assisted by a local committee composed of the matrons of hospitals in the area and local society ladies, the Principal Matrons ensured by their influence that the TFNS got the number of nurses required.

During the autumn and winter of 1908–1909, Miss Browne and Miss Haldane travelled around the country promoting the TFNS, speaking at meetings in hospitals and addressing local committees. They emphasised the value of the service to the country and to the individual nurse who joined, and nurses responded enthusiastically. A large meeting was held in the Mansion House in January, 1909, to establish the local committee for the TFNS in London. Miss Haldane addressed this meeting with support from Lord Esher, Chairman of the city's Territorial Force Association. The Mansion House Committee, as it became known, was appointed from the matrons of the large London hospitals and leading society ladies. Support from the matrons was essential for the success of the service, as only the large hospitals would be able to release sufficient numbers of staff at the outbreak of war. The four Territorial Hospitals in London required 480 nurses between them.

By the end of 1909 the staff of the 23 hospitals had been enrolled, with waiting lists in the case of some. The response to the service was due in large measure to the work of Miss Browne and Miss Haldane, but they were helped by the mood of the country. In the decade before the First World War, the feeling in the country was favourable to voluntary military organisations and women were determined to be involved. One of the attractions of the TFNS to nurses, and one which Miss Browne and Miss Haldane exploited in their recruiting speeches, was that it offered women the opportunity to take an active part in the defence of their country and at the time this privilege was unique to nurses.

Enthusiasm for the TFNS was maintained by regular meetings and badge presentation ceremonies. Each member received a silver badge in the shape of a 'T'. Presentation of the badges was usually performed by the Lord Lieutenant of the County, or a local member of the aristocracy, and either Miss Browne or Miss Haldane attended. Queen Alexandra presented the badges to the London TFNS in March 1910, and Sidney Browne, who had been appointed the Matron-in-Chief of the Service in January, was the first to receive her badge on this occasion.

The TFNS was confirmed as an integral part of the country's military nursing service when its members were allocated seats on the nurses' stand for the coronation of George V in 1911. Each of the 23 Territorial Hospitals was represented by five nurses. This was the first public appearance of the TFNS and, early in the morning of 23 July, they assembled in the grounds of the Middlesex Hospital, and marched to their position in the stand opposite Buckingham Palace.

Miss Browne, as Matron-in-Chief of the Service, was one of the four nurses allocated a seat in Westminster Abbey for the ceremony.

The Territorial Hospitals were under the control of the War Office and would be administered as military hospitals. Since the staff were all trained and experienced in civilian hospitals, the TFNS matrons required instruction in the procedures of the army nursing service. Between 1909 and 1914, each matron received one week's training at the larger military hospitals, though they all agreed that this was insufficient to master the numerous forms, reports and inspections required.

During the summer of 1914 the military authorities were preparing for war. The Matrons-in-Chief had been working continuously for several months to ensure that in the event of war, the mobilisation of nursing services would be swift. Miss Browne described the scene in the War Office on the eve of war: 'A quiet group of matrons spent the Sunday waiting in the electric atmosphere of the War Office for the news that meant so much for them as well as for the army'. War was declared on 4th August 1914 and, on August 5th, mobilisation orders went out to every Principal Matron of the TFNS with orders for every member of her staff. Within 10 days, the 23 hospitals, were ready to receive the wounded, and 3000 Territorial nurses were at their hospitals. By November the hospitals were all working to full capacity, dealing with wounded British and Belgian soldiers.

Three months after the start of the war there was concern about a possible shortage of trained nurses. The continuous demand for nurses at the front had taken up all the nurses in QAIMNS, approximately 200, and all the nurses in the Reserve, about 700, and by December over 2000 new recruits had been enrolled. For the first time in the history of the nursing service, nurses were sent to military stationary hospitals and clearing hospitals. More than half of the new recruits were sent overseas and, by the end of the year, members of the TFNS were also being sent to the front.

The War Office had delegated authority for the organisation of the voluntary medical and nursing services to the British Red Cross Society (BRCS). Medical and nursing personnel volunteered in their thousands, and supplies and premises were offered all over the country. The BRCS and the Order of St John of Jerusalem set up a Joint Committee in October 1914, to coordinate their work. A sub-committee was appointed to deal with the recruitment and organisation of the nursing work and Miss Swift, a former matron of Guy's Hospital (see chapter seven), was appointed Matron-in-Chief of the joint nursing department.

Auxiliary military hospitals were opened at home and in France, in private buildings and houses, staffed by nurses working for the BRCS and by nursing members of the Voluntary Aid Detachments (VADs). Since 1909 the VADs had been organised by the BRCS to give voluntary aid to the sick and wounded in the home territory. At the start of the war, there were 60,000 men and women partly trained in transport work, cooking, first aid and home nursing. The role of nursing members was to provide support for qualified nurses.

A special standing committee was formed at the beginning of 1915, to organise the work of the VAD nursing members, and it was composed of Miss Swift, Miss Browne, Miss Becher (the Matron-in-Chief of QAIMNS), the matron of the King George Hospital and two society ladies. The need for the committee arose from the nursing profession's increased concern about the lower standard of training accepted for nurses by the BRCS. Once again nurses saw the spectre of society ladies, with no formal nursing experience, running auxiliary hospitals for the sick and wounded with no professional nursing standards. One of the first tasks facing the Committee was to consider the conditions under which VAD nursing members could be employed in military hospitals. Up to this date they had been working only in the auxiliary hospitals run by the BRCS. The Committee's decision was that they must come under the control of the matron of the hospital, not the BRCS, they must live in the hospital, serve one month's probation, and serve for one year (this was reduced to six months in May 1915).

The original 23 Territorial Hospitals, with a total of 11,960 beds, proved hopelessly inadequate, and by spring 1915 it became necessary to double the number of beds. In most cases the hospitals were in educational or poor law buildings which had been taken over at the outbreak of war. Additional buildings were now requisitioned and no limit placed on the size of the hospital. The increase in the size of the hospitals meant a corresponding increase in the TFNS, and it was estimated that another 3000 nurses were needed. By March 1915, the shortage of nurses was officially admitted and the War Office called on married and retired nurses to return to work. The Director General of the Army Medical Services asked all civilian hospitals with training schools to make every effort to train for three or six months as many women as possible so they could be available for work under supervision in military hospitals. Most hospitals cooperated though it meant a great deal of extra work for the sisters.

As the size of her nursing force increased, so did Miss Browne's responsibilities. Although the TFNS was intended for service on the home front, by June 1915, over 400 were working in France and Belgium. Miss Browne was vigilant about the welfare of her nurses, inspecting all accommodation used and, with the expansion of the Territorial Hospitals, this involved considerable travelling. At the beginning of 1915 she crossed to France to inspect the nurses' quarters there. In all, about 25 per cent of the TFNS served overseas during the war as reinforcements to the regular army nurses in casualty clearing stations, in stationary hospitals and on hospital trains and barges. The number who wished to go abroad was always greater than the number selected and there was a certain amount of dissatisfaction among the experienced nurses working in the Territorial Hospitals at home, when they saw newly qualified young nurses joining QAIMNS and going abroad.

In March 1915, the War Office extended the age limit by 10 years and lowered the entry qualification for nurses joining QAIMNS and its Reserve, in future nurses up to the age of 45, who had three years training in hospitals of 50 beds or more would be eligible, previously the age limit had been 35 and the minimum number of beds acceptable was 100. In April, VADs were admitted to the wards of the military hospitals at home and abroad, three VADs being counted as equivalent to two trained nurses. The scheme worked smoothly in the Territorial Hospitals where they were given the same privileges as trained nurses and were subject to the same military discipline. For the rest of the war the number of VADs at the front increased while the trained nurses were concentrated on the home front where their services could be used more effectively.

Despite the official figures, the nursing profession was not convinced that the supply of trained nurses was exhausted. The employment of women with less than three years' training was a threat to the standards which the profession was working so hard to establish. The old prejudice against trained nurses seemed to be still prevalent in the War Office. Nursing leaders suspected that the considerable social influence attached to the VAD movement, which drew its support from the upper classes, had been used to put pressure on the War Office to admit VADs to the military hospitals before any alternatives had been considered seriously. Nevertheless, the need for nurses and women to train as assistant nurses continued throughout 1915. To meet the shortage the BRCS Joint Committee lowered its entry qualification to allow nurses with only two years general training to join their service to work as staff nurses under fully qualified nurses. By August 1915, the TFNS was advertising for nurses with a three year certificate of training from special hospitals, fever hospitals, womens' and childrens' hospitals, or nurses with two years' general training, to work as assistant nurses.

The call for nurses and for women to train in nursing continued throughout the winter of 1915–1916, and by the autumn of 1916 the War Office took steps to deal with the supply of nurses. A Committee was appointed to consider the system of recruiting nurses, and was known as the Supply of Nurses Committee, consisting of six lay men, four of whom were connected with the London Hospital, and one woman, Mrs Furse, the Commandant-in-Chief of the BRCS VAD Department, who was not a trained nurse. The announcement was received with disbelief and suspicion. The secrecy surrounding the appointment of the committee and the absence of a trained nurse from its membership, were guaranteed to provoke nursing leaders. The profession jumped to the conclusion that the committee was set up in the interests of the VADs. Why else had the matrons of the training schools been ignored and Mrs Furse included? Fully-trained nurses feared that the VAD nursing members would get a foot on the professional ladder by the recognition of their hospital experience as part of their training.

Nurses were not alone in condemning the membership of the committee. It was generally felt that the dismissive treatment of the profession was particularly insensitive at a time when nurses had been giving their services to the war without complaint. *The Daily Telegraph* commented:

> . . . skilled nursing has been the finest tribute that women have been able to offer to the gallantry of our splendid men, and it is not alone in the hospital wards, but wherever women are giving their strength and their endeavour in war work, that this most unhappily framed committee is regarded as a slight and a slur upon their willing acceptance of their share of duty.

Within two weeks, the Secretary for War appointed nine additional members to the committee, representing the military and civil nursing profession. They were the Matron-in-Chief of QAIMNS, the Matron-in-Chief of the TFNS, Miss Browne, the matrons of Guy's, St Thomas', St Bartholomew's, the Royal Free Hospital, the Royal Infirmary, Edinburgh, the President of the Poor Law Infirmary Matrons' Association and the Countess of Airlie. The committee's terms of reference were, 'to ascertain the resources of the country in trained nurses and women partially trained in nursing, so as to enable it to suggest the most economical method of utilising their services for civil and military purposes'.

The report was published in May, 1917, by which time many of its recommendations had already been implemented. It stated that there was no evidence to show that QAIMNS, the TFNS and the Joint War Committee had had any real difficulty in recruiting the number of nurses they required, but that many of these had been drawn from the civil nursing services which were now reduced to a dangerously low level. It was recommended that no more nurses should be obtained for military hospitals from institutions managed by the public health, lunacy or poor law authorities, nor from among district nurses, school nurses or health visitors. An appeal should be made to private nurses and their employers and to the Dominions, but the thrust of future recruitment should be aimed at newly qualified nurses as they left their training schools. The committee estimated that in 1917, the number of available probationers would be 2,400. The Supply of Nurses Committee was especially concerned about the annual wastage of trained nurses from military hospitals and the general understaffing of these hospitals. The strain on staff contributed to the exodus, and it was recommended that the number of staff in all military hospitals should be increased to allow regular holidays and emergency cover, with a maximum ratio of one nurse to 14 beds in ordinary hospitals, and one nurse to six beds in hospitals for officers.

The recommendations amounted to minor improvements in the nurses' conditions, with inducements for longer service. In addition, it was recommended that all VAD nursing members should be graded to distinguish those who had over one year's experience and, in an emergency, this pool of experienced nursing workers could be used as nurses to work under sisters. The report did not deal with the problem of the military service of the VADs being counted as part of their training if they went on to become nurses after the war. Nor did it address the mistrust felt by trained nurses towards the VADs, although it was admitted that many of the witnesses had referred to this.

In the spring of 1916, Miss Swift, the Matron-in-Chief of the BRCS, appealed to nurses to join together to found a College of Nursing. Her experience working for the BRCS, where she was receiving thousands of applications from nurses, qualified and unqualified, had convinced her that a uniform standard of training, examination and certification was the only way of bringing order to the profession. The time was favourable for such a development and the College of Nursing was launched in March 1916. Miss Browne supported the College and when, in December 1917, she was asked to become a member of the Council she accepted.

Her long administrative experience in the army was a great asset to the new organisation and until her retirement in 1927, she was a working member of several standing committees. Her financial abilities were especially appreciated and she was the first nurse to hold the position of Honorary Treasurer. She was responsible for the administrative work behind the Tribute Fund for Nurses which started as an endowment fund for the College and was so successful it was extended to include a benevolent fund for all nurses, whether or not they were members of the College.

## The Armistice and Retirement

In January 1918, Miss Browne, now 67, was awarded the distinction of a Bar to her Royal Red Cross, in recognition of her work as Matron-in-Chief of the TFNS. The two Advisory Boards, which dealt with QAIMNS and the TFNS respectively, were reconstituted as one Board in 1918, called Queen Alexandra's Army Nursing Board. The members of the Board were the Director General of the Army Medical Services, the two Matrons-in-Chief, a representative of the VADs, six lay women, including Miss Haldane, and six matrons of civilian hospitals. The joint board was a move towards greater uniformity in the two nursing services. The signing of the armistice on 11 November did not make any appreciable difference for several months to the work of the nursing services. An epidemic of influenza put the medical services under severe strain and the TFNS became involved in nursing children and repatriated prisoners.

Before the armistice, but when the outcome of the war had been decided, a committee representing women workers held a luncheon at the Trocadero Restaurant in London, in honour of the Matrons-in-Chief of the nursing services in England, France, Canada, Australia and New Zealand. The organisers included the Society of Women Journalists, the Women's Legion, the Association of Headmistresses, Queen Mary's Army Auxiliary Corps, the Ministry of Labour, and the Ministry of Munitions. Mrs Humphrey Ward, the novelist and reformer, was the guest speaker. She prefaced her remarks with the observation that nurses were not good at their own publicity, the tradition of the service was rigidly impersonal, and that not one of the names of the ladies gathered there would be found in the pages of *Who's Who*. She referred particularly to the work of Miss Browne, the most senior in age of the matrons present, and considered her largely responsible for the great expansion of voluntary aid training from which so much nursing manpower of the war had been drawn.

The wide involvement of women in war work, not only in the services and relief work, but in industry and agriculture where they had replaced men, had generated a spirit of unity among them. This spirit was celebrated at the Exhibition of Women's Work, held in the Whitechapel Art Gallery, during October and November, 1918. The exhibition was organised by the Imperial War Museum, which had appointed a Women's Sub-committee to record the contribution of women to the war effort. Miss Browne's role in this great channelling of women's energy was recognised and, in the hospital section of the exhibition, her portrait hung beside those of Dr Garrett Anderson and Dr Flora Murray. In the Times' *History of the War*, three chapters were devoted to women's war work, and Miss Browne was the author of the nursing section.

The demobilisation of nurses began in January 1919, under the direction of the Nurses' Demobilisation and Resettlement Committee. In the same month Miss Browne received the Grand Cross of the Order of the British Empire (Military Division), making her Dame Sidney Browne. Almost simultaneously, her health broke down and she was advised to rest. She spent several months on the Riviera and returned to London in May in time for the victory celebrations. One of her proudest moments was when the TFNS lead the Territorial Army in its victory parade through London. She selected 110 of the nurses to represent the service and carefully drilled them to march and take the royal salute. She was invited to view the parade from a stand beside the royal box, outside Buckingham Palace, and after the nurses made their salute, Dame Sidney was asked to speak with the Queen, and both the King and Queen congratulated her on the appearance and performance of the nurses of the TFNS. In August, she attended the King's Garden Party for war workers and presented the Principal Matrons of the TFNS, and of Canada, Australia and New Zealand, to the King. A week later she received her insignia of the Grand Cross at the Palace, and afterwards was received by Queen Alexandra at Marlborough House for a private conversation.

At the end of 1919, Dame Sidney gave up her role as representative in England of Lady Minto's Indian Nursing Association, a role she had performed for more than ten years. The Committee of the Association presented her with a gold wrist watch in gratitude. In December, 1919, she announced that she would retire from the post of Matron-in-Chief of the TFNS the following March. The Principal Matrons of the Service held a farewell dinner for her at the Grosvenor Hotel. The Countess of Minto, President of the service since 1909, presided, and the 33 guests included Dame Sidney's old friend Sir Alfred Keogh, as well as her brother, Dr Langley Browne and his family. The table was decorated with scarlet geraniums and white heather, the colours of the TFNS, and the music was provided by Mrs Steed's Ladies Band.

After the formal toasts, Miss Cox-Davies, Principal Matron of the First London General Territorial Hospital, who had known Dame Sidney since the war in South Africa, paid tribute to her as a matron and a friend. Dame Sidney's great wealth of human sympathy, she said, had won her the respect and love of the hundreds of women who had served under her. Recalling an incident which for her summed up Dame Sidney's varied life and wonderful character, she told how one evening in South Africa, when she was homesick and weary from long hours nursing hopelessly ill soldiers, she had met a Superintending Sister wearing a battered panama hat and faded dusty uniform, who invited her to sit down and have a chat. Miss Cox-Davies remembered how that friendly chat with Dame Sidney had lifted her despondency and inspired her to continue.

Dame Sidney became the first woman to receive the Freedom of the Borough of West Bromwich and at the ceremony, which took place in November 1921, the Mayor thanked Dame Sidney for the honour she had bestowed on the town. In accepting the Freedom of the Borough, Dame Sidney said that she had lived in many countries since living in West Bromwich, but she still loved the town. She accepted the honour as a representative of all the women who had done such good work during the war. The University of Leeds conferred an Honorary Nursing Diploma on her in 1925 and in July, 1927, she was awarded the International Florence Nightingale Medal by the League of Red Cross Societies.

She continued her active work for the profession until 1927, attending the meetings of the Association of Hospital Matrons and of the College of Nursing. The Association of Hospital Matrons had been founded in 1919 as an alternative to the Matrons' Council which had refused to work with the College of Nursing. In 1922, when the Council of the College decided to appoint a president, Dame Sidney received the honour of being the first to hold the office. When the College set up a Department of Education to develop postgraduate courses for nurses, Dame Sidney made a gift of £300 to establish a course on the nursing of tropical diseases. In 1927, she decided to move out of London and to leave her home in Hampstead, where she had lived for many years. She moved to Cheltenham where she shared a house with her great friend Miss Hoole. She retired from the office of Honorary Treasurer of the College and was appointed a Vice-President. Throughout the remainder of the 14 years of her life, she maintained an interest in nursing matters, particularly the welfare and progress of the military services.

*Fig 9. Sidney Browne, first President of the College of Nursing, 1922–1923*

On 13 August, 1941, she died at the age of 91. The funeral took place on 16 August at St Stephen's Church, Cheltenham, and was attended by many friends and admirers, including representatives of the army and medical corps. A message of sympathy was sent by Queen Mary. Six sergeants from a regiment stationed in the locality carried the coffin and a bugler sounded the Last Post. A Red Cross flag, made by army sisters and flown over their quarters at Springfontein and Rondebosch in the South African War, was draped over the coffin, and a cross of Haig poppies lay on top.

The Matron-in-Chief of the British Red Cross Society, Miss R. E.

Darbyshire, wrote a personal appreciation of Dame Sidney for the nursing press

> Everyone who worked with Dame Sidney was impressed with the fact of her great human understanding. She was delightful to work with, and she had a sincere appreciation of the responsibilities carried by trained nurses, and the arduous and important nature of their work. Her whole heart and soul were concentrated upon doing the very best possible for the soldiers. She never let an opportunity slip which would improve the nursing in the military hospitals, and she always insisted upon a proper status being given to the matrons and sisters working under her.
>
> *Nursing Times*, 23 Aug 1941, p. 675

## Conclusion

Miss Browne was a religious person and it is easy to understand why she was attracted to nursing with a father and a brother in the medical profession. Her career in the army nursing service lasted 23 years during which she worked in all the large military hospitals at home and abroad and served in three military campaigns. By 1902, she had 19 years experience of nursing in the army and was considered the obvious choice for the new position of Matron-in-Chief. Her work was respected by her medical colleagues within the army medical services and among her civilian nursing colleagues and, although she had only four years before her retirement to establish Queen Alexandra's Imperial Military Nursing Service, she left the new service with the professional standards associated with her work.

When she took on responsibiity for the new Territorial Force Nursing Service, in 1908, she can hardly have imagined that this would prove to be the most demanding position of her career. With the outbreak of war in 1914, she became responsible for approximately 6000 nurses, and found herself in one of the key nursing posts in the War Office. Her commitment to the TFNS was total and, at the age of 65, she travelled all over Britain and France, under war conditions, inspecting the nurses' accommodation and boosting their morale, and was twice mentioned in despatches for her bravery.

The demands of the war on the nursing profession were great and like many of her contemporaries, Miss Browne found herself faced with the need to compromise professional standards in the interests of the sick and wounded soldiers. She was an active supporter of the campaign for the state registration of nurses and had demonstrated her commitment to the three years' qualification for trained nurses in the conditions she had imposed on QAIMNS and the TFNS. However, as a member of the War Office Committee to organise the work of the VADs, she was party to the introduction of VADs to military hospitals. Similarly in 1916, she was a member of the controversial Supply of Nurses Committee, appointed by the War Office to assess the strength of existing and potential nursing manpower. The Committee was criticised by the nursing press for its failure to address the most important issue of the day, the relationship of the VADs to the profession, but the contribution of Miss Browne and the other seven matrons, was probably one of damage limitation.

Like many of her contemporaries, Miss Browne believed that it would be a better world after the 'great war' and had great hope in the League of Nations. She wrote about the League on several occasions in the nursing press and urged nurses to support it. In her last Christmas letter to the members of the Territorial Force Nursing Service, in 1918, she wrote

> This is the happiest Christmas we have had together since the war began . . . We are all feeling the strain of these long years of war . . . It will be a renewed, better world to which we return, we hope. There is to be a 'League of Nations' to make peace as permanent as it can be on earth . . . You have done your work splendidly in this war, and won the respect and admiration of all with whom you have come into contact . . . I am very proud of the records which have been sent to me, but more than all of the knowledge that you think little of what you have done and do not desire any praise or reward; but what you appreciate most is to know that you have helped thousands of our men, whose poor wounded bodies you have tended with such gentleness and skill, and inspired them with fresh courage and hope. Put a high ideal before you, and do your future service in a greater strength than your own, and your life will be for the betterment of the world.
>
> *Nursing Mirror*, 4 Jan 1919, p. 205

During the 10 years of active work Dame Sidney gave to the profession after the war, she was awarded all the tributes due to an elder statesman, the Grand Cross of the Order of the British Empire, the Freedom of her town, an honorary degree, the office of president of the College of Nursing, and the International Red Cross Medal. Her outstanding quality was kindness, which combined with her commitment to nursing and her administrtive abilities, made her a great Matron-in-Chief.

## Sources

### Public Record Office
WO25/3955 Military Nursing Establishment, Nursing sisters nominal rolls, 1869–1891
WO25/3956 QAIMNS Register, 1903–1926
WO30/114 Reorganisation of the Royal Army Medical Corps and Nursing Services, correspondence and papers, 1901
WO30/133 Advisory Board for Army Medical Services, reports on military hospitals in Great Britain, 1902–1904
WO 145 Register of Royal Red Cross

### QARANC Museum, Aldershot
Papers of Sidney Browne, correspondence from South Africa, photographs, cuttings

### Royal College of Nursing Archives
*Nursing Record/British Journal of Nursing*, 1894–1902
*Nursing Times*, 1905–1924, 1941
*Nursing Mirror*, 1910–1919, 1941
*Army Nursing*, Sidney Browne, in The Science and Art of Nursing, Chapter IX, Cassell and Co., London, 1910

### Imperial War Museum
*Times' History of the War*, Vol IV, chap LXXI
*Times' History of the War*, Vol XVII, chap CCLXI

 5

# Rebecca Strong
## Pioneer of University Education for Nurses
### (1843–1944)

*Nightingale Training School, 1867; Matron, Glasgow Royal Infirmary 1879–1885, 1891–1907; pioneer of preliminary training for nurses, 1893; member Royal British Nurses' Association and Matrons' Council; founder Scottish Nurses' Association 1909, President 1912–1930; Fellow, British College of Nurses; OBE.*

REBECCA THOROGOOD was born on 23 August 1843, in Aldgate, East London, where her father was the proprietor of the Blue Boar Inn. She married young and had one daughter before she was 20. Little is known about her husband other than his name, Strong, that he died within a couple of years of their marriage, and was buried in Liverpool. Shortly after becoming a widow, Rebecca decided to do something with the rest of her life and, through the influence of a close friend who was a midwife, she chose to take up nursing. She was aware of the work of Florence Nightingale and applied to the Nightingale Training School, which had started in 1860 at St Thomas' Hospital, and was accepted as a probationer, starting her training in 1867, at the age of 23.

The training at the Nightingale School was still in an early stage, consisting of one year's practical work in the wards of St Thomas' with a certain amount of instruction in basic nursing practice. In later life Mrs Strong described the training

> Very little was expected from us . . . kindness, watchfulness, cleanliness . . . A few stray lectures were given . . . There was a dummy on which to practise bandaging . . . The principal resident Medical Officer took a great interest in the pupils, and would occasionally ask for notes

to be taken of some particular case, and from that would point out mistakes and omissions, which was most excellent teaching.

The probationers at the Nightingale School signed a contract for six years service. On completion of their year's training, the nurses were generally posted to another hospital where they were expected to introduce good nursing practices. Mrs Strong was sent to the new hospital at Winchester, with five other Nightingale nurses, in 1868. Miss Nightingale preferred to send several nurses together to a hospital, a group having a better chance of introducing reforms than one nurse on her own. At the Winchester Hospital one nurse was assigned to each of the five wards and Rebecca Strong volunteered to do night duty, as she thought this work would be more interesting. She enjoyed the work at Winchester and was disappointed when, in November 1869, she was recalled and sent to the new British Army hospital at Netley, Southampton.

Miss Nightingale had selected five nurses to go to Netley with the Superintendent Mrs Deeble, and she held a personal interview with each prior to their departure. Rebecca recalled with pride the privilege of the bedside interview with Miss Nightingale, an invalid at the time, and the two books which Miss Nightingale presented to her, Scott's *Poetical Works* and Charlotte Yonge's *The Heir of Radclyffe*, a popular work of fiction with a high moral tone. She also recalled Miss Nightingale's advice to take with her high ideals, and to work on in hope.

The Royal Victoria Hospital at Netley had been built on a grand scale after the Crimean War. The five nurses were responsible for six to eight wards each and the wards contained an average of eight beds. The majority of patients were received from troopships and once the acute cases had been attended to, there was little nursing required by the convalescents, and this work was done by the medical orderlies. Rebecca found the work monotonous and in 1872, she decided to leave Netley and return to Winchester. This decision was in breach of her contract with the Nightingale School and she was almost dismissed. Nevertheless she did return to Winchester, and finished her six years' service there.

Through the influence of friends, Mrs Strong was appointed matron of the Dundee Royal Infirmary, in 1874. There she found a Medical Superintendent, Dr Sinclair, who had modern ideas about nursing. He had already persuaded the Infirmary managers of the need to improve the standard of nursing and to provide the nurses with separate bedrooms. Mrs Strong was able with the support of the managers to improve the nurses' conditions further and to introduce new nursing practices. Nurse training was still the traditional method of learning by experience on the wards, and at the time, Mrs Strong believed that an average intelligent woman could learn all that was required of a nurse by working on the wards, under the instruction of a medical man.

## Matron of Glasgow Royal Infirmary, 1879–1907

The Glasgow Royal Infirmary advertised for a matron in 1879 and Mrs Strong was encouraged to apply by William Macewen, a surgeon on the staff of the Glasgow Royal Infirmary, who was impressed by her work at Dundee. She was attracted by the challenge – the Glasgow Royal Infirmary was the largest voluntary hospital in Scotland with 570 beds, and a nursing staff of 62 nurses and 29 probationers. Mrs Strong was appointed and started on a salary of £120 per annum. She was shocked by what she described as the backward conditions of work. Nurses were divided into day and night nurses, one of each class being assigned to each ward, and they worked exclusively for the physician or surgeon of that ward, never transferring to another ward unless the medical staff requested a change of nurse. Until 1877 the nurses had also been responsible for cleaning the wards, but in that year scrubbers and cleaners had been employed.

Probationers' training consisted of two years' work on the wards where they worked as assistants, one in each ward and the more experienced were selected to cover for the regular nurses who were on leave or sick. They received £12 a year while training, £20 when qualified, rising by £2 a year until it reached £30. The year before Mrs Strong was appointed, lectures on medical and surgical nursing had been introduced by two members of the medical staff and this had proved so successful it was decided to continue the practice. These lectures were open to the public on payment of a fee and, on Mrs Strong's recommendation, it was decided that in future no nurse would be allowed to take charge of a ward without having attended the lectures and passed an examination on the subject.

The Infirmary managers asked Mrs Strong for her opinion on the introduction of fees for the training of nurses from outside institutions. At the time, 1882, she did not consider that the training at the Infirmary was sufficiently established for such a step, pointing to the lack of adequate living accommodation for the nurses and the lack of a certificate. She thought that if they asked payment for the instruction they were giving they would lose the probationers they already trained for Miss Harland in Edinburgh and for the Prison

*Fig 10.  Rebecca Strong, Matron of the Royal Infirmary, Glasgow*

Gate Mission, London. Mrs Strong outlined her plans for the training school in the future

> By transferring our nurses to other hospitals, we shall gradually establish our position as a 'School' and in time we should turn our attention towards making it a more remunerative part of our work and should have a fee attached . . . This, however, you will not be able to accomplish until you are in a position to provide each pupil with a separate sleeping apartment and also an ordinary comfortable sitting room. These things are now provided in all recognised Schools of Nurses.
>
> GGHB HB14/1/15, 1 Jun 1882

Mrs Strong found herself fully occupied with running the nursing department of a large, busy hospital, and because the nursing staff were overworked she frequently took on nursing duties to relieve them. William Macewen, surgeon to the Royal Infirmary since 1876 and who had encouraged her to apply for the post of Matron, was one of the pioneers of modern surgery. He was in charge of three wards in the Infirmary where he worked continuously, taking very little rest, and demanding a continuous supply of good nurses. Macewen had been one of the first surgeons to adopt Lister's antiseptic methods in surgery, and had developed the technique further. He perfected a method of osteotomy of the lower limbs, to counteract the bone deformities associated with rickets, a condition prevalent among the poor in Glasgow at the time. In 1880 he had published an account of his work on femoral osteotomy, which was translated into six languages and brought him international recognition.

In his current work, developing a method of brain surgery, Macewen had to rely on the nurses for continuous observation of his patients when he was away from the wards and for this he required intelligent nurses who understood the significance of the slightest change in a patient. As matron, Mrs Strong had to intervene regularly in his wards to ensure that the nurses were given some rest. She appealed to him to allow the night nurses to leave the wards at the end of their duty in the morning and not when he had finished his rounds, ' . . . night duty is not what it used to be, there is no taking of sleep during the night, . . . they have to be on the alert the whole night, 12 continuous hours, from 10 to 10' (RCPSG 10, 11 Feb 1882).

Mrs Strong and Macewen worked well together but not without friction and this caused her a good deal of trouble in the performance of her duties as matron. He needed highly trained nurses and Mrs Strong responded by producing nurses capable of, what was then, advanced nursing practice. She found her orders, concerning the allocation of nurses to wards, contradicted by the junior resident staff and when she complained to the Superintendent, who was her direct superior, he failed to support her. In a letter to Macewen, Mrs Strong objected to the invidious position in which he had placed her

I think it almost a mistake on your part to ask me to make arrangements for the nursing of your patients beyond supplying you with ten nurses, . . . I think it would be much better if you would arrange the work with your assistant, and leave him to give the orders [to the nurses]. I would not like to subject myself a third time to having my orders contradicted.

RCPSG 10, 15 Apr 1882

On several subsequent occasions the Superintendent overruled the matron in favour of the junior medical staff and, in consequence of his lack of support, Mrs Strong found her authority as matron undermined. In August 1882, Mrs Strong gave notice of her resignation from 1st December following, as she considered her position as matron was no longer tenable. The managers of the Infirmary appointed a sub-committee to investigate her complaints which found that the Superintendent and Mrs Strong had different opinions on several matters of house government. The Superintendent believed Mrs Strong did not make sufficient allowance for the youthfulness of the resident medical staff, while she considered his management too slack, leading to insubordination. The committee agreed with Mrs Strong's view, and decided that the Superintendent had not adequately supported her position and authority and recommended that the distribution of the nurses and probationers should be in the hands exclusively of the Matron, with power of review only with the Superintendent. Since this was the arrangement which Mrs Strong had requested, she agreed to withdraw her resignation.

However, by November (1882) she was again on the point of resignation believing that the job was becoming too much for her. This decision was made when she was unwell and following a disagreement with Macewen. After taking a fortnight's rest away from the Infirmary, she reconsidered and withdrew her resignation. Nevertheless, her health was suffering from the constant pressure of the work and in April, 1883, she again gave notice of her resignation, writing to Macewen 'I heartily pity the poor wretch who comes after me and I hail my own exit with delight.' The Infirmary nurses drew up a memorial, signed by 92 of them, asking the managers not to accept her resignation. The post was advertised and 30 applications received before Mrs Strong asked for permission again to withdraw her resignation. A statement from her doctor said that she had recovered from her 'mental depression' and was anxious to continue her work at the Infirmary. The House Committee unanimously agreed to allow her to remain.

The struggles with Macewen continued, as he demanded more nurses for his pioneer brain surgery while Mrs Strong worried about the constant strain on the nurses. There were no nurses available to do extra work or to cover for holidays, and day nurses often had to do night duty after a day's work. The main problem was the shortage of accommodation for the nurses which prevented the managers from increasing the staff. The old Dispensary was converted in 1883 and provided 19 bedrooms for nurses but there were still 42 nurses and 10 probationers sleeping in small rooms off the wards throughout the hospital. In January 1884, Mrs Strong reported that a new nurses' home was a necessity. The managers accepted her report but were reluctant to build the new nurses' home out of hospital funds, the estimated cost being £5000. They decided to raise the money by subscription, but by the end of 1886 they found that the money was not forthcoming and announced that the building of the home would commence in the summer of 1887. By this date, Mrs Strong had already left the Infirmary. Believing that her health could not stand another year in the post, in June 1885, she gave three months' notice and left the Infirmary in October. The nurses' home, which provided 88 additional bedrooms, was opened in August 1888.

On leaving the Royal Infirmary, Rebecca Strong maintained her professional partnership with Macewen and opened a private nursing home in Glasgow. They both realised the need for nursing to keep pace with advances in medicine and surgery. His reputation as a leading surgeon was well established but he never forgot that the success of his work depended on good nursing. Before her departure from the Infirmary in 1884, Macewen attended an international conference on medical sciences in Copenhagen, where he received a standing ovation. He wrote to Mrs Strong describing the warm reception he had received from his colleagues

> I know you will be pleased to hear them [congratulations], as you are so mixed up with everything I do in the surgical way. I look on you and the nurses as part of myself and honour which might be conferred on me is something which should be shared with you.
>
> RCPSG 10, 24 Aug 1884

## Education of Nurses

Macewen was the first to suggest to Mrs Strong the possibility of a uniform method for the technical instruction of nurses. Her own experience of training, 20 years earlier, learning largely from her mistakes, had convinced her that a probationer should have a basic knowledge of anatomy, physiology and hygiene before she was allowed to undertake practical nursing in the wards. After her experience at the Glasgow Royal Infirmary, she believed that the amount of knowledge required by a nurse in the 1880s, in order to carry out technical instructions intelligently, had become too great to expect a probationer to attend lectures, study, and simultaneously work in the wards. Macewen proposed that nurses attend lectures in the medical schools, attached to the teaching hospitals, before they began their practical training in the wards.

Asked to speak on the subject of nurses and nursing, Macewen first made public his ideas on the education of nurses at the Annual New Year meeting of the managers and nurses of the Royal Infirmary in 1891. After paying tribute to the nurses and matrons of the hospital, with whom he had worked for over 10 years, he said how he hoped to see nursing make further progress. Good nurses were the exception, the mass remained an untutored host. He asked why was nursing not a distinct profession, with an entrance examination, theoretical and practical instruction, teachers, examiners and a diploma? He then proposed that the medical school of the Royal Infirmary, St Mungo's College, set up a Faculty of Nursing and outlined what he considered were the subjects a nurse should study before beginning her practical training. Anatomy, physiology, bacteriology, hygiene, and cookery, he listed in addition to the need for an understanding of the principles of therapeutics, medicine, and surgery. Every candidate for nursing should have passed an examination in these subjects before she was allowed to work in a ward, and later in her training she should attend a second course of instruction, in clinical nursing, before she was awarded her final Diploma.

Mrs Strong's successor as matron at the Royal Infirmary, Miss Wood, had found the post equally troublesome and in July, 1891, she gave notice of her resignation. She had asked that the nursing staff be increased by eight as, due to the increased duties required of the nurses in the surgical and medical wards, the three nurses assigned to these wards were no longer sufficient. The managers had responded by placing a wardmaid in each ward. An unpleasant controversy ensued when a letter written by a probationer was printed in the *North British Daily Mail* (2 September 1891) describing the poor accommodation, long hours and inadequate food which the nurses at the hospital were forced to accept. Several more letters followed from nurses, medical staff and subscribers and eventually 70 nurses supported the charges. The medical staff petitioned the Directors to hold an inquiry into the nurses' conditions.

*The Nursing Record* took up the cause and the editor, Mrs Bedford Fenwick, visited Glasgow to see for herself. With characteristic decisiveness, she declared that the facts had been understated rather than exaggerated.

> The first principle seems to be, economy at any cost . . . The Managers, it would seem, have striven to show as large a number of patients, at as small an expenditure in pounds, shillings, and pence as

possible . . . economy at the expense of efficiency, when life and death are concerned, is the most ridiculously wasteful policy possible.'
*The Nursing Record*, 1 Oct 1891, p. 170

Mrs Fenwick recommended the reorganisation of the Infirmary's nursing department, the appointment of a nursing committee which would have full control over the department and to which any nurse could make a direct complaint, an improvement in the nurses' diet, the separation of day and night duty, at least two nurses on duty on every ward at a time, three hours off duty every day, a half day off once a fortnight and three consecutive weeks' holidays each year for the nurses and probationers.

The sub-committee appointed to investigate the complaints interviewed witnesses including 23 nurses and when the report was published, it exonerated the managers from any blame. The report listed the improvements which had been made in the nurses' conditions over the last 20 years, it stated that the food was adequate, the hours of work not unreasonable, and the ratio of one nurse to five beds as good as in other hospitals. The report did recommend an improvement in the nurses' holidays, increasing them to a month's leave, with at least 14 days in the summer. The appointment of a nursing committee to supervise the nursing department was also approved.

The managers were not as complacent as the report suggested, and when the House Committee considered the appointment of a new matron, Rebecca Strong was the only candidate nominated and was elected unanimously. Despite her previous experience of the post, she was attracted by the opportunity to develop her ideas on the education of nurses and, after a holiday in Switzerland, she commenced her duties in November, 1891. *The Nursing Record* (15 November 1891) reported that she returned to the Royal Infirmary as a dictator, and on the understanding that drastic reforms would be introduced in the nursing department.

## Matron of Glasgow Royal Infirmary, 1891–1907

The main problem facing Mrs Strong on her return to the Royal Infirmary was the severe understaffing of the wards. The nursing staff numbered 106, but a ward of 20 beds was still staffed by one staff nurse and one probationer during the day, and at night by one probationer. Probationers of six or eight months' experience were put on night duty and kept there, sometimes for as long as two years. The managers approved plans to build an additional storey to the nurses' home, providing 22 bedrooms, and when that was ready, the nursing staff was increased. Mrs Strong was able to assign four nurses to each ward and to rearrange the hours of duty so that continuous night duty was abolished and replaced by a rotation of three months.

Mrs Strong and Dr Macewen did not waste time before proposing the reform of the nurses' training. In April 1892, Macewen put their plans to the House Committee, which unanimously agreed that the scheme would be of benefit to the Infirmary. After a joint meeting of the Medical Committee and the House Committee had discussed the proposals, the details were worked out and arrangements made to inaugurate the new course in January 1893. The scheme consisted of three months' compulsory instruction and training before candidates began their practical work in the wards. Unless holding a Leaving Certificate of the Scottish Education Department, candidates were required to take an entrance examination in grammar, composition, spelling and arithmetic. The preliminary training consisted of two courses of six weeks each, the first comprising 12 lectures and demonstrations in anatomy, 12 in physiology and 12 in hygiene. After passing the examination in these subjects, candidates were eligible for the second course consisting of 20 lectures and demonstrations on surgical cases and 20 on medical cases, 10 practical lectures on ward work, and 10 in cookery. The lectures were given in the medical school, St Mungo's College, and in the Infirmary, by five members of the medical staff, and were open to the public foı a fee of £5. Ward work and cookery lectures were given by the Matron, and candidates were responsible for their own board and lodgings during the three months, estimated at approximately £12.

After passing the examinations of the second course, candidates were admitted as probationers for two years' training in the wards for which they were paid £12 in the first year, £20 in the second year, and received free board and lodging. At the end of their second year, probationers took a final written and practical examination, and if successful, received certificates as trained nurses.

The scheme was a new departure in nurse education in several ways. It pioneered the block system by dividing the nurse's training into blocks of lectures, followed by blocks of practical ward work. It introduced the idea of compulsory theoretical instruction and examination before probationers entered the wards, and inaugurated a systematic theoretical instruction iṅ nursing. It set an educational standard for entry to the training, and initiated the practice that nurses should pay fees for their instruction. Most innovatively, it

*Fig 11. The Royal Infirmary, Glasgow, 1900*

placed nurses' education in the medical college, making nurses potential students.

When the prospectus was published certain aspects of the scheme were criticised by nursing commentators, namely the length of the training and the amount of clinical instruction. Two years' practical training in the wards was considered too short, three years having been adopted as the ideal by the supporters of state registration. The six weeks' clinical instruction was considered inadequate and given too early in the training for the nurse to benefit from it.

Mrs Strong was invited to give a paper to the first meeting of the Matrons' Council in London, in November 1894, on the new training scheme at the Glasgow Royal Infirmary. Her theme was the need for uniformity of education in nursing and in her opinion nursing, at that time, had no definite position. Despite the advances in medicine and the demand for well trained nurses, there was as yet no standard or general examination to test the qualifications of a nurse. After almost two years of the new training scheme, she was pleased with the results, but emphasised that it was only a tentative beginning in the development of nurses' education, and she did not hold up their syllabus as a model for other schools.

There had been no shortage of candidates of suitable educational standard applying for the preliminary training scheme. One of the main aims had been to separate class work from ward work because like other training schools, the Glasgow Royal Infirmary had increased the number of lectures until they became a serious hindrance to the work of the wards. The examinations had become a constant worry for probationers, who did not have time to study after 10 hours a day in the wards. For probationers on night duty, attendance at classes had meant an interruption to their sleep in the middle of the day. Mrs Strong especially welcomed the fact that under the new system all probationers received the same instruction and the ward staff knew what standard to expect from the new probationers. When speaking to the Matrons' Council, the first probationers to train under the scheme had not completed their two years in the wards and the arrangements for the final examination had not been made. Mrs Strong optimistically hoped that a central examination by an independent body, similar to the General Medical Council, perhaps the Royal British Nurses' Association, might replace the need for local examinations. Mrs Strong considered that the success of the new training scheme was due to the full cooperation of the medical staff, who had already noticed an improvement in the nurses' work. She hoped it would be possible to extend the training scheme to three years in the near future, with 18 months spent in the medical wards and 18 months in surgical wards, and divided equally between male and female wards.

The paper was published in *The Nursing Record* (November 1894) and in *The Trained Nurse*, an American journal (January 1895) with the title 'Education in Nursing . Although Mrs Strong had emphasised the experimental nature of the Glasgow syllabus, it became the model for many nursing schools in America, where nurse education was developing more rapidly than in Britain. The article was published in the influential *American Journal of Nursing* in February 1901, and in the following issue, Adelaide Nutting, Superintendent of Nurses at the Johns Hopkins Hospital, Baltimore, and one of the leaders in the development of nurse education, paid tribute to the lead which the Glasgow Royal Infirmary had given to schools of nursing in all countries. In her article, Miss Nutting pointed out that the development of a systematic course of theoretical instruction for nurses, brought nursing into line with all other branches of education, whether in art, trade or the professions.

The number of patients being treated in the Royal Infirmary was steadily rising and new departments were required. The Managers drew up plans for a rebuilding programme in 1899 and Mrs Strong was asked to specify the nursing and domestic requirements. The nursing staff had reached 134 and the accommodation available for nurses within the Infirmary was full; the additional nurses had to be housed in various lodgings in the neighbourhood. The new building programme included a nurses' home to accommodate 90 nurses, with sitting-rooms, dining-room, kitchen and sick room, a servants' house, the matron's and housekeeper's apartments, which were to be within one of the main buildings, a large dining-room for the nursing staff, a large general kitchen and a kitchen attached to each ward.

That same year, Mrs Strong recommended an increase in the nurses' pay to encourage the trained nurses to remain on the staff. In future the maximum salary of £30 per annum would be reached after five years' service, instead of seven, and in 1901 the maximum was raised to £35.

Mrs Strong, like a number of other leading nurses of the day, travelled to America in September, 1901, to attend the first congress of the International Council of Nurses in Buffalo, New York. On her way to the Congress she visited the leading teaching hospitals in Baltimore, Philadelphia, Washington and Boston. Her intention was to read a paper at the congress on 'The Preparatory Instruction of Nurses', but she became ill in Philadelphia and was unable to present the paper herself. It was read by another delegate and published in the transactions of the congress. It gave a more considered assessment of the Glasgow preliminary training scheme than she had been able to give earlier. The training period had been extended to three years and she was confident that the scheme had been a step in the right direction. She saw the development of preliminary training as a progression not a revolution. The aim of Professor Macewen and herself had been to rescue nursing from the chaotic state it was in due to the proliferation of training schools operating independently with different standards of training and examination. They hoped to place nursing on a sound base of systematic education, leading to final examination, under the control of the State.

Mrs Strong believed the advantages of a preliminary training were many, but she thought it particularly valuable that when the probationers entered the wards they were in a position to enjoy the work. They were familiar with basic nursing practice and terminology, had passed an examination which had weeded out the unsuitable candidates and, after three months together, they had formed friendships which helped to diminish the strangeness of living in a big institution. She wished to see the cost of the preliminary training to the candidate reduced. If all hospitals insisted that proba-tioners passed an examination in anatomy, physiology and hygiene, the increased attendances at these lectures, which could be run by established medical schools, would reduce the fees. The second part of the preliminary training, the clinical instruction, she felt, should be given in the individual hospitals, with candidates paying a fee to cover the lectures but receiving board and lodging free. Her paper concluded by comparing the system of training at the Glasgow Royal Infirmary to that developed by Miss Nutting, at the Johns Hopkins Hospital, Baltimore. Training at the latter consisted of six months' preliminary instruction and two and half years' practical training, encompassing many specialised areas of nursing. Mrs Strong believed that any specialisation should be undertaken as postgradu-ate training, after a nurse had gained her certificate in general nurs-ing. She wanted it to be illegal for a woman to take up a specialised area of nursing, including midwifery, without first acquiring a cer-tificate in general nursing.

In January 1907, Mrs Strong was granted three months' leave of absence on health grounds and her absence from the traditional New Year Meeting of the staff and managers was noted with regret by the Lord Provost of the city. He paid tribute to her pioneer work to improve the education of nurses, and welcomed the large attendance of nurses at the recently inaugurated postgraduate lectures. When she returned from leave, Mrs Strong gave notice of her intention to retire, saying that she found the work too fatiguing and could not face another winter of work. Before leaving the Infirmary in August, 1907, she attended the laying of the memorial stone of the new buildings which she had helped to plan. Miss Melrose, her deputy, succeeded her as matron.

When she retired, Mrs Strong went to live with her sister in West Kirby, and remained there until 1912 when her sister died. Her daughter had married Adolph Geyer, the minister of the German Protestant Church in Glasgow, and was settled there with four children. Mrs Strong received a pension of £120 per annum from the Infirmary and in 1908 she was left a legacy of £6000 by the late Dr McCowan of Glasgow, who had been impressed by her work at the Infirmary. Her ideas on the education of nurses and the need for a state examination made her a natural supporter of state registration for nurses and she had joined the Royal British Nurses' Association

(RBNA) and the Matrons' Council in the 1890s. Her commitment to the professional organisation of nurses continued after her retirement and, in 1909, she was elected to the General Council of the RBNA and appointed a member of the executive committee. In 1910, she was made a Vice-President of the National Council of Trained Nurses.

A Scottish branch of the RBNA had been formed with its headquarters in Edinburgh in 1895, the impetus coming from members of the medical profession. Miss Shannon, the matron of the Western Infirmary, Glasgow, was one of the matrons who gave evidence to the House of Commons Select Committee on State Registration of Nurses in 1905. She stated that there was little support for state registration among nurses in Glasgow, and that the medical men there did not support it. This is surprising as William Macewen had moved to the Western Infirmary in 1892, when he was appointed Regius Professor of Surgery at Glasgow University.

When Mrs Strong was appointed a member of the RBNA Bill Committee for state registration in 1905, her priority was to ensure that the profession was self-governing. This meant that the composition of the proposed nursing council must have a majority of independent nurses. In November of that year, she held a meeting of Scottish matrons at the Infirmary to discuss state registration and to ascertain the opinions of the other matrons.

## Scottish Nurses' Association 1909

By 1909 support for state registration was growing in Scotland and an Association for the Promotion of the Registration of Nurses in Scotland was formed at a meeting in Edinburgh in March. The Association was well supported by matrons, the medical profession and hospital managers, but some supporters were in favour of a separate Bill for Scotland. This was in response to an English Registration Bill which excluded Scotland. Mrs Strong and Professor Macewen were strongly opposed to separate legislation for Scotland as they believed that the interests of the profession and the public would best be served by one Act covering the whole country.

Professor Macewen was a long-time member of the Society for the State Registration of Nurses and, in May 1909, was part of the delegation from this Society to the Prime Minister. In July, 1909, he and Mrs Strong formed the Scottish Nurses' Association (SNA), the objective being to work for a single system of state registration for nurses in the whole country. They had been prompted to take this initiative by the publication of a Bill for the Registration of Nurses in Scotland which received considerable support. They hoped the SNA would provide nurses with a professional voice in Scotland and would represent the opinions of nurses, rather than that of doctors and hospital managers, who dominated some of the existing regis- tration organisations. At the first Annual Meeting, in November 1909, Macewen, now Sir William and the first president of the Associ- ation, gave the address and spoke of the need for the SNA to promote the dignity of nursing as a profession and to obtain a distinguishing title for its graduates. He drew attention to the unsatisfactory position of nurses in Britain compared to the colonies and on the continent, where state registration was already in practice.

In 1912, after her sister died, Mrs Strong moved back to Scotland and took a more active role in the activities of the SNA, becoming a frequent speaker at the meetings. She was appointed President and in this capacity represented the association on the executive commit- tee of the Society for the State Registration of Nurses. When the first world war started and the shortage of trained nurses became a matter of public concern, Mrs Strong recognised that the need for a standard qualification for nurses was more urgent than ever. However, she was one of the strongest critics of the move to establish a College of Nursing in 1916, to her anything less than state registration, with a statutory General Nursing Council, was not good enough. Like many of the leading campaigners, she saw the College of Nursing as yet another voluntary system of registration, promoted by hospital authorities, and denying nurses professional independence.

The promoters of the College of Nursing held a conference at the end of February 1916, to clear the air and dispel rumours concerning the aims of the College. One of the critics of the College at this conference was the representative of the Scottish Nurses' Associ- ation, Dr McGregor-Robertson. In contrast, Miss Graham, the Sec- retary of the Association for the Promotion of State Registration of Nurses in Scotland and Honorary Secretary of the Scottish Matrons Association, both organisations being based in Edinburgh, supported the College of Nursing. Dr McGregor-Robertson said that the SNA stood by the decision of the 1914 representative conference of nurses, which had agreed the essential principles of any Bill for state regis- tration. The SNA did not see why the promoters of the College could not accept this decision.

At a subsequent meeting between the promoters of the College and the representatives of the nurses' organisations, Dr McGregor- Robertson said that they were not against any action being taken, provided it was along the right lines. Mr Stanley, for the College, said that where they differed was in the question of procedure. He considered it a mistake to ask Parliament to sanction something that they could do themselves and pointed to the hopeless record of Private Members' Bills in the fight for women's suffrage. Nurses could set up a voluntary system of registration and if they then applied for state registration, Parliament would know exactly what was involved. He was prepared to accept the fundamental principles of any nurses' Bill, state registration, a uniform curriculum of education and a single portal examination, and to add to these, that the College of Nursing must be governed by nurses. The meeting agreed to set up a committee to draft a joint Bill for state registration.

The College of Nursing was established at the beginning of April, 1916, and the Scottish Board of the College was set up the following September, in Edinburgh. Negotiations on the joint Bill were in the final stages, but they still had to agree upon the constitution of the General Nursing Council, which would govern the profession. The composition of this body was regarded by many pro-registrationists, including Mrs Strong, as fundamental to the future independence of the profession. At the Annual Meeting of the Society for the State Registration of Nurses, in June 1916, she proposed a resolution which was carried unanimously, that the joint Bill must make provision for the direct and adequate representation of nurses themselves on the governing body.

That autumn, Mrs Strong gave the opening address at an open conference in London, held by the National Union of Trained Nurses. She welcomed the impetus which the arrival of the College of Nursing had given the long-standing cause of uniformity in nurses' education. Nevertheless, she criticised the proposed rules of the College which would accept nurses for registration from recognised training schools and leave the majority of the smaller schools ostracised. Her contention was that a minimum standard of theoretical knowledge should be set by examination, so that the training in hospitals, large or small, could be tested and a common diploma awarded, thus placing all hospitals on the same footing. Her preference was for the term 'graduate in nursing' rather than registered nurse.

The negotiations between the College of Nursing and the Central Committee for the State Registration of Nurses to produce a joint Bill broke down in November, 1916. The two parties decided to proceed with separate Bills, but no progress could be made until the Government lifted the ban on Private Members' Bills, introduced at the start of the war. At its Annual Meeting in 1916, the SNA voted to federate with other nurses' societies and organisations which shared their objectives. Mrs Strong spoke in support of this motion, saying that the hour for nurses' legislation had come and it was the duty of nurses to fight for it and to make their profession worthy of its name.

In March 1919, following the restoration of Private Members' Bills, the Bill for State Registration promoted by the Central Committee was introduced in the House of Commons and, in May, the College of Nursing's Bill was introduced in the House of Lords. Both Bills had their supporters and their critics in the two Houses. The Association for the Promotion of Registration of Nurses in Scotland issued a memorandum, signed by 59 matrons and nurses, criticising the Central Committee's Bill as partisan and attacking the Scottish Nurses' Association as a local Glasgow society with no following in Edinburgh. The College of Nursing also criticised the Central Committee's Bill for the unjust representation it gave on the proposed general nursing council to the various nurses' societies. No agreement had been reached when Parliament rose in July and, when it resumed in the autumn, the Minister of Health introduced a government Bill for the registration of nurses. The Nurses' Registration Act 1919 was passed in December, with a separate Act for Scotland and Ireland.

In Scotland and Ireland the nurses' organisations protested against the setting-up of three separate Registers. The government maintained that separate legislation was necessary because the administration of public health in the three countries was distinct. At a meeting of the SNA in Glasgow, Sir William Macewen carried a resolution which expressed the Association's anger with the Government's legislation, ' . . . no Nurses' Registration Bill will be satisfactory which does not provide a single nursing authority for the United Kingdom, a single standard of training, a uniform examination qualifying for registration, and a single register.'

The Nurses' Registration Acts set up General Nursing Councils for England and Wales, Scotland and Ireland. The members of the first Councils were nominated by the Minister of Health and their first task was to inaugurate the registration of nurses, by compiling a register of trained nurses. The nominated Councils ceased to exist on 30 November 1922 and were replaced by elected Councils, elected by the nurses on the Register. The second General Nursing Council for Scotland consisted of nine elected members and six nominated by the Secretary of State. Eighteen candidates stood for election, nine nominated by the SNA and nine nominated by the College of Nursing. The nine elected candidates were all College of Nursing nominees, two of whom had also been endorsed by the SNA. The two unsuccessful independents were a male mental nurse from Lanarkshire and a public health nurse from Stirlingshire. Eighty per cent of the nurses on the register voted, 1,787 of the 2,237.

The Scottish Nurses' Association was highly critical of the new Council, instead of being a true general nursing council representing all classes of nurses, the Council would be dominated by the point of view of hospital matrons, since eight of the nine elected members were matrons. What was needed was a progressive Council with public health nurses and those engaged in the preventive nursing of the future, instead the Council would be controlled by a clique of College matrons, out of touch and out of sympathy with nurses outside of hospitals. For Mrs Strong the result of the election was disappointing. For 25 years she had urged Scottish nurses to prepare themselves for registration, to understand the issues involved and to appreciate the importance of professional independence, which she now considered was compromised.

The election manifesto of the SNA had emphasised that only their candidates would protect the interests of Scottish nurses, only they were independent of London-based organisations. This appeal to Scottish independence was contrary to the aims of the founders of the Association, Professor Macewen and Mrs Strong, who in 1909, had wished to promote the unity of the profession throughout the kingdom. By 1922, the Association had become the opposition party in nursing politics in Scotland, which meant it stood against the College of Nursing. The election results reflected the division between the supporters of the SNA based in Glasgow, and the College of Nursing based in Edinburgh. They also showed the superior strength of the College of Nursing.

## The Scottish Nurses' Club

In March 1917, on the initiative of Mrs Strong, the SNA took rooms at 103 Bath Street, Glasgow, which it opened as a meeting place for all nurses, trained or in training, on payment of a small subscription. Mrs Strong, who was now living in St Fillans, Perthshire, moved to Glasgow to supervise the refurbishment of the rooms. One room would be used as an office by the Association and the other as a reading and writing room for nurses. The rooms proved very popular, over 400 nurses joined within a few months, and the idea of extending the accommodation to provide a proper nurses' club was considered. The Lord Provost of Glasgow, Sir Thomas Dunlop, offered his official help and an appeal was launched as the City's tribute to nurses for their war work. Over £10,000 was raised within six months and the trustees of the fund were able to purchase premises at 205 Bath Street, which became the home of the Scottish Nurses' Club for many years.

The club consisted of a drawing room and a dining room, which could be combined to provide a lecture room, a library, 21 bedrooms which were intended for nurses on holidays or passing through Glasgow, and a kitchen and store in the basement. At the official opening, in December 1918, the Lord Provost, now J. W. Stewart, handed over the keys of the club to Mrs Strong as the doyenne of Scottish nursing. In her speech she spoke to the nurses themselves, saying that she hoped this noble gift would be as much an educational centre as one of recreation. She would like to see the club used for nurses' postgraduate education, with lectures given by members of the medical profession, and one evening a week devoted to the study of politics and general subjects so that when women got the vote nurses would use it intelligently. Mrs Strong was associated with the Club for many years, both as a trustee and as a welcome speaker.

At the age of 76, Mrs Strong set off alone on an extended journey to the Middle East and India. She left London in October 1919, travelled through France, crossed to Egypt, where she stayed for several months, and on to Jerusalem where she became involved in running a nurses' home. In August, 1920, she sailed for India and Ceylon where she spent four months, returning to England in January 1921.

The following December, Mrs Strong was chairman at a gala dinner in the Athenaeum Restaurant, Glasgow, to inaugurate the Glasgow Royal Infirmary Nurses' League. The dinner was attended by nurses from each generation of Infirmary nurses since 1879, when Mrs Strong was first appointed matron. The guests included members of the Board of Governors of the Infirmary and members of the medical staff. In replying to the toast to 'one of the greatest pioneers in the nursing profession', Mrs Strong said she was proud that the Glasgow Royal Infirmary was the first hospital in Scotland to establish a nurses' league. She considered nursing to be at a watershed, poised to reap the benefits of the long struggle for state registration and she paid tribute to the work of her friend Mrs Bedford Fenwick, without whom state registration would still be a dream. Her advice to the nurses of 1921, was the same advice that she had received from Florence Nightingale in 1869, 'Do not lose your ideals . . . keep your souls as well as your bodies'. After the speeches, the nurses queued up to obtain the autograph of Rebecca Strong.

In July 1925, Mrs Strong travelled to Finland to attend the Congress of the ICN at Helsinki, the first ICN Congress since 1912. She travelled with the official British party, which included eight Scottish delegates, via Copenhagen and Stockholm, where they were welcomed by the Danish and Swedish national associations of nurses. The Helsinki congress was remembered by all who attended it as an unique experience. Nurses from countries which had been at war were eager to meet their colleagues, and all were motivated by their experience of the suffering caused by the war to strengthen international links and help to avoid future wars. At the congress, Mrs Strong spoke briefly at the opening dinner on the first night.

In July 1927, at the interim conference of the ICN in Geneva, Mrs Strong was invited to give the closing address. She spoke of her envy of the young nurses of the day who had such splendid opportunities opening up before them in the development of the profession. She had sympathy for them too, there was so much to learn in the short time they were in training. She repeated her strongly held view that all nurses should receive a general training before they specialised in a particular field of nursing, as was the practice in medicine. She referred to the introduction of the Sister Tutor in nurse training schools, which she regarded with regret, believing that a subject should only be taught by qualified experts, as she had pioneered with the lectures given at the Glasgow Royal Infirmary in 1893.

At the congress in Finland in 1925, the ICN had accepted the invitation of the Nurses' Association of China to hold its next quadrennial congress in Peking. Mrs Strong wrote to the Nurses' Association of China in 1926, in reply to their invitation, indicating that she was planning to attend the congress in 1929. However, the revolution in China in 1927 forced the Chinese nurses to withdraw their invitation, and instead the 1929 congress was held in Montreal. Mrs Strong sent a message to the Chinese nurses, which was printed in their journal

> I feel sure that if nations only knew each other better there would be no wars or rumours of wars. At heart we are one, but unfortunately our different languages and manner of expressing ourselves lead to misunderstanding. We are so surprised when we meet to find our common brotherhood. Nurses have a great responsibility, being in such close contact with mankind in its weakened condition, and easily influenced. Then is the time to sow good seed, not so much by the spoken word, but by the daily life showing forth good will to men, and always a good word for his fellow creatures, never imputing wrong words or thoughts.
> The Nursing Times, 25 Jun 1927, p. 762

The ICN congress in Montreal was the last one which Mrs Strong attended and her presence, at the age of 86, was appreciated by the new generation of nurse educators in North America. The problems facing the nursing profession, following the war, and the need for changes in the training of nurses to meet the new demands on the profession, were recognised earlier in North America than in Britain. Their response to the situation was the development of a university-based training and the leaders of this movement acknowledged Mrs Strong as their pioneer—from her lead in the 1890s they had developed university degrees in nursing. Annie Goodrich, Dean of the School of Nursing, at Yale University, wrote to Mrs Strong after the congress, to express the gratitude which the nurses of America felt towards Mrs Strong

> . . . every member of the International Congress with whom I have come in contact since that memorable meeting have [sic] expressed the inspiration, encouragement and admiration born of your attendance at the Congress and your wonderful presence and address. It was a never to be forgotten episode of our history of nursing.
>
>                                                           GGHB HB14/6/97

## Retirement 1927–1944

In 1926 Mrs Strong became involved in setting up the British College of Nurses, an academic institution founded by Mrs Bedford Fenwick to provide nurses with a postgraduate college. Membership of the College was to be by examination but a number of founder fellows were elected, among them Mrs Strong. As a loyal supporter of Mrs Bedford Fenwick, Mrs Strong threw her influence behind the British College of Nurses. She encouraged members of the Scottish Nurses Association to join and she addressed meetings of nurses explaining what the role of the College would be, providing postgraduate courses for nurses with scholarships and bursaries. The first 'Diploma Day' was held on 29 April 1927 when the founder fellows were presented with their certificates. The certificate awarded to the fellows was decorated with the names of those who had rendered outstanding service to nursing and nurses, among them was the name of Rebecca Strong. Mrs Strong made a short speech at the ceremony, in which she said nurses were on the threshold of their career when they qualified and registered, for those who wished to specialise the College offered opportunities of postgraduate education beyond that provided by hospitals.

In 1930, Mrs Strong moved to Edinburgh where she lived until 1939. She was not as active as before but her international reputation ensured that she had contact with the nursing world through correspondence and visits. Her friends and admirers were anxious that she should be appointed an OBE and several times petitioned on her behalf. They were told that their lack of success was due to the opposition of St Thomas' Hospital. Mrs Strong sympathised with the stand taken by St Thomas', in a letter to a friend in August 1938, she wrote

> After nearly 85 years since Miss Nightingale's memorable work in the Crimea, followed by her arrangement with St Thomas' Hospital for the reception of pupils . . . then in 1893 to be eclipsed by the Royal Infirmary Glasgow, introducing a system for the preliminary instruction of nurse students . . . with St Thomas' powerful influence, it would not sacrifice its prestige to any authority.
>
> GGHB HB14/6/97

Within four months of writing this letter, she was made an OBE. It was announced at the New Year Meeting of the staff and managers of the Glasgow Royal Infirmary when, at the age of 96, Mrs Strong took her place on the platform beside the Lord Provost and Sir James Macfarlane, Chairman of the Infirmary Managers. She addressed the meeting in a firm, clear voice, speaking with confidence of the future of nurse education and its place in the medical colleges. This was her last public appearance.

In 1939, Mrs Strong moved back to Glasgow and lived in Hyndland until her home was destroyed by a bomb in March 1941. She was persuaded then to move to Chester to live with her great-nephew and his wife. In 1942, Dr J. Macewen, son of Professor Macewen (who had died in 1924) and a surgeon at the Glasgow Royal Infirmary, decided to mark the 50th anniversary of the inauguration of the preliminary lectures for nurses at the Glasgow Royal Infirmary in 1893, and to commemorate the work of his father and Mrs Strong. He commissioned two medals which were to be awarded annually, one bearing the bust of his father, to be awarded to the nurse who was considered the best practical surgical nurse in her year, and one bearing the bust of Mrs Strong, to be awarded to the best practical medical nurse in the year.

Mrs Strong welcomed the renewed contact with the Macewen family and the Royal Infirmary. She wrote to Dr Macewen and his sister, in January 1942

> . . . it was nice to hear even your name, having suffered much from depression the old name is like a bit of inspiration putting fresh life into me.

And in February

> Your letter is invaluable in helping to raise me out of my desponding
> condition and perverted view of things, it is deplorable, treatment for
> anaemia of the brain is still going on, my own opinion is that it is old
> age—ninety-nine in August.

And after the first medals ceremony, in January 1943

> I am greatly indebted to you for all you have done for me and wish Sir
> William was here to see the reward of your great efforts for the Royal
> Infirmary to give stability to the preliminary class work for pupils.
> RCPSG 10

In August 1943, Mrs Strong celebrated her 100th birthday with a
personal message from Queen Mary, besides the usual telegram from
the King and Queen. The nursing press paid tribute to the pioneer
of nursing education. The local newspapers of Glasgow and Chester
carried congratulatory articles on the 'centenary of a Nightingale
nurse' and the Glasgow Royal Infirmary and the Nightingale Fellowship of St Thomas' Hospital presented her with bouquets. To mark
the occasion, the BBC recorded a message by her to old friends and
to younger nurses, which was broadcast on radio. She died eight
months later, on 24 April 1944, in Chester.

## Conclusion

Mrs Strong's outstanding characteristics were her spirit and vision.
This strength of character was demonstrated early when, faced with
widowhood in her twenties, she decided to train as a nurse at a
time when nursing was still regarded as unsuitable for respectable
women. Her decision to train in a hospital, rather than practise
nursing among the poor of her neighbourhood as many widows did,
involved separation from her daughter who can only have been three
or four years old at the time. Again, by choosing the Nightingale
School when Miss Nightingale was still a national hero and the
school an experiment showed spirit and, later, her decision to leave
Netley Hospital, contradicting the orders of Miss Nightingale and
Mrs Wardroper, was the act of an independent person.

It is significant that it was in Scotland that Mrs Strong was able to
fulfil her potential. It would have been unusual for a woman with
her working-class background to have been appointed matron of a
large voluntary hospital in England. Macewen, a pioneer in surgery

with an international reputation, was the first to recognise her abilities. He was a difficult man to work with, he did not like to work in a team and demanded the complete dedication of his assistants and nurses. Mrs Strong recalled that at her interview for the position of matron of the Glasgow Royal Infirmary she lost her temper with him when, despite the fact that he had encouraged her to apply, he gave her a difficult time. The combination of their two personalities produced the partnership which led to the great step forward in nurses' education in 1893.

Mrs Strong did not enjoy her first term as matron of the Glasgow Royal Infirmary. She considered the nurses' working conditions backward but was torn between the conflicting demands of the sick poor, the nurses, and the medical staff, particularly Macewen whose pioneer work in surgery she wished to aid and support. On top of these problems, there was the unhelpful personality of the Superintendent and the financial constraints of a voluntary hospital. Her strong character eventually gave up the struggle and, after threatening to resign three times within a year, she finally did because she feared for her health.

The conditions at the Glasgow Royal Infirmary about which she had protested were the cause of the nurses' revolt in 1891, and it is an indication of the impression she had made on the Infirmary managers that they turned to their former troublesome matron to reform their nursing department. Mrs Strong could not resist the challenge. Her second term as matron of the Infirmary was one of the happiest times of her life. These were the years 1892–1907, when she was developing the preliminary training scheme and building up the reputation of the training school. Macewen had created the right atmosphere for Mrs Strong to reform the nurses' training and, within a few months of her return to the Royal Infirmary, he moved to the Western Infirmary, in Glasgow, demonstrating his confidence in her ability to carry out the reforms.

Her ideas about the professional status of nurses were a natural development of her theories on nurses' education. Macewen and Mrs Strong differed from Mrs Bedford Fenwick and the leaders of the campaign for state registration of nurses in their view of the fight. To the former, it was a battle to raise educational standards, by placing the education of nurses in universities they believed professional status and independence would automatically follow. For Mrs Bedford Fenwick and her supporters the priority was the statutory recognition of a minimum standard of training for nurses, thus defining the term 'trained nurse', and excluding all who did not meet the standard.

Mrs Strong was always open to new developments in nursing and in her speeches she often advised the younger generation to keep an open mind, describing nursing as progressive, the facts of today yielding to the knowledge of tomorrow. This openness of mind is echoed in her enthusiasm for travelling which she took up when she was in her eighties, at a time when travelling was still something of an adventure.

Her attitude to women's role in society was fairly traditional, she believed women were morally superior and that they had a duty to influence mankind for good. In the case of nurses, this duty was even more onerous. However, she was a strong supporter of women's suffrage and of equality in education, believing that intelligent women who lived unproductive lives were wasting their talents.

Her reputation as a pioneer in nurse education was always greater in North America than in Britain. This was partly due to the conservative approach to nurse training in Britain in the 1920s and 1930s, and partly to the imbalance in nursing politics at the time caused by the long and acrimonious campaign for state registration which left the losers, Mrs Bedford Fenwick and her supporters, excluded from policy decisions.

Rebecca Strong had a modest view of her contribution to nursing, when she was eventually persuaded to write her *Reminiscences*, published in 1937, she started with an apology

> One's own little bit is very insignificant when compared with the multitude of women who have freely given their lives not merely to nursing, but to other branches of work . . . scattered over the world working steadily on from day to day in obscure corners under the most adverse conditions.

## Sources

### Greater Glasgow Health Board Archives
HB14/1/14–21 Glasgow Royal Infirmary, Managers Committee, minutes 1871–1908.
HB14/6/97 Miscellaneous papers relating to Rebecca Strong 1894–1942.
HB14/10/1 Register of Nurses 1902–1942.

### Glasgow Eastern College of Nursing and Midwifery Library
GHB35/1/9 Collection of pamphlets, cuttings, correspondence, and photographs relating to Rebecca Strong and nursing at the Glasgow Royal Infirmary, 1893–1967.

### Royal College of Physicians and Surgeons of Glasgow
RCPSG 10 William Macewen Collection, correspondence between Macewen and Strong, and Macewen's family and Strong, 1882–1884, 1942–1943.

**Royal College of Nursing Archives**

*Education in Nursing*, Rebecca Strong, 1895, printed 1927, (Historical
     Pamphlets Collection 11B)

*Reminiscences*, Rebecca Strong, [1935] (Historical Pamphlets Collection 3B)

RCN 4 Papers relating to State Registration

*Nursing Record/British Journal of Nursing*, 1891–1927, 1943

*Nursing Times*, 1905–1927, 1943

6

# Margaret Huxley
*Pioneer of Scientific Nursing in Ireland*

(1856–1940)

*Matron of Sir Patrick Dun's Hospital, Dublin, 1883–1902; founder of the Dublin Metropolitan Technical School for Nurses 1893; founder member of the International Council of Nurses 1899; co-founder of the Irish Matrons' Association 1903, and the Irish Nurses' Association 1904; Vice-President National Council of Nurses of Great Britain and Ireland 1908; Vice-President Society for the State Registration of Trained Nurses 1914; member of the first Irish General Nursing Council 1920–1923; Hon. M.A. Dublin University 1928.*

MARGARET RACHEL HUXLEY was born in 1856, yet little is known about her until she went to St Bartholomew's Hospital, London, to train as a nurse. She was a niece of Professor T. H. Huxley, the scientist, and when she started her training, in November 1880, her home address was 47 Stockwell Park Road, South London.

The training at St Bartholomew's when she arrived consisted of two years' practical work on the wards with one evening lecture a week, on medical and surgical nursing. A few months after she started her training, Ethel Manson, the future Mrs Bedford Fenwick, became matron of St Bartholomew's. She had been matron for two days when Miss Huxley asked for an interview to discuss a grievance concerning her professional status as a probationer. The new matron was happy to rectify the problem, and Miss Manson was also impressed by the 'strong young woman', who was some months older than herself. The two women became friends.

On completion of her training in October, 1882, Miss Huxley received her certificate and immediately took up the post of matron

*Fig 12. Margaret Huxley*

of the National Eye and Ear Infirmary in Dublin, a small hospital of 60 beds in Molesworth Street. After less than a year, she was appointed matron of Sir Patrick Dun's Hospital, where she was to remain for the next two decades.

## Matron of Sir Patrick Dun's Hospital, 1883–1902

Sir Patrick Dun's Hospital was a small general hospital, serving a working class area of Dublin, on the south side of the Liffey. Miss Huxley replaced Mrs Stevenson who had been matron for 33 years. The nursing system in the hospital had been reformed in 1867 when the governors had entered into an agreement with the Dublin Nurses Training Institution. By this arrangement the institution could use the hospital as a training school, provided no additional expense was incurred by the hospital, and the governors agreed to select at least half of their staff from the Institution's nurses. A Lady Superintendent was appointed to take responsibility for the nursing staff, at a salary of £60 per annum, £20 to be paid by the hospital and £40 by the Institution. The governors had found it necessary to terminate this agreement in 1883, due to the refusal of the Lady Superintendent to train probationers who were not Church of England or Church of Ireland. The governors appointed their own Lady Superintendent and from that date the probationers were selected by the governors without reference to religion. When this Lady Superintendent resigned, Miss Huxley indicated to the Board that she was anxious to take over the responsibility for training the nurses. The governors accepted her proposal and for the next 18 years Miss Huxley held the combined post of Lady Superintendent and Matron.

The training of probationers at Sir Patrick Dun's consisted of one year's practical work in the wards. Miss Huxley drew up a new training scheme of three years, with an examination at the end carried out by the medical staff of the hospital. Probationers had to be between 25 and 40 years and they must be able to read and write well. They had to serve a three months' trial period in the hospital and, if they were accepted, they would be provided with uniform and receive a salary of £10 per annum. At the end of one year they were considered competent and were required to serve for two years on the hospital staff, either in the wards, nursing the poor in the district or nursing private cases. During their second year the nurses were paid £12, and in the third year £14. On completion of their third year they received their certificates. Provision was made for lady probationers to be taken on for periods of not less than three months, at a fee of 13 guineas, although they were expected to do the same duties as the regular probationers. In 1886, Miss Huxley introduced a six month series of weekly lectures on elementary anatomy and surgery, given by the House Surgeon. After two years of this arrangement, she took over the lectures herself.

The growing demand for trained nurses to nurse private patients prompted the governors of the hospital to increase the nursing staff in 1885. They rented a large house near the hospital, at 98 Upper Mount Street, to provide additional accommodation, and in the annual report for that year they confidently stated that they expected the nurses' home to become a source of income through the fees earned by the additional private nurses. The terms on which the nurses were supplied to private cases were one guinea per week, or part of a week, and 10s 6d per day, or part of a day. By 1887 the income earned by the private nursing staff was £558 9s 6d and the annual report stated, . . . the perfection of hospital management would be to provide trained nurses to attend external cases in private families, to such an extent as to pay for all the nursing required for the hospital, for patients who are unable to pay'.

The shortage of skilled nursing available for private patients persuaded Miss Huxley to open a nursing home in 1890. The home, which was later called 'Elpis', was the first in the country to provide private patients with medical and surgical nursing care. It started in a house near the hospital, at 48 Lower Mount Street, and Miss Huxley employed a trained nurse from the hospital to run the home. She made an arrangement with the governors of the hospital, so that probationers spent two months of their training working in the home and thus gaining experience in private nursing, 'the benefit received and gained would be about equal'. After a few years the nursing home needed additional accommodation and moved to 19–20–21 Lower Mount Street, where it became one of the most popular nursing homes in Dublin.

The governors of Sir Patrick Dun's were pleased with the nursing arrangements under Miss Huxley and in their annual report for 1890, they invited subscribers to visit the wards and see the arrangements for themselves, 'the excellence that has been attained has been chiefly due to the zeal and skill of Miss Huxley, and to the attention of the skilled staff of nurses trained under her'. Her salary was increased in 1891, from £100 to £125 per annum, and in 1895, the staff nurses' salary was increased from £20–£25 per annum to £25–£30.

The rules governing the training of probationers were amended in 1892, the minimum entrance age was lowered to 23 and the maximum age to 30. The length of training was increased to 18 months and the probationer's contract to four years, so that on completion of her training, the nurse had to work on the staff of the hospital for a further two and a half years before she received her diploma and was free to leave.

The income from the estates of Sir Patrick Dun in County Waterford collapsed in 1893, and the governors had to appeal to the public for funds. The hospital was expanding in all departments, medical, surgical and gynaecological, it now had 80 beds and the number of admissions, in 1893, was 1,034, the number of out-patients 17,454. The Friends of the hospital, assisted by the medical staff and Miss Huxley, organised a fête in aid of the hospital in 1895, which raised £7,784. The event was held in the grounds of the Royal Dublin Society in Ballsbridge and was a major social occasion involving Dublin society.

Minor alterations were made to the nurses' training in 1895, notably increasing the period of training from 18 months to two years; this did not affect the overall contract which remained at four years. The Annual Report for 1896 stated

> The system of teaching probationers their work is now complete and thorough. Judging from the number of applications to be trained at Sir Patrick Dun's, the continued and increasing demand for our nurses for private work, and the fact that many when trained are appointed to responsible and important positions in various institutions, the Governors believe that the training school is in a very high state of efficiency, and that it is turning out nurses second to none.

As the number of nurses on the staff increased, the nurses' home at 98 Lower Mount Street, at the rear of the hospital and connected to the hospital by a covered bridge, was extended by leasing the adjoining houses.

In January 1902, Miss Huxley gave notice of her resignation to the governors. This was not unconnected with a dispute which arose between her and Arthur Macan, the gynaecologist of the hospital and Professor of Medicine at Trinity College, Dublin. The midwife probationers at Sir Patrick Dun's were a separate class to the general nurse probationers, their training was shorter and they were not under the supervision of the Lady Superintendent. In 1900, she wrote to the governors listing three specific cases of maternity nurses describing themselves as Sir Patrick Dun's nurses and obtaining employment as general nurses. She pointed out that this would diminish the reputation of the general medical and surgical nurses trained by her. The governors referred the matter to the medical staff who recommended that a distinction between a general nurse and a maternity nurse should be indicated on the certificate of each. The issue continued over the next two years, and in 1902 the governors discontinued granting certificates to maternity nurses. Dr Macan, supported by the Royal College of Physicians, opposed the move on the grounds that a maternity nurse trained at Sir Patrick Dun's had a right to call herself a Dun's nurse. In the end the Maternity Department of the hospital, which had been in existence for over 30 years, was discontinued.

Margaret Huxley refused to reconsider her decision to retire, but did concede that she would remain in post until a suitable successor was found. She left on 31 August and was replaced by Miss Haughton, who had trained at Guy's Hospital. The past and present nurses of Sir Patrick Dun's subscribed £50 as a tribute to Miss Huxley and she used the money to inaugurate the Margaret Huxley Memorial Medal, to be awarded every second year, to the best nurse.

After her retirement, Miss Huxley became more involved in the running of her private nursing home, 'Elpis'. She shared the management of the home for many years with Mrs Frances Manning, a Dun's nurse, and they continued the arrangement with the hospital whereby the probationers spent two months of their training working in the nursing home. The reputation of the nursing home grew, bringing credit through association to Sir Patrick Dun's and in 1912, Miss Huxley was appointed the first woman governor of the hospital.

## Dublin Metropolitan Technical School for Nurses

Miss Huxley's reputation as the pioneer of scientific nursing in Ireland was based on her role in introducing theoretical lectures to nurses' training. Ten years after her arrival as Matron of Dun's in 1893, she organised a meeting in the National Eye and Ear Infirmary, Molesworth Street, to consider a scheme to improve the education of nurses in Dublin. The meeting was attended by 11 matrons of Dublin hospitals and eight members of the medical profession. Miss Huxley proposed the establishment of a central school where nurses from different hospitals could attend weekly lectures, given by a qualified lecturer. The proposal was accepted and a sub-committee appointed to draw up a syllabus. The sub-committee, which consisted of three doctors and three matrons, including Miss Huxley, reported back after a month, in January 1894.

They proposed that all hospitals and nurse training institutions in the city should be invited to participate and that the governing body of the school should consist of the matron and one representative of the medical staff of each participating hospital. The cost of providing the lecturers and examiners, estimated at £100 per annum, would be provided by the hospitals in direct proportion to the number of probationers they sent to the school. The probationers would be required to pass an entrance examination in general education and the instruction would consist of three terms each year, with twelve lectures in each term. The same lecture would be delivered on two separate days each week.

The school was named the Dublin Metropolitan School for Nurses, Miss Huxley was made the Honorary Secretary and the Presidents of the Royal College of Physicians and the Royal College of Surgeons were appointed patrons and ex officio members of the governing body. The school opened in September 1894 with 72 pupils, 52 probationers and 20 trained nurses. The participating institutions were, Sir Patrick Dun's Hospital, Dr Steeven's Hospital, Usshers Quay

Nurses Training Institution, the House of Industry Group of Hospitals (the Richmond, the Hardwicke Fever Hospital and the Whitworth), the Orthopaedic Hospital and the National Eye and Ear Infirmary.

The first course comprised six lectures in anatomy, six in physiology and six in hygiene and invalid cookery. Dr Ninian Falkiner was appointed the lecturer in medical subjects and the cooking demonstrations were given by Miss Hetherington, in the National Training School, Kildare Street. The fee for the course was one guinea and the lectures were open to any trained nurse on payment of a fee. Nurses who passed the examinations received a diploma which was distinct from the certificate which they received from their hospitals for practical training.

The governing body applied to the Head of Dublin Technical Schools for a grant in November 1894, stating that an increased income would enable the committee to extend the usefulness of the school since present income was only from students' fees, 'The importance to the public of having a reliable standard of education for nurses cannot be overestimated, especially as to the management of infectious diseases and other matters relating to the public health' (DMTSN Minute Book). Although it is not recorded, the application would appear to have been successful as the word 'technical' was added to the name of the school.

Dr Falkiner was succeeded by Dr E MacDowel Cosgrave, lecturer until 1906, when he was succeeded by Dr Ella Webb who continued the lectures until 1915, when Dr Percy Kirkpatrick took over. Miss Huxley proposed that additional lectures be given in medical and surgical nursing in 1897, and four extra lectures in each of these subjects were added. In 1905, four lectures on 'drugs and their actions' were added to the syllabus, and these were later increased to six. The reputation of the school grew as the number of participating hospitals increased and by 1899 *The Irish Times* carried the examination results and recommended the school's diploma to all nurses. The average number of probationers attending the lectures in these years was 50. In 1900 the lectures were transferred from the National Eye and Ear Infirmary to the Royal College of Surgeons.

## The Irish Nurses' Association 1890–1905

The professional status of the trained nurse was an issue which Margaret Huxley took seriously, and dated back to her training days at St Bartholomew's Hospital. Her friendship with Mrs Bedford

Fenwick drew her into the group of matrons, active in London, in the campaign for the state registration of nurses. Miss Huxley was one of the original members of the British Nurses' Association, founded by Dr and Mrs Fenwick, and travelled to London to attend the meetings. During the 1890s, when the executive committee of the Royal British Nurses' Association (RBNA) was taken over by an anti-registration faction, Miss Huxley protested and finally, in 1897, when asylum attendants were admitted as members, she resigned on the grounds that the Association had been founded for nurses with three years general training. She was also a member of the Matrons' Council and was present at the historic meeting in 1899, and seconded the proposal by Mrs Fenwick, to establish an International Council of Nurses (ICN).

When Queen Victoria visited Dublin in the spring of 1900, the matrons of the Dublin hospitals were presented to her at the Vice Regal Lodge. The Queen spoke to Miss Huxley, as the senior matron, before passing along the line of matrons. An address of welcome was presented to Her Majesty, thanking her for her interest in promoting the progress of trained nursing. After the royal visit there was a balance left in the fund which had been collected for the address, and it was decided to put the money towards the establishment of a club for nurses in Dublin. The object of the club was to provide a meeting place and reading rooms for nurses, where all branches of the profession could meet and discuss professional matters. A committee of six matrons was appointed to manage the club and Miss Huxley was elected president. The subscription was set at one guinea per annum for voting members and five shillings for ordinary members.

The inaugural meeting of the Dublin Nurses' Club was held in the club rooms, 3 St Stephen's Green, in December 1900. The majority of the Dublin hospitals participated in the scheme and the club opened with over 400 members. Miss Huxley chaired the meeting which was attended by approximately 25 matrons, 250 nurses and sixty medical men. The President of the Royal College of Surgeons of Ireland gave the inaugural address, welcoming the initiative taken by the nurses, and promising the support of the medical profession. He paid tribute to Miss Huxley's role in raising the standard of nursing in Ireland, saying

> She had introduced methodical system, regular training and habits of discipline, educated and trained intelligence into the wards of the hospitals, and her pupils now held very high and honourable positions in the nursing profession.
>
> *The Nursing Record*, 22 Dec 1900, p. 499

The club rooms, which were rented from the DBC (Dublin Bread Co.), comprised a sitting room, writing room, committee room and cloakrooms. The principal daily and nursing papers were taken and a series of lectures was held in the spring of 1901. The club proved very popular and at the first Annual General Meeting, in November 1901, Miss Huxley reported that the membership was over 500 and that approximately 4000 visits had been made to the Club. The Club was the first venture into professional organisation taken by Irish nurses and its success prompted the members to consider forming themselves into an association. At a meeting in January 1904, they decided to change the name of the club to the Irish Nurses' Association (INA). It was hoped that the change of name would encourage trained nurses all over the country to join and that the INA would unite Irish nurses to protect their professional interests.

At the same meeting in 1904, the two Bills for the state registration of nurses, which were to be introduced in parliament by the RBNA and the Society for the State Registration of Nurses, were discussed. Miss Kelly, matron of Dr Steeven's Hospital, described the Bills and urged Irish nurses to appoint representatives who would guard their interests and keep them informed of the progress of the Bills.

The inaugural meeting of the INA was held on 26th January 1904, at 86 Lower Leeson Street, the home of Miss MacDonnell, matron of the Richmond Hospital, who had offered the association the use of two rooms on the ground floor of her house. It was decided at the meeting to form committees throughout the country to promote the association and to stimulate interest in the state registration of nurses. Details of the two Bills for state registration were studied by a sub-committee and an open meeting was organised at the Royal College of Physicians to discuss the question. Over 400 nurses and matrons, 50 members of the medical profession, and Mrs Bedford Fenwick attended. The meeting voted in favour of the principle of state registration for nurses and called for a Select Committee of the House of Commons to inquire into the whole nursing question. This demand was taken up by the nurses' associations in England, and supported by medical opinion and Members of Parliament, with the result that a Select Committee was appointed in June, 1904, 'to consider the expediency of providing for the registration of nurses'.

During Mrs Fenwick's visit to Dublin, Miss Huxley held an 'At Home' for her to meet the members of the INA and the Irish Matrons' Association, founded in December 1903. Ethel Fenwick spent a week in the city during which time she visited the main hospitals and addressed the meeting on state registration. She also spoke to the INA about the International Council of Nurses, which was holding its second congress in Berlin in the summer. Four members of the INA attended the congress, including Miss Huxley.

## Select Committee on the Registration of Nurses 1904–1905

When the committee commenced its proceedings in London in July 1904, Miss Huxley was one of the first witnesses to give evidence. She described the system of training nurses at Sir Patrick Dun's Hospital, and it is clear that she considered it unfair to the nurses. They were contracted for four years' service, but only the first two years were regarded as their training period, in the following two years they were regarded as part of the trained staff of the hospital. The result was that they were ineligible for many positions which now required nurses to have had three years' training. Until a statutory nursing council defined a nurse's professional education in content and length, it was her opinion that hospital governors would continue to act independently and this injustice to young women would continue. She spoke strongly in favour of a three years' training, during her matronship of Sir Patrick Dun's the training had been increased from one year to 18 months, and then two years. Only after she had retired, it had been increased to three years.

Miss Huxley's emphasis was on the need for an independent nursing council to regulate the profession in the interests of nurses and of the public. She was in favour of nurses paying for their training if that was necessary to raise the standard of their education, and she felt the minimum entry age for probationers could be lowered to 18, with a minimum of 21 for the final examination. She submitted a copy of the Rules and Regulations of the Dublin Metropolitan Technical School for Nurses to the committee, and commented that the school was useful as it ensured that the nurses who attended the lectures at the school, and passed the examinations, had proper instruction and knew their work, but it did not go far enough. It was limited to the nurses' technical instruction, the standard of the practical training in the hospital wards was just as important, and this remained unregulated. After taking evidence from 33 persons, 23 of whom were in favour of state registration and Miss Huxley among them, the committee reported in favour of registration.

Another initiative arose in 1905 when a company calling itself 'The Society for Promoting the Higher Education and Training of Nurses' applied for a licence (see chapter three). Miss Huxley attended the hearing at the Board of Trade in London, as the delegate of the

INA and the Irish Matrons' Association. Previously she had called a meeting, on 24 February, to consider the appropriate response to the proposed society from Irish nurses and found them eager to protest against it. Miss Huxley read a petition, which she had drawn up against the incorporation of the society, and it was resolved to send the petition to the Board of Trade. It was also decided to write to the 'seven gentlemen who had taken it upon themselves to improve the education of nurses', and to notify the Irish Members of Parliament of the opinion of the INA. Miss Kelly, Lady Superintendent of the City of Dublin Nursing Institution, drew attention to the fact that no reference was made to Ireland in the Memorandum of the Society, that Irish nurses would have no control over the rules for the regulation of their profession.

The hearing took place on 5th May and Miss Huxley and the other representatives of the various nurses' associations spoke against the licence application. Mr Swansea, Vice-President of the Royal College of Surgeons, Ireland, also spoke against the application, criticising the unrepresentative nature of the constitution of the proposed society. Sir Victor Horsley, for the British Medical Association, said that the time had gone for private persons to group themselves into voluntary societies for the registration of nurses, his association was in favour of state registration. The Board of Trade refused the licence.

Miss Huxley continued to work in Ireland for the establishment of the INA, believing in its value as an organisation to raise professional awareness among nurses. At a meeting at Queen's College, Belfast, in January 1906, to consider setting up an Ulster branch of the Irish Nurses' Association, she gave two recent examples of the consequences of lack of professional organisation among Irish nurses. First, the inadequate rules for nurses drafted by the Local Government Board, which defined a qualified nurse as having two year's training; this qualified the nurse to work only in poor law infirmaries. The second example was the Midwives' Act (1902) which had not applied to Scotland or Ireland, and now meant that Irish midwifery pupils had to travel to England for examination. Had Irish midwives been organised they could have used their united strength to ensure that the Act was extended to Ireland. Miss Huxley's campaigning was successful and the meeting voted to establish a branch of the INA in Ulster.

The Irish Nurses' Association affiliated to the National Council of Trained Nurses of Great Britain and Ireland, formed in 1904 to represent British and Irish nurses in the ICN. Miss Huxley was elected one of the six delegates of the INA and attended the meetings and congresses of the ICN in this capacity. In June 1907, she travelled to

Paris for an interim conference with two other Irish delegates, Mrs Kildare Treacy, Lady Superintendent of the City of Dublin Nursing Institution, and Miss Carson Rae, Matron of the Cork Street Fever Hospital. Mrs Kildare Treacy, as President of the INA, was one of the speakers on professional organisation and Miss Huxley was asked to speak on the work of the Dublin Metropolitan Technical School for Nurses. She did not speak at the conference but her paper appeared in the proceedings of the conference under the title 'A Central Preparatory Course for Nurses'.

As a Vice-President of the National Council of Trained Nurses of Great Britain and Ireland, she attended the ICN Congress in London in July, 1909, and took part in the ceremony of affiliation for the new national councils of Canada, Holland, Finland and Denmark. Following the Congress, the distinguished American nurse Lavinia Dock, Honorary Secretary of the ICN, visited Dublin. The Irish Matrons' Association held a reception in the Café Cairo to mark the occasion, which was also a farewell to Miss Haughton, who was leaving Sir Patrick Dun's Hospital, after seven years, to take up her appointment as matron of Guy's Hospital, London.

In January 1910, the executive committee of the INA decided that the membership of the association, which stood at 789 and was concentrated in Dublin and Cork, should be increased to make the association more representative. They reduced the subscription from 5/- to 2/6 per annum for ordinary members and to 1/- for probationers and country members. They sent out an appeal to all Irish nurses to join the association so that it could effectively defend their interests. In 1912, the constitution was amended to allow all members to vote at meetings, with the provision that not more than three members from the same institution could vote. Every hospital and nursing institution could have a representative on the executive committee provided that the united subscriptions of the institution amounted to one pound.

Miss Huxley proposed the formation of a nurses' hostel in Dublin, to be run on cooperative lines. The Irish Matrons' Association took up the idea and the Nurses' Hostel Co. Ltd. was formed with its premises at 34 St Stephen's Green. The large Georgian house was refurbished and opened in February 1911. At the first meeting of the shareholders, Miss Huxley spoke about the aims of the undertaking which were the well-being and comfort of the nurses connected with it. The INA took one of the rooms in the hostel for their lectures and meetings, and at its Annual General Meeting that year, a vote of thanks was given to Miss Huxley for her part in setting up the hostel.

The National Council of Trained Nurses of Great Britain and

Ireland accepted the INA's invitation to hold its annual conference in Dublin in 1913. Miss Huxley was appointed President of the Association for the year and took on the task of organising the conference. It opened on 3 June with a reception at the Royal College of Surgeons, to which many prominent Dublin people were invited to meet the delegates. The reception was followed by a pageant of nursing, and during the conference an exhibition of nurses' work and equipment was held in the Mills Hall, Merrion Row. The proceedings of the conference were spread over three days, at the Royal College of Physicians, Kildare Street, and the subjects discussed were training, state registration, the nurse and insurance law, venereal disease, poor law nursing and midwifery. Mrs Fenwick was the principal speaker at the session on state registration, and her resolution, seconded by Rebecca Strong, affirming the meeting's commitment to state registration and urging the Prime Minister to allow a second reading of the Nurses' Registration Bill at the earliest possible date, was carried by a large majority. The conference closed with a garden party at the Zoological Gardens in the presence of the Lord Lieutenant, and on the same evening, a banquet in the Mansion House, chaired by Miss Huxley. She received many tributes for the success of the first nursing conference in Ireland.

In July 1914, a civic exhibition was organised in Dublin to promote the better housing of the poor, a question of great concern to the city since the riots of 1913. Miss Huxley took a particular interest in the housing of the poor and under her influence, the INA took part in the exhibition, fitting out a room as a ward and giving lectures and demonstrations on nursing and hygiene.

## Ireland and State Registration

In the autumn of 1908, the pro-registration lobby succeeded in getting a Bill for Registration introduced in the House of Lords, however, it excluded Ireland from its provisions. The INA formed an emergency committee, under the guidance of Miss Huxley, to consider what action to take. A conference was organised, with the support of the medical institutions, and resolutions in favour of state registration for nurses and the inclusion of Ireland in the Bill were passed unanimously. The strength of feeling in Ireland was communicated to Lord Ampthill, responsible for the Bill in the Lords, and to the Irish members of the Lords, who by their united efforts succeeded in having the clause which excluded Ireland removed.

The Bill was successfully carried in the Lords on its second reading but the government failed to take any action on the Bill, and the INA held a special meeting in February 1909 to consider further action. Miss Huxley proposed sending a resolution to the Prime Minister and to the Chief Secretary of Ireland calling on the government to introduce the Bill as a non-contentious measure in the Commons. This was done, and in May 1909, Miss Huxley took part in a deputation to the Prime Minister, Mr Asquith, led by Lord Ampthill, which asked the government to allow the Nurses' Registration Bill to be debated in the House of Commons. Speaking as the representative of Irish nurses, Miss Huxley said that Irish nurses were united in their desire for registration and they had worked hard for inclusion in this Bill. The deputation included Sir Victor Horsley, representing the British Medical Association, and representatives of the leading nurses' societies. Mr Asquith's response was that the government had to consider whether this Bill was the best method of introducing a system of registration, he had received lists of names, including 100 doctors in London and 120 in the provinces, 49 matrons in London and 109 in the provinces, who were opposed to this piece of legislation. The result of this unsuccessful deputation was the formation of the Central Committee for the State Registration of Nurses, consisting of representatives of all the pro-registration societies, with the aim of promoting a joint Bill. Back in Ireland, the INA held a general meeting to consider further action, and elected Miss Huxley to represent them on the Central Committee. She opened the meeting by saying that Irish nurses wished to let Mr Asquith know that they would not give up their desire for registration until it had been achieved. Mrs Kildare Treacy, referred to the figures quoted by Mr Asquith regarding the opposition to the Bill and said that Irish nurses could not rest content while they were coerced by a small autocracy of, for the most part, London matrons and doctors.

In February 1914, the Central Committee succeeded in having a revised Bill introduced in the House of Commons, which was passed on its first reading. At its Annual General Meeting in March, the INA passed a resolution, to be sent to the Irish MPs, thanking them for their unanimous support for the first reading of the Bill and urged them to use their influence to secure its second reading. The start of the First World War in August put paid to the success of this particular registration Bill.

## The War and Irish Nursing

Within days of the declaration of war, the INA set up courses in First
Aid for its members so that they would be able to give classes around
the country. They also formed a Nursing Corps under the St John
Ambulance Brigade, and within a few months had 75 members.
Some of the Corps were sent to the front under the War Office or to
France with the French Flag Nursing Corps, other members served
at base and military hospitals. In October, 1914, a branch of the
British Red Cross Society (BRCS) was set up in Dublin to organise
volunteer work. At first the executive committee did not include a
nurse, but following a protest from the INA, they invited the association to nominate three members and Miss Huxley, Miss Cunningham, the President, and Miss Sutton, matron of St Vincent's Hospital, were appointed.

Miss Huxley took on the matronship of the Dublin University
Women's VAD Hospital in 1915. The women students of Trinity
College, who had formed one of the first Voluntary Aid Detachments
(VADs) in 1911, leased a large house at 19 Mountjoy Square which
they equipped as a hospital for the wounded. It contained four wards
of 24 beds each, and an operating theatre. The staff comprised Miss
Huxley, two trained nurses, and several Belgian refugees employed
to work in the kitchen. During the rebellion, which took place in
Easter week 1916, all Dublin hospitals opened their doors to the
wounded, including the Trinity VAD hospital. Miss Huxley's private
nursing home 'Elpis', in Lower Mount Street, and Sir Patrick Dun's
Hospital, were in the centre of one of the trouble spots on Easter
Monday, and Miss Huxley joined the staff of the two institutions
ferrying the wounded from the street to the hospital, a task which
took them from four in the afternoon until midnight.

## Ireland and the College of Nursing

A scheme to establish a College of Nursing was proposed in February
1916, by Miss Sarah Swift (chapter seven), the Matron-in-Chief of
the BRCS and the Honourable Arthur Stanley, its chairman. The aim
was, through the voluntary support of the profession, to introduce
a uniform system of training nurses, with a standard examination and
certificate. Many of the large teaching hospitals which had previously
opposed the registration of nurses were in support of the proposed
College. The pro-registration lobby, of which Mrs Fenwick and Miss
Huxley were two leaders, was dismayed that once again they had to

contend with a scheme for voluntary rather than statutory registration.

In Ireland, the Royal Colleges of Physicians and Surgeons set up a joint committee to consider the College of Nursing scheme, and received a deputation from the INA, which included Miss Huxley, protesting against it. The joint committee sent Mr Stanley a resolution informing him that unless Irish nurses were given one-fifth of the council seats of the College, they could not recommend that they join.

Speaking at a meeting in Dublin in July, 1916, Dr de Courcy Wheeler, RCSI, a prominent medical man, said that Irish nurses' attitude to the College was, rightly, one of caution. Full Irish representation on the council of the College was essential for Irish cooperation. The training in Ireland differed from that in English schools, and any attempt to make the Irish schools conform to the English system would result in chaos. He was confident that the College would never receive statutory powers without Irish cooperation.

The Irish Matrons' Association and the INA were opposed to the College for the same reasons that the registration lobby opposed it. Both associations had been part of the original registration group which had campaigned for over 20 years to achieve statutory recognition for the profession. They could not accept Mr Stanley's argument that state registration was as far away as it had ever been, believing that once the war was over the government would be forced to give the Registration Bill a second reading. The extent of the immediate support for the College of Nursing among English nurse training schools shocked the pro-registration lobby.

The College of Nursing was founded in April 1916 and within weeks the founders accepted that state registration was desired by the majority of its members, and made it one of the aims of the College. Initially they entered into negotiations with the Central Committee for the State Registration of Nurses in an attempt to produce a joint Bill, but when negotiations broke down in October, 1916, both parties promoted their own Bills. The Irish Matrons' Association appealed to the Irish Members of Parliament to block the College of Nursing Bill and to support the Bill promoted by the Central Committee. In response to the conditions laid down by the Joint Committee of the Royal Colleges of Physicians and Surgeons, the College of Nursing had offered Irish nurses a sixth representation and an Irish Board based in Dublin. The INA held an extraordinary general meeting, on 25 November 1916, to consider the position but no decision was taken although some of the leading medical and nursing personalities felt that the proposal could be of value to Irish nurses.

Early the following year, the secretary of the College of Nursing, Miss Rundle, and Miss Cox-Davies, matron of the Royal Free Hospital, London, and a member of the College council, visited Ireland to address meetings in Dublin and Belfast on the aims of the College. The meeting in Dublin was held in the Royal College of Physicians, with the president Dr J. O'Carroll in the chair. Miss Rundle explained the objectives of the College and the powers of the proposed Irish Board. A Scottish Board had already been formed with representatives on the Council, and there were still six places left for the Irish nurses. If the Irish nurses would join and add their names to the College register, they would strengthen the hands of their representatives promoting the Bill for registration in Parliament.

Miss Rundle and Miss Cox-Davies addressed a second meeting in the Nurses' Hostel, 34 St Stephen's Green, at which Miss Huxley asked who would appoint the Irish Board. Miss Rundle explained that the first Board would be self-appointed and carry out the work until there were enough Irish nurses on the register to hold an election. The Board would have full powers to regulate the Irish training schools and the examination of Irish nurses. The INA discussed the proposed Irish Board at its executive committee meeting in February and decided that there was still no advantage to Irish nurses in joining the College. Mrs Fenwick, writing in the *British Journal of Nursing* (17 Feb 1915, p. 121) on the Irish situation, commented that as an honorary member of the Irish Matrons' Association she would like to see a College of Nurses of Ireland, in touch with the Royal Colleges of Physicians and Surgeons of Ireland, as the headquarters of nursing education in Ireland. Her suggestion was that such a College would bear the same relation to a General Nursing Council, set up by Act of Parliament, as the Medical Colleges do to the General Medical Council.

The Irish Board of the College of Nursing held its first meeting on 29 March 1917. The first Board consisted of 22 members, composed of nurses and representatives of the medical profession and lay people. The nurse members were:

Miss Bostock, Royal Victoria Hospital, Belfast;
Miss Chisholm, Irish Branch, Queen Victoria's Jubilee Institute of Nursing, Dublin;
Miss Coffey, Barrington's Hospital, Limerick;
Miss Curtin, Mater Hospital, Belfast;
Miss Eddison, Royal City of Dublin Hospital;
Miss Egan, President Irish Matrons' Association;

Miss Hill, Adelaide Hospital, Dublin;
Miss McDowell, County Infirmary, Waterford;
Miss McGiveney, Mater Hospital, Dublin;
Miss O'Brien, 67 Lower Leeson Street, Dublin;
Miss Phelan, South Dublin Union;
Miss Reed and Miss Shuter, Ivanhoe, Lansdowne Road, Dublin.

In the same month, the Royal Colleges of Physicians and Surgeons, with the support of the INA and the Irish Matrons' Association, proposed the formation of an independent Irish Nursing Board. The original object was to confer diplomas on trained nurses but this scheme was rejected by the Physicians. The Surgeons, however, went ahead with the formation of a nursing board, 'drawn up and entirely controlled by professional experts in Ireland'. It was launched in May, 1917, and its aims were to promote the education of Irish nurses, to examine trained nurses, to grant certificates to nurses passing the examination of the Board, and to make and maintain a register of such nurses. The Board consisted of 22 nurse members, and four representatives elected by the Royal College of Surgeons. The initial Board would resign in July 1918 and the nurses on the register would elect a new one. The nurse members of the first Board included:

Miss L. Bradburne, Meath Hospital;
Miss Bradshaw, Royal Hospital for Incurables;
The Honourable Albinia Brodrick;
Miss E. Hezlett, Richmond Hospital;
Miss M. Huxley;
Miss J. Jordan, Mercer's Hospital;
Miss K. Kearns, Nurses' Insurance Society;
Miss M. Keating, National Maternity Hospital;
Miss M. O'Flynn, Children's Hospital, Temple Street;
Miss A. Carson Rae, Secretary, Nurses' Hostel;
Miss L. Ramsden, Rotunda Hospital;
Miss A. Reeves, Dr Steeven's Hospital;
Miss A. Rhind, Cork Street Fever Hospital;
Miss E. Sutton, St Vincent's Hospital;
Miss M. Thornton, Sir Patrick Dun's Hospital;
Miss D. West, North Dublin Union.

The College of Nursing and the Irish Nursing Board competed for the support of Irish nurses and each held open meetings in Dublin to explain their aims and objectives. At the College of Nursing meeting, in the Royal College of Physicians, Miss Vera Matheson, the Secretary of the College's Irish Board, described the constitution of the College, the role of the Irish Board, and reported that the membership of the College was just short of 8000 members, increasing by several hundred a month. The advantages to Irish nurses of being part of a larger movement, encompassing English, Scottish, Welsh, Irish and colonial nurses, who were nurses first and foremost, with the needs and responsibilities of nurses whatever their nationality or political opinion, were many. She criticised the Irish Nursing Board for being too narrow in conception. A nurse never knew where her work would take her, she needed a certificate which would carry weight all over the world, and no matter what happened to Ireland politically, Irish nurses would always look for work in England. She appealed to Irish nurses to unite, 'Why will you degrade a noble profession by allowing political considerations to interfere or to bias you?' (*The Hospital*, 3 Nov 1917, p. 102).

At the alternative meeting held by the Irish Nursing Board, in the Royal College of Surgeons, the Honourable Albinia Brodrick, sister of Lord Middleton and a trained nurse, spoke about the aims of the Irish Nursing Board. She emphasised that the Board was Irish and democratic, its objectives were to organise nurses' training and education in Ireland. A series of speakers followed her including Miss Huxley, who spoke of the need for a uniform curriculum so that all nurses started on an equal footing. Dr O'Carroll, the chairman and President of the Royal College of Physicians, moved a vote of thanks and said that Miss Brodrick had hit the nail on the head when she said that Irish nurses were not going to be governed by England.

The Irish correspondent of the London journal *The Hospital*, who wrote under the pseudonym 'Ierne', reported these meetings in detail, and was not sympathetic to the Irish Nursing Board. Commenting on Miss Brodrick's statement that Irish nurses did not want to be governed by England, she wrote

> I am not aware that nurses want to be governed at all, either in England or in Ireland, the Irish Nurses' Association, out of which the Irish Nursing Board has grown, and of which Miss Brodrick was a distinguished member, never did anything else than 'govern' the Irish nurse . . . these women, preaching democracy and practising autocracy, have succeeded in adding to the difficulties that lie in the way of reform by creating faction'.

*The Hospital*, 22 Dec 1917, p. 256.

The two sides of the Irish nursing world cooperated to establish and promote the Tribute Fund for Nurses in 1918. Sir Arthur Stanley had initiated the appeal in England to establish a fund for the welfare of nurses whose health had been broken by war service. A proportion of the fund was to endow the College of Nursing. To procure the support of all Irish nursing opinion, and public support, it was decided to earmark all money raised in Ireland for the benefit of Irish nurses.

In each county the wife of the County Lieutenant was asked to organise a local committee, and with one or two exceptions they accepted this responsibility, with the Marchioness of Waterford as president. An executive committee was appointed, consisting of representatives of all Irish nursing organisations, including Miss Huxley and chaired by Lady Arnott. The aim was to raise £10,000 to establish a hostel for nurses in need. Sir Arthur Stanley visited Dublin to officially launch the fund in June 1918, and addressed a large meeting in the lecture threatre of the Royal Dublin Society. It was attended by the leading members of Dublin society, and presided over by Sir James Campbell, the Lord Chancellor of Ireland.

The Lord Chancellor, in introducing Sir Arthur, paid tribute to the achievements of Irish women in the war, and especially to the work of Irish nurses. Sir Arthur said that the fund was not a charity but a debt owed by the nation to the nursing profession. Through the Red Cross he employed a large number of nurses and two things struck him, the lack of organisation among a profession so old and honourable, and the lack of financial provision for those nurses who were unable to work through ill-health. The Red Cross had set aside £10,000 to help Red Cross nurses, and the government had promised compensation to nurses working in the services. But there was still a vast army of nurses working for the civil population who would receive no help from the government or the Red Cross. Nursing was hard work and many nurses found they could not continue working up to late in life. Moreover, the pay of nurses, which was inadequate for the service they rendered, did not allow them to provide for their retirement.

He referred to the request from the Irish executive committee that the money raised in Ireland should be spent on Irish nurses, and said that if the Irish committee could take on the responsibility of providing for all Irish nurses, then he could assure them that the organisers of the Fund in London would be very grateful. The Irish Fund would be independent of the College of Nursing and would be administered by commissioners appointed in Ireland. Within a year £5000 had been raised by the counties and the remainder of the sum was collected in Dublin. The fund was named the Nation's Tribute to Nurses, and it gave assistance to all nurses in need. Miss Huxley served on the executive committee for many years.

## Conditions of Irish Nurses

The poor economic conditions of Irish nurses became the dominant problem facing the various nursing organisations in 1918 and 1919. It was generally accepted that their conditions were worse than those of English nurses. A pamphlet, published anonymously at the beginning of 1919, called 'A Plea For Irish Nurses by one of them', stated that the Irish nurse worked an average of 16 hours a day, 83 hours a week, with one day off a month. Their average salaries were, for a staff nurse £30 per annum, for a sister £35 per annum, private nurses earned £40–£50 per annum, while Irish working men were striking for a 44 hour week and a typist or clerk earned £200 per annum. The author called on the employers of nurses to face the facts and act now before the nursing service degenerated.

Dissatisfaction among nurses gave rise to the Irish Nurses' Union, set up in 1919 as a branch of the Irish Women Workers' Union (IWWU). At a meeting in the Mansion House, attended by over 500 nurses, Miss Louie Bennett, the organising secretary of the IWWU, made the case for a nurses' trade union. She described the nursing profession as one that 'in return for great skill of the most valuable kind offers a wage less than that of a railway porter' (*Nursing Times*, 22 Mar 1919, p. 270). At the meeting Miss Matheson, the secretary of the College of Nursing Irish Board, spoke against trade unionism for nurses, as did the representatives of the Irish Matrons' Association and the INA. The general view of the Irish nursing establishment was that the Irish Nurses' Union was a 'Larkinite movement', although Miss Bennett maintained from the start that a nurses' strike was inconceivable.

In response to the growing discontent, the INA wrote to the governors of the majority of the Dublin hospitals asking them to abolish probationers' fees, to introduce a 56 hour week, a three years' training, to increase probationers' salaries to £10 in the first year, £12 in the second and £14 in the third year, and to pay staff nurses a minimum of £36 per annum and sisters £45. The Irish Board of the College of Nursing recommended a minimum salary for a trained nurse of £50 per annum, and a maximum of 56 hours a week, with one day off a fortnight. The Irish Nurses' Union claimed, on behalf of its members in the Dublin Union Hospital, an eight hour day or night, a forty-eight hour week, and a minimum salary of £100 per annum, rising to £160. Some of the Dublin hospitals introduced reforms in response to public opinion, Dr Steeven's and the Adelaide abolished probationers' fees, reduced the number of hours the nurses worked, and increased their salaries.

In May 1919, a Nurses' Conference was held at the Royal College
of Surgeons to discuss the formation of a joint committee to represent
all the different nursing associations in Ireland. The conference was
attended by six delegates from each of the existing societies, except
the Irish Nurses' Union which declined the invitation. It was decided
to form an Advisory Body consisting of three representatives of each
society.

## Nurses' Registration Acts 1919

When the government introduced its Nurses' Registration Bill in
early November 1919, the Irish nursing world was alarmed that it
did not include Ireland. The INA, the Irish Matrons' Association and
the Irish Nursing Board sent a deputation to the Chief Secretary,
who was the Minister of Health for Ireland. The deputation was
received by Dr Coey Bigger, the chairman of the Irish Council of the
Ministry of Health, who accepted the case for a similar registration
Bill for Ireland and reciprocity between the three countries.

The Irish Bill was published on 26 November and provided for a
General Nursing Council of ten persons, of whom six would be
nurses and would be appointed by the Chief Secretary in consultation
with the nursing profession. The Irish nurses' associations wished
to make several amendments to the Bill but they were advised against
it if they wished to achieve reciprocity with English and Scottish
nurses. The only substantial amendment which was made to the
Irish Registration Bill was to increase the size of the Council from
ten to 15 persons, and the *Nurses' Registration (Ireland) Act* became
law on 23 December 1919.

Miss Huxley held a celebration dinner in the Bonne Bouche restaurant in Dawson Street, to mark the passing of the *Nurses' Registration Act*. The guests included the matrons and nurses who had
worked for the cause over the years. In her speech, Miss Huxley said
that she had promised herself this celebration at least 20 years ago,
' . . . though our success has not come exactly in the way we hoped
it would, at least we may congratulate ourselves that our determination in the past was a strong factor in the framing of this broadly-
conceived Act'. She took up the point made by Dr Addison, Minister
of Health for England and Wales, in a recent speech, that nurses
should be citizens first and professional women second. She felt that
nurses needed to improve their education so that as a professional
body they were in a position to assist the Minister in making the
nation healthy. She suggested that the Irish Matrons' Association

plan a course of lectures in 'sanitation, hygiene, preventive medicine, and child welfare, and also lectures giving a working knowledge of the various Acts of Parliament affecting public health . . . ' (*British Journal of Nursing*, 7 Feb 1920, p. 82).

Miss Huxley's speech was followed by several which outlined the future for nurses under registration. Finally, her colleague from the early days of the registration movement, Miss Carson Rae, paid tribute to Miss Huxley's role in the achievement of registration in Ireland. From the beginning Miss Huxley had worked on behalf of Irish nurses, that they might take their place as equals among English and Scottish nurses under the Act. Every year she had attended meetings in London, crossing the Irish Sea in all weathers, often at great inconvenience and always at her own personal expense. They all owed her a great debt of gratitude, not least for asking them to celebrate this evening the great event in the history of nursing.

Miss Huxley returned to the theme of the nurse's role in public health at a meeting of the Statistical and Social Inquiry Society of Ireland, in February 1920. Dr Ninian Falkiner gave a paper on 'The Nurse and the State', and in the discussion of the issues raised, Miss Huxley spoke of the role which the nurse could play in improving the standard of health of the public. She had been involved in caring for the health of the working people of Dublin since her days as matron of Sir Patrick Dun's Hospital, and she was familiar with the conditions in which the poor lived.

## The General Nursing Council for Ireland

The first General Nursing Council for Ireland held its initial meeting on 25 February 1920, at the offices of the Minister of Health, 33 St Stephen's Green. There were nine nurse members and five representatives of the medical profession. Miss Huxley, Miss Reeves, Miss Michie and Miss O'Flynn represented the Irish Nursing Board, and Miss Matheson, Miss Curtin and Miss Bostock from the College of Nursing Irish Board. The other two nurse members were Miss Walshe, Matron of the Union Infirmary, Waterford, and Mrs Blunden, Matron of Mosaphir Private Nursing Home, Cork. The medical representatives were Dr Coey Bigger of the Irish Public Health Council, who was elected chairman, Sir Arthur Chance, FRCSI, Chairman of the Irish Nursing Board, Col William Taylor, FRCSI, R. J. Johnstone, Royal Victoria Hospital, Belfast, P. T. O'Sullivan, South Charitable Infirmary, Cork. The fifteenth member was the Countess of

Kenmare, Vice-President of the Queen Victoria Jubilee Institute (Irish Branch) for Nurses.

Miss Huxley was appointed a member of the committee which drew up the rules for the conduct of the council's business, the formation, maintenance and publication of the register of nurses, and the conduct of examinations. The Committee met seven times before reporting back to the Council in June. The following committees were appointed, a general purposes committee, a finance committee and a registration committee, and Miss Huxley was elected a member of the finance committee and the registration committee. The rules for the admission of existing nurses to the register were:

1. nurses who were for at least three years before 1 November 1919 engaged in approved practice as nurses;
2. nurses who had spent a period of at least one year's training in a recognised hospital would be accepted as having adequate knowledge and experience;
3. nurses who had already been admitted to the register of the Irish Nursing Board or of the Irish Branch of the College of Nursing.

The period of grace for existing nurses to register was two years from the date of the promulgation of the rules. These rules were in general conformity with the rules made by the English and Scottish General Nursing Councils. The three councils were keen to have reciprocal agreements to enable nurses to transfer from one country to another without having to sit additional examinations. The negotiations between the councils were protracted, due to the conditions laid down by the English council for 'existing nurses', but full reciprocity was achieved in 1925.

After the passing of the *Government of Ireland Act*, 1920, the government of the country was divided between Belfast and Dublin. The six counties of Northern Ireland were to be governed from Belfast, and the remaining 26 counties from Dublin, both parts of the country would be represented at Westminster. The members of the Irish General Nursing Council unanimously decided that it was in the interests of Irish nurses to retain one General Nursing Council for the whole of Ireland and asked the Irish Public Health Council to convey this to the English Government. However, the Dublin government did not accept the provisions of the Government of Ireland Act and eventually, in 1922, the 26 counties were recognised as a separate state, the Irish Free State, by the British government. The Northern Ireland government set up the Joint Nursing Council for Nurses and Midwives to take over the role of the Irish General

Nursing Council in the six counties and, in November 1924, the two Irish nursing councils agreed on complete reciprocity.

The first Irish General Nursing Council, which had been nominated by the British administration, went out of office on 31 December 1923. The new council was elected by a postal ballot of the nurses on the register before 15 November 1923. The number of nurses who had registered by July 1923 was only 2,289 and although it was felt that the political uncertainties surrounding the future of the Irish General Nursing Council had discouraged nurses from registering, the election went ahead. Practically all the members of the first council lost their seats, including Miss Huxley.

The first council and its committees had met 95 times, it had set up the register and the registration process, agreed on an examination syllabus, and started the process of approving hospitals as training schools. Miss Huxley had been appointed one of the three examiners to examine existing nurses who had failed to register during the period of grace, which had been extended to 31 March 1923, and who were required to pass an examination before being admitted to the Register of Nurses. She continued to act as an examiner for several years after losing her seat on the council.


## Irish Nursing Organisations after 1923

After 1920 the INA found its role in Irish nursing politics diminished. The Irish Nurses' Union, founded in 1919, had become the representative voice of nurses and the General Nursing Council had taken on the responsibility of improving and enforcing standards of training. In May, 1923, the executive committee voted to suspend the work of the association. The Irish Nurses' Union seceded from the Irish Women Workers' Union in 1928, when it had a membership of 220 nurses and 324 midwives. It was thought that a nurses' organisation existing in its own right would be more attractive to nurses and it subsequently changed its name to the Irish Nurses' Organisation. The Irish Board of the College of Nursing was dissolved in 1925, when it had a membership of over one thousand.

The Irish Matrons' Association continued to meet until 1959 and Miss Huxley was a regular attender of the quarterly meetings up to 1937. In the 1920s and 1930s, the Association was closely concerned with the work of the Irish General Nursing Council and made recommendations to the Council, including the syllabus of training, the standard of education for entry to training, the value of training in small and special hospitals, which was important in Ireland where many of the hospitals were under 100 beds, and the conduct of the examinations. In discussing the syllabus of training which should be adopted by the General Nursing Council, the Association recommended that the three year syllabus of the English Council should be adopted in principle, with slight alterations. The syllabus of the Dublin Metropolitan Technical School for Nurses was amended in 1920 and 1921 to include second and third year lectures. Miss Huxley remained the Honorary Secretary of the school until her death and attended the meetings of the executive committee until 1938.

The Irish Matrons' Association proposed in 1924, when Miss Huxley was president, that Ireland should affiliate to the ICN in its own right. Previously it had formed part of the National Council of Trained Nurses of Great Britain and Ireland. The National Council of Trained Nurses of the Irish Free State was therefore established in March, 1925, and affiliated to the ICN at the congress in Helsinki that summer. This was the last ICN congress which Miss Huxley attended and it gave her some of her happiest memories. The congress was a unique celebration by the nurses of the world, in the aftermath of war, of the peace and optimism which they felt about the future development of their profession and their role in the peace and health of the world. At the congress, Miss Huxley was made an honorary member of the Finnish Nurses' Association.

## Tributes and Death

In 1928, when she was 72, the Senate of Dublin University conferred an Honorary Degree of Master of Arts on Margaret Rachel Huxley, in recognition of her pioneer work for scientific nursing in Ireland. The Irish Matrons' Association gave a dinner at Mills' Hall, Merrion Row, to celebrate the occasion and a letter of congratulations was read from Princess Arthur of Connaught, President of the Royal British Nurses' Association. In acknowledging the congratulations of her colleagues, Miss Huxley said she felt that the university in honouring her had honoured all nurses and she hoped they would continue to deserve the good opinion of their work.

Miss Huxley lived to the age of 83. She never lost interest in the development of the nursing profession and attended meetings of the Irish Matrons' Association, the Dublin Metropolitan Technical School for Nurses, the National Council of Nurses and the ICN until well into her seventies. At this stage, Miss Huxley admitted that she was disappointed that Irish nurses had failed to realise the advantages of professional organisation. She also continued her association with

*Fig 13. Honorary Degree, University of Dublin, 1928*

work for housing the poor of Dublin and a crescent of houses in the Coombe area of Dublin was named after her. She died at 'Elpis', on 10 January 1940, and her funeral was held on 13 January, at the Unitarian Church, Dublin, and she was buried in Mount Jerome cemetery.

## Conclusion

There is no record of what influenced the young Margaret Huxley to take up nursing, nor any evidence to suggest why she went to work in Ireland and, more unusually, why she decided to stay there for the rest of her life. It is possible that her family were not keen on her chosen work, they were a highly intellectual family and Margaret undoubtedly had had a good education. The date and place of her training were an important influence in her life as it brought her into touch with Miss Manson, the future Mrs Bedford Fenwick, and we know from the latter's own writings that the two young women immediately became friends.

Within months of completing her training, Miss Huxley arrived in Ireland for her first job, at the age of 26, and the following year she was appointed matron of Sir Patrick Dun's Hospital where she remained until she retired. Sir Patrick Dun's Hospital was not a large hospital, even by Dublin standards, and it is slightly surprising that this intelligent and highly competent English woman did not wish to take on a more challenging post in one of the large London hospitals. The 19 years that she was matron of Sir Patrick Dun's Hospital, from 1883 to 1902, were years of hard work, building up the standard of nursing in the hospital and the reputation of the training school. The high standard she achieved was recognised by all her contemporaries, the governors of the hospital, the medical staff, and her nursing colleagues at home and abroad. Speaking of this period of her life, Miss Huxley said that her greatest reward had been the good work done by the many excellent women she trained and their appreciation of her method of training. Her nurses remembered her as a strict disciplinarian, who always did three ward rounds every day and knew every patient.

Miss Huxley's most far-reaching accomplishment was the introduction of theoretical instruction to the training of Irish nurses. She first introduced lectures in the training of Sir Patrick Dun's nurses and, after ten years, the improvement in the standard of nursing was so great that she took steps to extend the benefits to the nurses of other Dublin hospitals. In 1893, she founded the Dublin Metropolitan

(Technical) School for Nurses, a central school for nurses which was suited to the needs of the many small hospitals in Dublin. The school operated successfully for over 60 years and Miss Huxley was the Honorary Secretary from its foundation until her death.

Miss Huxley retired from paid employment at the age of 46 but she continued to be involved in nursing work through her private nursing home. This home was very successful and appears to have provided Miss Huxley with a comfortable income. After her retirement from hospital work, she became more involved in the professional development of nursing and nurses in Ireland. She was the main force behind the foundation of the Irish Nurses' Association and the Irish Matrons' Association which were the first professional voice of Irish nurses. Although these organisations were never representative of the majority of Irish nurses, they raised the professional awareness of nurses in the country, and the status of the nurse in the community.

Miss Huxley's long association with the campaign for the state registration of nurses, and her friendship with Mrs Fenwick, meant that she opposed the College of Nursing. It was inevitable that the opponents of the College of Nursing in Ireland should, in 1916, adopt an anti-British argument. Miss Huxley's sympathies were never nationalist, her opposition to the College was on professional grounds. Through their membership of the London based professional organisations, Miss Huxley and a handful of other Irish matrons had maintained a link between Irish nurses and the wider nursing world, particularly the ICN. In her obituary of her friend, Miss Alice Reeves wrote that Miss Huxley preferred deeds to words and this is borne out by the amount of committee work which she undertook and the total absence of any surviving written work. She remembered her as a woman of very simple tastes, unostentatious and self-disciplined. She disliked any publicity for herself and refused to accept the award of a Royal Red Cross for her work during the war, as she considered her work had not been of sufficient importance to merit public recognition. Her influence was far-reaching and she was consulted on all matters concerning nursing by the medical and nursing professions in Dublin. The two causes to which Miss Huxley dedicated her life, the care of the sick, both rich and poor, and the professional development of nursing, reflected the philanthropic and intellectual traditions of her family.

## Sources

**Royal College of Physicians of Ireland**
Records of Sir Patrick Dun's Hospital
1/6–9 Board of Governors, minutes 1877–1909.
Annual Reports, 1883–1899.

**Royal College of Surgeons of Ireland, Faculty of Nursing**
Dublin Metropolitan Technical School for Nurses, minute book 1893–1952.
Irish Matrons' Association, minute book 1910–1938.

**An Bord Altranais**
General Nursing Council of Ireland, minutes 1920–1943.
Rules Committee, minutes 1925–1946.

**Royal College of Nursing Archives**
House of Commons Select Committee on Registration of Nurses, minutes
of evidence and report, 1904–1905.
*Nursing Record/British Journal of Nursing*, 1890–1940.
*Nursing Times*, 1905–1924.
*The Hospital*, 1917–1918.

 7

# Sarah Swift

## *A Supreme Organiser*

(1854–1937)

*Matron of Guy's Hospital 1901–1909; Matron-in-Chief of the
British Red Cross Society, 1914–1935; Founder of the College
of Nursing 1916, President 1925–1927, Vice-President
1928–1937, Hon. Treasurer 1928–1937; Lady of Grace of the
Order of St John of Jerusalem; Florence Nightingale Medal
1929; RRC, GBE.*

S ARAH ANNE SWIFT was the second child and only daughter of
Robert and Mary Swift. She was born on 22 November 1854 at
Kirton, near Boston, Lincolnshire, where her father's family had been
independent farmers for over a century. Her parents' first child, a
son, had died in infancy, and a second son followed Sarah. When
she was about two years old, the family moved to Donington, near
Boston, where she grew up and attended school.

At the age of 22, in May 1877, Sarah went to the Dundee Royal
Infirmary to train as a nurse. The matron at the Infirmary at the time
was Rebecca Strong (see chapter five) who had been appointed in
1873 to reform the nurse training on the Nightingale School model.
The training consisted of two and a half years' practical work on the
wards under the supervision of sisters and medical staff. Before
completing her training, Miss Swift was asked to stand in as Matron
when Mrs Strong left for the Glasgow Royal Infirmary in June, 1879,
and before her successor was appointed in August. The minutes of
the hospital board record their thanks for the able way Miss Swift
carried out the duties. On completion of her training in October,
1879, she became Sister-in-Charge of the Home for Incurables in
Dundee, a post she held for six years. She then left Dundee and
spent under a year in Liverpool, as a Ward Superintendent at the
City Hospital, before moving to London. There she worked at the

London Fever Hospital, Islington, as Night Superintendent, for a year and then took time off to travel.

She went first to America to study nursing practices in New York and later to Constantinople where she worked in the British Seamen's Hospital. She returned to England at the end of 1890 with a fever and on recovery went to Guy's Hospital, London, in December, as a paying probationer. Paying probationers were accepted by many of the training schools for one year's training. They were also known as lady-pupils as they tended to be girls from well-off families. They received the same instruction as the ordinary probationers but did not have to undertake the heavier domestic tasks or night duty and they lived in separate accommodation. The practice arose when the training period for probationers was one year, hospital authorities were happy to receive the additional income and matrons found lady-pupils had a good influence on the ordinary probationers. By the 1890s, the appointment of these lady-nurses to positions of authority over nurses who had had three years' training was unusual and attracted criticism. It became the practice for a paying probationer wishing to qualify as a nurse, to transfer to the ordinary training for the second and third year, and to take the final examination to obtain a certificate.

At the age of 36, and with over ten years' experience of hospital nursing, Sarah Swift was not a usual paying probationer. It is likely that she wished to benefit from the lectures given by the medical staff to the probationers at Guy's since her training at Dundee had not included any theoretical instruction. The training scheme at Guy's had been reorganised in 1879 to provide three years' practical work with weekly lectures given by members of the medical staff.

## Guy's Hospital 1891–1901

On completing the one year's course in December 1891, Miss Swift was appointed Assistant Matron at Guy's. A year later the matron, Miss Victoria Jones, retired and was succeeded by Miss Nott Bower, previously the Lady Superintendent of the private nurses' department of the hospital. Miss Swift was promoted to Miss Nott Bower's former position, and thereby became responsible for Guy's Hospital Trained Nurses' Institution. The Institution employed only nurses trained at Guy's, candidates signed a four and a half year contract and during the first three years were trained with the other probationers in the wards of the hospital. After obtaining their general certificates, the nurses served as private nurses for one and a half years after which they were granted a further certificate.

As head of the Institution from 1893 to January 1901, Sarah Swift was in charge at a time when the demand for private trained nurses was growing rapidly. The Institution had started in 1885 with five nurses, when Miss Swift became the Lady Superintendent there were 62 nurses and when she left the post the staff numbered 100 nurses, yet the number of applications for nurses always exceeded the supply. Charges for private nurses were one and half guineas a week for ordinary cases of illness, two guineas a week for surgical cases and cases of fever, two and a half guineas a week for small-pox cases, and for infectious cases an extra fee of one guinea was charged to defray the cost of disinfection.

The income of the Institution in 1893 was £5,057. The nurses were paid £25 the first year they were on the staff, their first year after training, £30 the second year, £35 the third year and £40 in subsequent years. In 1894, a bonus scheme for the nurses on the staff of the Institution was introduced, the surplus profits were divided among the nurses who had been on the staff for four years after completing their training. The share of profits depended on how long they had been on the staff and it was not paid directly to the nurse, but invested in the Royal National Pension Fund for Nurses.

Miss Nott Bower retired from the post of Matron in 1899, and was succeeded by Miss Esther Young, the Assistant Matron at Guy's for the previous three years. She resigned 12 months later, and, on the recommendation of several of the sisters, the governors appointed Sarah Swift as Matron. She inherited a well run nursing department and a well established training school. Miss Nott Bower had introduced many improvements in the conditions of the nurses, especially in the amount of off-duty time and holidays. The average day had been reduced to eight and a half hours taken over a four week period, and all nurses had a half day off each week. The sisters had a weekend off twice a month, from 4 pm on Saturday to 10 am on Monday. These improvements had been achieved by increasing the number of the nursing staff to 197, while the number of beds in the hospital was 650. The reputation of the training school was in keeping with the standing of the hospital, over 3000 applications were received annually for approximately 90 training places.

A new nurses' home was opened in 1902, increasing the accommodation available for nursing staff and allowing Miss Swift to make several improvements, the most important being the introduction of a preliminary training school. The new nurses' home was called the Henrietta Raphael Nurses' Home after Mrs Raphael whose husband had made a gift of £20,000 to the hospital in memory of his wife. It was described as 'the largest and most complete of its kind in the country', and provided separate bedrooms for 213 nurses, each with hot and cold water, and a bathroom to every ten rooms. Sisters were provided with bedsitting rooms, and there was a large general sitting-room in addition to kitchens, dining rooms, a sick room and, in the basement, a swimming pool. Before this home was built, the nurses had lived in dormitories at the top of the hospital buildings. The gala opening of the home was attended by the Prince and Princess of Wales, and the royal couple were received by the governors, the Treasurer Mr Cosmo Bonsor, the Matron Miss Swift, and members of the medical and surgical staff.

The Preliminary Training School (PTS) opened in October 1902, in accommodation within the nurses' home. The school took 15 pupils for a six week course in practical housework and instruction in elementary anatomy, physiology, hygiene, bandaging, the making of dressings and sick room cookery. During their preliminary training probationers had no contact with the hospital, the fee for the course was six guineas, which included board and lodging in the nurses' home. At the end of the course the pupils had a practical examination and the Matron decided which pupils could continue their training as probationers. Before being accepted as a full-time probationer, however, the candidate still had to complete a trial period of two months in the wards. If the Matron was satisfied with the sisters' reports on her work and attitude, the candidate's place was then confirmed and the probationer signed an agreement binding herself to three years' service.

During the first year the probationers attended 12 lectures on anatomy and surgical nursing, 12 lectures on physiology and medical nursing, given by members of the medical staff, followed by lectures on nursing given by one of the sisters. The second year included classes in pharmacy and dispensing given by the hospital pharmacist, and examinations on all subjects were given at the end of the two years. Failure to pass in any subject meant termination of the probationer's contract. In her final year the nurse was given more responsibility and on successfully completing the year she received her certificate. Miss Swift introduced a new form of certificate which showed the degree of credit with which each examination was passed.

Her matronship was a very successful period for the nursing department of the hospital. The number of patients being treated in the hospital showed an annual increase – in 1900 the number was 7,320 and the number of out-patients 90,617. By 1908, the figure was

8,565 patients and 132,288 out-patients. Over the same period the number of nurses increased to 276, consisting of the Matron and Assistant Matron, 32 sisters, 60 head nurses, 167 probationers, and 15 preliminary pupils. By extending the matron's house in 1904, Miss Swift was able to increase the number of paying probationers taken per year to 30, and since the fee was 13 guineas per quarter, this represented a significant increase in income to the hospital. In addition the income from the PTS, with approximately 100 pupils passing through at six guineas each a year, added another 600 guineas to the funds.

Miss Swift was able to improve the pay and conditions of the trained nurses, off-duty consisted of two half days and one whole day in four weeks and five weeks' annual holidays. During training, the nurse was paid £8 in the first year, £12 the second year, and £18 the third year. As a trained nurse, her salary was £25 during her fourth year of service, £28 in the fifth year and thereafter, £30. The sisters' salary rose from £30 to £50 per annum. In addition, the governors of the hospital provided a pension for all the nurses of £11 5s per annum at the age of 50, and the nurses were expected to take out a pension, at the same age, for £7 10s.

Sarah Swift conformed to the stereotype of the matron of her day, usually described as a strict disciplinarian. She was short in stature, about 4'10", and spoke slowly and deliberately in a quiet voice. When describing her attitude to the nurses she said, 'My idea is to make nurses undertake their own education as grown-up women, not as children; if they choose to disregard the rules, they bring their own punishment upon themselves, and if they are persistently wilful they must go' (*Nursing Times*, 24 Mar 1906, p. 247).

Despite a strict approach to discipline, she gave a high priority to the development of recreational and social facilities for the nurses. She established the very successful Guy's Hospital Past and Present Nurses' League in 1902. The purpose of the league was to promote social and professional intercourse among all Guy's nurses, and to provide the present nurses with better facilities for mental and physical recreation. The league took over the existing nurses' sports clubs, which included cycling, tennis, swimming and gymnastics, and the choral and literary societies. The hospital governors encouraged the league by providing sports facilities and a club house at Honor Oak Park near Dulwich. Subscription to the league was one guinea per annum and membership was compulsory for sisters joining the staff after 1904. Miss Swift used the League to develop professional awareness among the nurses and, in 1903, she started postgraduate lectures for league members. In keeping with her attitude of treating nurses as adults, she allowed the nurses in the choral society to join the medical students in the Musical Society to give concerts in aid of the hospital, a practice which was considered very liberal by her contemporaries.

Miss Swift published a handbook for members of the League in 1903, known as *A Nursing Guide*, which contained information useful to nurses and incorporated a list of past and present Guy's nurses. It was updated and reissued regularly, and by the time Miss Swift retired from Guy's in 1909, membership of the League was just under 1000. She had been the Honorary Secretary since its foundation and on retirement was appointed a Vice-President. She continued to attend the annual meetings for the rest of her life. In July 1909, Miss Swift gave notice of her intention to resign in September. She would be 55 in November and had been 19 years on the staff of the hospital. Her administrative abilities had served the hospital well, not only had her efficient organisation of the nursing staff produced the lowest average cost per nurse of the London hospitals, but the reputation of the Guy's nurse was of the highest standing throughout the world. Her skill in financial matters was recognised outside the hospital and much of the work which she undertook in her retirement was connected with the financial welfare of nurses.

## Professional Organisation

Miss Swift shared the growing awareness among nurses, at the turn of the century, of the new potential of nursing as a profession. Her views on the development of the profession were associated with raising the standard of nursing education and practice. There is no record of her membership of either the Royal British Nurses' Association (RBNA) or the Matrons' Council, although in 1901, she made a request to the House Committee of Guy's Hospital for a contribution towards the expenses of the English delegate attending the nursing conference in Buffalo, the first conference of the International Council of Nurses (ICN). When Sidney Holland, Chairman of the London Hospital, gave evidence to the Select Committee on the Registration of Nurses, in 1904, he said that there were only three matrons in favour of registration, one of them being the matron of Guy's Hospital, Miss Swift.

In 1905, Mr Cosmo Bonsor, Treasurer of Guy's Hospital and a director of the Bank of England, and C. H. Goschen, a governor of Guy's, were among the promoters of The Society for Promoting the Higher Education and Training of Nurses. The aims of the proposed society were many but its primary purpose was to raise the standard of education and training of nurses by promoting a uniform curriculum of training. It proposed to recognise approved training schools and to grant certificates of proficiency in nursing to those nurses who passed the prescribed examinations, and it would maintain a register of nurses to whom certificates had been granted.

The promoters of the scheme were all city financiers who were also hospital governors and associated with the Royal National Pension Fund for Nurses. They included Lord Rothschild, E. A. Hambro and Henry Burdett. The nurses' organisations, led by Mrs Bedford Fenwick, took exception to the scheme on the grounds that it proposed to set up a voluntary system of registration, controlled by a council which would consist of persons appointed by the promoters of the Society. It was inevitable that trained nurses who were campaigning for professional independence, should oppose such an unrepresentative body setting itself up to govern nurses. The timing of the Society was also inopportune; it coincided with the sitting of the House of Commons' Select Committee on the State Registration of Nurses, a time when the state registration lobby was more than usually optimistic. The significance of the proposed Society was in its relationship to Guy's Hospital and, in particular, to Miss Swift. There is no record that she publicly supported the scheme, yet contemporaries clearly understood that she had been involved in the drafting of it. This suggestion is supported by two facts, her close involvement with the promoters of the scheme through Guy's Hospital and her work for the Royal National Pension Fund for Nurses, and by the close parallels between this scheme and the College of Nursing, proposed by Miss Swift in 1916. The Memorandum and Articles of Association of the two bodies are almost identical.

Miss Swift's interest in the welfare of nurses involved her in several schemes for their benefit. One of these was the Junius Morgan Benevolent Fund, run by the Royal National Pension Fund for Nurses. This fund had been set up in 1890 to provide financial relief to nurses who were members of the pension fund and who were in distress. It also granted annuities to nurses who were unable to provide for themselves after the age of 60. In 1908, Miss Swift was appointed Chairman of the Advisory Committee which administered the fund.

Miss Swift's connection with the Royal National Pension Fund for Nurses also involved her with the Nurses' Memorial to King Edward VII. As Prince of Wales, the King had been the first patron of the pension fund. On his death in 1910, the fund announced an appeal for donations to set up one, or more, retirement homes for nurses as a memorial to the late King. Miss Swift was appointed Honorary

Secretary of the Memorial Committee. The appeal raised £12,200 and two homes were opened. The first opened in 1912, in Victoria Road, Clapham, providing accommodation for 23 nurses, the second home was opened in 1914, in Holland Park, London.

## Matron-in-Chief, Joint War Committee

At the outbreak of war, on 4 August 1914, Miss Swift was on holiday with friends at Spa, Belgium. She returned to London and helped to convert a wing of a large house into a home for Belgian refugees. She offered her services to the St John Ambulance Association and to the British Red Cross Society (BRCS). The former accepted her offer and appointed her to their nursing committee which was enrolling nurses for work in France and Belgium. She was also appointed as a nursing representative, along with Mrs Bedford Fenwick, to the Queen's Special Ladies Committee which was organising comforts for the sick and wounded.

In October 1914, the St John Ambulance Association and the BRCS formed a Joint War Committee to coordinate their work. When the Matron-in-Chief of the St John Ambulance Association, Miss Claridge, retired in November, Miss Swift was appointed to succeed her and became the Matron-in-Chief of the Joint War Committee's nursing department. The amalgamation of the nursing departments of the two organisations involved bringing under one system the thousands of records of all the women volunteering for nursing work. The offices of the St John Ambulance Association's nursing department were at St John's Gate, Clerkenwell, and those of the BRCS at Pall Mall. For 12 months, Miss Swift carried on the work of her department at both locations, but in October 1915 all the work was transferred to Pall Mall.

The War Office had delegated the responsibility of selecting nurses from all the women who volunteered for service to the BRCS. The work of the Nursing Department involved checking the qualifications of nurses who volunteered, interviewing and selecting candidates, and dispatching them to home hospitals or hospitals abroad administered by the Joint War Committee, or to serve with the French Red Cross in Anglo-French hospitals. The department was also responsible for checking qualifications of nurses going abroad to serve in hospitals unconnected with the Joint War Committee. This measure was introduced as a result of the situation which arose at the beginning of the war when many women volunteering for nursing work abroad were found on arrival at their destination to be untrained and an embarrassment to the authorities. From January 1915, the Foreign Office would not issue passports to nurses going to work aboard until their qualifications had been checked by the Joint War Committee's nursing department.

The qualifications required by the Joint War Committee for nurses were three years' training in a general hospital of not less than 50 beds, and a good reference from the matron. All candidates were personally interviewed by the selection board and three references taken up. Nurses with less than three years' training, or training in a special hospital, were accepted as staff nurses at a lower salary than those employed as sisters. All nurses selected had to agree to serve in a home hospital for six months after which they would be sent on foreign service when a suitable vacancy arose.

At the start of the war nurses were engaged at a salary of two guineas a week. In January 1915, it was decided that as this was more than most nurses earned in hospital or private work, when the initial six month contract expired, the salary would be one guinea a week. After one year's service, the pay was increased by ten pounds a year. In March 1915, the BRCS and the Order of St John set aside £1000 each for pensions to nurses who were disabled through war work. Miss Swift was appointed to the committee, known as The Nurses' Relief Fund Committee, along with the matrons of Guy's Hospital, St Mary's Hospital, St Thomas' Hospital and the Middlesex Hospital. Also on the committee were several representatives of the Royal National Pension Fund for Nurses.

In February, 1915, the BRCS appointed a special standing committee to deal with the work of its VADs. These were women members of Voluntary Aid Detachments who were employed as assistant nurses in the BRCS hospitals. The members of the committee included several society ladies associated with the work of the Red Cross, and Miss Swift, Miss Becher, the Matron-in-Chief of Queen Alexandra's Imperial Military Nursing Service, and Miss Davies, Matron of the King George Hospital. The nursing press welcomed the move by the BRCS to involve the profession in the organisation of the VADs. For the first six months of the war, the BRCS had ignored the demands of nursing leaders to maintain a professional standard of nursing in their hospitals by employing VAD members to nurse only under the supervision of trained nurses. The appointment of this special committee, with three leading matrons among its members, was seen as an attempt to put the whole organisation on a sound basis, with a general 'rounding-up' of the untrained. This move added to the work of the nursing department of the Joint War

Committee which became responsible for interviewing VADs and reporting on their suitability for nursing work.

One of the most demanding aspects of Miss Swift's work as Matron-in-Chief was the regular inspection of the 1500 auxiliary hospitals run by the Joint War Committee. These hospitals, which varied from 25 beds to 2000 beds, were scattered all over the country. Miss Swift inspected a county at a time and reported on conditions to the War Office, and made recommendations for improvements where necessary. She also inspected the hospitals in France and Belgium, run by the Joint War Committee, and the hotels and hostels used by nurses in transit. In October 1916, she was asked to go to Italy to inspect the arrangements of the BRCS hospitals there. She undertook the journey despite the dangers of travelling at the time, and was received by the Queen of Italy, who was a leading figure in the Italian Red Cross.

At the end of the war Miss Swift stayed on at the Joint War Committee to help with the demobilisation of nurses. Her department had been responsible for the employment of over 6000 trained nurses during the war, 4,730 in the home auxiliary hospitals, 762 in France and Belgium and 666 on other fronts. The nurses employed by the Joint War Committee were the first to come back from France, and Miss Swift and her department did their best to fit them to the jobs available. On demobilisation, the nurses received a payment which varied from four weeks' pay for those with under six months' service to 20 weeks' pay for those with four years' service. A large part of the work was concerned with looking after the interests of nurses and VADs in pursuing claims for disabilities, pensions, honours and resettlement.

The BRCS and St John Ambulance Association decided to continue the joint working of the two organisations in peace-time and a Joint Council was set up to include members of the war-time committee. The BRCS extended its charter to include peace-time objectives which the League of Nations had decided to delegate to the national Red Cross organisations. These were the promotion of health, the prevention of disease and the mitigation of suffering throughout the world. A League of Red Cross Societies was formed and Miss Swift was appointed the nursing representative of the British Society. She was also appointed a member of the Council and the Executive Committee of the BRCS and represented the society's nursing interests on several committees, including the United Services Relief Committee, which provided assistance for nurses who had suffered in the war. She was awarded the Royal Red Cross, first class, in 1916, and in 1919 was

awarded the Order of the British Empire Dame Grand Cross and
made a Lady of Grace of the Order of St John of Jerusalem.


## The College of Nursing

Miss Swift's work for the Joint War Committee brought her into
contact with thousands of nurses. Each day, she and her staff
checked the qualifications of nurses, trained in large teaching hospitals, provincial hospitals, voluntary hospitals, poor law institutions,
fever hospitals, children's hospitals, special hospitals, some with
certificates of training, some with no training but years of experience,
but all considered themselves 'qualified' as nurses. By the end of
1915, Miss Swift had come to the conclusion that the state of nurses'
training was chaotic and something would have to be done to stan-
dardise it. She approached Arthur Stanley, the Chairman of the
BRCS, and asked for his help in founding a College of Nursing. Mr
Stanley agreed to her proposal and they enlisted the support of the
matron of St Thomas', Alicia Lloyd Still, the matron of the Royal
Free Hospital, Rachel Cox-Davies, the Matron of Guy's Hospital,
Miss Haughton, and Sir Cooper Perry, the Medical Superintendent
of Guy's.

On 30 December 1915, Arthur Stanley wrote to the matrons and
managers of the large training schools and hospitals in the country
setting out the need for cooperation among the nurse-training
schools and the proposal for a College of Nursing. After receiving a
favourable response, the scheme for the establishment of a voluntary
College of Nursing was announced in the *Nursing Times* at the beginning of January 1916. The aims of the founders were:

- to promote the better education and training of nurses;
- to promote a uniform curriculum for the training of nurses;
- to recognise approved training schools and to grant certificates of
  proficiency in nursing to persons who passed recognised examinations;
- to make and maintain a register of nurses who had received certificates of proficiency;
- to promote Bills in Parliament for any object connected with the
  interests of the nursing profession and, in particular, with nurse
  education, organisation, protection, or for their recognition by the
  state;
- to promote the advancement of nursing as a profession in all or
  any of its branches.

The scheme for the College of Nursing was immediately opposed by the supporters of state registration for nurses. They were the most organised and most articulate group within the profession, although they remained a minority of the total number of nurses in the country. They believed that it was only a matter of time before the government accepted the necessity of state registration for nurses. They recognised that the situation created by the war had altered the conditions of modern nursing, but they saw this as further evidence of the need for state registration. They regarded the College of Nursing scheme as a distraction from this main objective and distrusted the motives of its promoters.

Miss Swift and the other founders of the College of Nursing did not believe that the government had any intention of introducing a Bill for the registration of nurses. They held that the profession would be in a much stronger position after the war if it organised itself on a voluntary basis first; then when the government came to look at the question it would be able to see what was being asked for. In an interview in the *Nursing Times* in January 1916, Miss Swift addressed the suspicions of the opponents of the scheme. The opposition focused on three issues, the motives of the promoters, the position of state registration in the priorities of the College, and the relationship between the College and the VADs.

The leaders of the state registration movement suspected the motives of the promoters of the College because one of the cornerstones of their campaign was that the profession should be self-governing. Their aim was the establishment of a representative council of nurses, elected by the nurses on the statutory register. The College of Nursing scheme proposed that the first council of the College would be appointed by the promoters. To Mrs Bedford Fenwick this was unacceptable 'lay interference'. She was convinced that her old rival, Sir Henry Burdett, was behind the scheme. She drew attention to the similarities between the scheme for the College of Nursing and the 1905 scheme for registration, proposed by Burdett and other hospital governors, when they attempted to launch the Society for Promoting the Higher Education and Training of Nurses.

Miss Swift explained that the promoters would fade into the background once they had appointed 10 or 12 members of the Council. This Council would then coopt additional members, up to 25 or 30. The members of this first Council would be representative of all branches of nursing work and also of the medical profession. This nominated Council would retire between 1918 and 1920, a third each year, and would be replaced by representatives elected by the members of the College. Miss Swift did not accept the criticism that the College represented employers rather than nurses. In her opinion, matrons had a duty to look after the interests of their nurses, who at that time were scattered all over Europe on military service. To wait until after the war would be too late. On the question of state registration, Miss Swift said that the majority of the promoters of the College were in favour of it. She did not think, however, that the establishment of the College should be dependent on the passing of the Bill for State Registration. The organisation of the profession could go ahead with the cooperation of the training schools and the nurses. She emphasised that the scheme was still fluid and the College could move in any direction which was in the interests of the profession.

The third point worrying many nurses about the College was the connection between Mr Stanley and Miss Swift and the BRCS and the VADs. Trained nurses were very concerned about the economic effects of these 12,000 uncertificated women on the profession after the war. Miss Swift dismissed the suggestion that she and Mr Stanley intended to allow VADs to be members of the College of Nursing. The decision as to who should be a member of the College, the standard of training required for recognition as a trained nurse, and similar questions, would be decided by the Council of the College which would have a majority of members who were trained nurses. It was her concern for the interests of the trained nurses for which she was responsible as Matron-in-Chief, which had led her to propose the College of Nursing.

The National Council of Trained Nurses of Great Britain and Ireland held a meeting in the premises of the Royal Society of Medicine, in February, to consider the scheme for the establishment of a College of Nursing. This organisation had been founded in 1904, as the body through which British and Irish nurses' societies could affiliate to the ICN. At the meeting, all speakers were unanimous in condemning a voluntary system of registration. Mrs Bedford Fenwick described the proposed College of Nursing as a scheme for the government of nurses by their employers, and against all the interests of nurses. Miss Musson (see chapter eight), matron of the Birmingham General Hospital, said the scheme was the child of certain matrons of London hospitals, and regretted that the representative bodies of the profession had not been consulted. Resolutions were carried authorising the National Council of Trained Nurses to oppose the College of Nursing. Copies of the resolutions were sent to all Members of Parliament, to members of the Joint War Committee, and to nurse-training schools.

The promoters of the College of Nursing had anticipated opposition from the state registration movement and they were prepared to meet the leaders of the various societies to discuss common ground. Three meetings were held between the two parties in February and March 1916. At the first meeting, held at the offices of the BRCS in Pall Mall, Mr Stanley explained that the College would be a democratic body, governed by nurses, but that it was necessary to start with a nominated council. Miss Haughton, Matron of Guy's Hospital, said that every profession had to attain a certain measure of organisation from within before it gained legal recognition from Parliament. Membership of the College would be confined to trained nurses, and the Council of the College, elected by the members, would be a professional body competent to deal with the training of nurses and their professional relationship with other groups of workers.

Mrs Bedford Fenwick spoke for the Central Committee for State Registration. She wanted to know who were the men behind the College. She did not understand why they had not consulted the existing nurses' organisations, which represented 6000 nurses. She did not consider that a licence from the Board of Trade qualified anyone to speak for her or the nurses she represented. Many of the matrons present, nevertheless, expressed sympathy with the scheme. Miss Seymour Yapp, representing the Poor Law Officers' Association, said she did not see why the College should be inimical to state registration. She was an ardent registrationist, but she did not mind how it was achieved.

Dr Comyns Berkeley, a prominent gynaecologist and member of the Royal British Nurses Association (RBNA), said that the objects of the College appeared to be similar to those of the RBNA and he felt sure that the Association would give the scheme a sympathetic hearing. However, he wished Mr Stanley would assure the meeting that one of the first objectives of the College would be to set up a committee to draft a Bill for state registration, which would have the approval of all the nurses' societies.

The second meeting was held at the Royal Automobile Club, Piccadilly, at the beginning of March. The Central Committee for the State Registration of Nurses had prepared a detailed memorandum which was read by Dr Goodall, who represented the British Medical Association on the Central Committee. The Committee felt strongly that the action of the promoters of the College was untimely. The memorandum set out the case for waiting until the war was over before attempting to organise the nursing profession. The Committee considered it an anomaly that a voluntary scheme for registration should be proposed when the Central Committee's Bill for State Registration, which had received a majority in the House of Commons on its first reading in 1914, was only waiting for a second reading.

Mr Stanley repeated the reasons why he considered it essential to act now in view of the large number of untrained women who would compete with trained nurses after the war. He hoped that at a time of very great issues, nurses would be more inclined to sink their smaller differences and work for a common end. He believed that the difference between the position of the Central Committee and of the promoters of the College was one of procedure. He did not give much weight to the argument that the Central Committee's Bill was half-way to becoming legislation. Anyone who had been in the House of Commons as long as he had knew that nine-tenths of all Bills did not have a division on their first reading, being purely a formal stage. The fact that there had been a division at all on the first reading showed that there was opposition to the Bill.

The representatives of the Central Committee asked the promoters of the College to hold a further meeting to discuss a joint Bill. They agreed to this but said they would go ahead with the foundation of the College since they considered that the College was more necessary than state registration and they were not prepared to make the College dependent on the passing of the Bill. They did agree to postpone the foundation of the College for three weeks to allow consultation over the drafting of a joint Bill.

The third meeting was held at the end of March in the offices of the BRCS. On this occasion there was a significant shift of opinion among the state registration parties, led by the RBNA, to support the establishment of the College. Mr Stanley said that he now regarded state registration as settled, they were all agreed that it must be achieved as soon as possible. The first duty of the College would be to appoint a committee to draft a Bill and he thought an agreed Bill could be got through parliament as a war measure.

Mrs Bedford Fenwick wanted the meeting to appoint a committee to draw up a Bill which would embody state registration and a College of Nursing, but Mr Stanley said that such a committee would have to be postponed until after the formation of the College. Major Chapple, who had fathered the Central Committee's Bill in the Commons since 1914, eventually said that he was prepared to tear up the old Bill and to allow Mr Stanley to draw up a new Bill. He recognised that the time had come for a new phase of action. The result of the meeting was that both sides, with some notable exceptions, agreed on the fundamental principles for the organisation of the profession and on the priorities of the College. These were state registration, a uniform curriculum of training and a one portal system of examination. This last point meant that there should be only one certificate of general training for all nurses wherever trained. It was considered essential, in the interests of professional solidarity, that the certificates awarded for training at the best hospitals and infirmaries should not be regarded as superior to those awarded for training at poor law institutions and smaller hospitals.

The College of Nursing was registered as a limited company on 27 March 1916, with an address at 83 Pall Mall, the offices of the BRCS. The signatories of the Articles of Association were Mr Stanley and six members of the BRCS. They appointed the first 15 members of the Council of the College, which included Sarah Swift, and this Council held its first meeting on 1 April. A further ten persons were coopted on to the Council and of the 25 members, 15 were matrons. The Council appointed five standing committees, including one to deal with the question of state registration, and Miss Swift was appointed a member of all the standing committees.

A circular letter was sent to all the main hospitals in the country announcing the establishment of the College and inviting representatives of the hospitals and training schools to a meeting in London, on 7 April. The purpose of this meeting was to form a Consultative Board and an Examination Board of the College. These boards would act in an advisory role to the Council and would consist of representatives of the medical profession, matrons, trained nurses, managers of hospitals and infirmaries, and persons interested in the relations between nurses and the public. The founders of the College knew that the success of the College in setting up a uniform standard of training and examination depended on the cooperation of the nurse training schools. At the time, the nurses who trained at the best hospitals and infirmaries were able to make a living on the reputation of the certificates they held from these schools and they would have little inducement to enter for a further qualifying examination. By appointing the two consultative boards, the Council of the College involved hospital managers and matrons of training schools in setting up the scheme, thus giving them an interest in its success.

The College's first office was a room in Guy's Hospital. In June, 1916, the first Secretary, Miss Mary Rundle, took up her duties and it moved to offices in Vere Street where she began the task of enrolling members. A leaflet was published setting out the aims and objectives of the College and this was sent to nurses at home and abroad. The response was overwhelming, applications for membership poured in and the Secretary and the one clerk had to call in voluntary helpers to assist.

Throughout 1916, Mr Stanley, Miss Swift and the other founders

*Fig 14. Sarah Swift, founder of the College of Nursing, 1916*

travelled around the country addressing meetings to promote the College. They encouraged nurses to join by pointing out that the larger the number of names on the register when it was presented to Parliament with the Bill for state registration, the more likely was the success of the Bill. In Miss Swift's words, 'The nurses who are not in England, as well as those who are, who fill in their forms and are entered on the Register now, will have the honour of having their names sent to Parliament applying for an Act to release their profession from the bonds under which it labours today' (*Nursing Times*, 12 August 1916, p. 938).

At the annual dinner and meeting of the Guy's Hospital Nurses' League, in May 1916, Miss Swift took the opportunity of speaking about the College. She explained that it was her work as Matron-in-Chief for the Joint War Committee that had opened her eyes to the chaotic state of nurses' training and the urgent need for action to protect the interests of nurses. To wait until the end of the war would be to wait too long. After the war, conditions would be utterly changed and trained nurses must prepare themselves to contend against the dangers which threatened their position. The 12,000 VADs employed as assistant nurses would return with experience and knowledge, having seen the best surgery there is without having gone through the mill of a recognised training. The College of Nursing would be in a position to protect the trained nurse but it needed the support of the nurses themselves. Therefore, she hoped to see every Guy's nurse a member. She, Miss Swift, was number one on the membership roll of the College, and there were already over 2000 names on the roll.

Negotiations between the College and the Central Committee for State Registration on a joint Bill initially went well. The two parties were in agreement about fundamental principles and the *Nursing Times* wrote, ' . . . if the one aim is kept in view and personal considerations discarded, it is quite possible that State Registration is almost as near as the Daylight Saving Bill' [a Bill which had only two or three opponents in the Commons] (13 May 1916). By July the negotiations had reached an impasse over the composition of the provisional Nursing Council which would be set up to govern until the first election of Council members could be held. Negotiations on this point continued until November, when the Central Committee decided to withdraw and to proceed with its original Bill.

A year later, in July 1917, Mr Stanley (now Sir Arthur Stanley) reopened negotiations with the Central Committee for the State Registration of Nurses, informing the Committee that the College was prepared to accept the Committee's point about who should nominate the Provisional Council. Major Chapple, who was in parliamentary charge of the Central Committee's Bill, and Sir Arthur drafted a new Bill but, in December 1918, the Central Committee decided that its own Bill was a better Bill and asked the College to support it. The College refused to do this, as the Bill did not fulfil the promise which the College had given to its members, that at least two-thirds of the proposed General Nursing Council should be elected by the nurses on the general register. The negotiations were again broken off and both organisations proceeded with separate Bills.

Throughout the summer of 1916, representatives of the College were also negotiating with the RBNA on the amalgamation of the two organisations. By the end of October, an agreement had been drawn up for the establishment of the Royal British College of Nursing. As a body incorporated by Royal charter, the RBNA had to obtain the approval of the Privy Council for the necessary amendments to its charter for the establishment of the new body. Accordingly, the amended charter and bye-laws were sent to the Privy Council at the beginning of 1917. The amalgamation of the two bodies was supported by Princess Christian, the President of the RBNA. A petition against the amalgamation was lodged by the Society for the State Registration of Trained Nurses. The Privy Council made certain changes to the supplemental charter and after months of negotiations, the Council of the RBNA decided that they could not accept the alterations and withdrew the application for a supplemental charter.

The decision of the Council of the RBNA was interpreted by the Council of the College as a signal that the Association no longer wished for amalgamation. On 3 November 1917, the Secretary of the College wrote to the Secretary of the Association in the following words

In view of the delay and inconvenience resulting from the course of action pursued by your Council, the Council of the College has carefully considered whether it is now in the interests of its members to proceed further with the scheme for the amalgamation of the two Associations. After nearly a year's experience of the dilatory manner in which proceedings have been conducted by your Association with the privy Council, my Council has reluctantly reached the conclusion that there is at the present time little evidence of any real desire on the part of your Council to amalgamate with the College .. . .

It was undoubtedly of some importance to the College in its early days to seek to ally itself with your Association, just as it was of importance for your Association to obtain enlarged powers, the new infusion of energy, and increased membership, which would have come about by the establishment of the amalgamated bodies as the Royal British College of

> Nursing; but as the College of Nursing has now become well known, . . . the advantage to the College of amalgamation becomes less obvious . . . I am instructed to ask your Council to refrain from incurring further expenditure, which, as you will no doubt remember, the College has to find, and . . . to regard negotiations as practically at an end.
>
> College of Nursing Minutes, 1 Nov 1917

This breakdown in amicable relations between the established nurses' societies and the College of Nursing was fatal. The leaders of the nurses' societies displayed their hostility towards the College at public meetings and in the nursing press. The founders of the College regretted this animosity, and maintained that the College stood for the unity of the nursing profession. They had tried to achieve an agreed Bill for State Registration but negotiations had been broken off by the Central Committee, and they had tried to amalgamate with the RBNA but the Association had withdrawn from the process.

Despite the hostility of the nurses' societies, the College flourished. By December 1917, the membership had reached 8000, the membership of the RBNA at the time was 4000 and not all the members were nurses. In the spring of 1918, when the first one third of the nominated Council retired, and were replaced by elected councillors, over 100 nominations were received for the 12 places. By April 1919, when the second election took place, there were over 13,000 members voting, and in 1920, when the whole Council became elected, the figure was over 17,000.

The economic future of the College was set on a more secure basis when, in the spring of 1918, the British Women's Hospital Committee agreed to raise a fund for the endowment of the College. Sir Arthur Stanley had been closely associated with the work of the British Women's Hospital Committee, which had grown from the war-time activities of the Actresses' Franchise League. The Committee had just finished collecting over £220,000 for the building of the Star and Garter Home, Richmond, for disabled soldiers. The Honorary Treasurer of the Committee was Lady Cowdray, who had been involved in work for the welfare of nurses for over 30 years. The Council of the College and the Committee agreed to launch an appeal, with the title 'The Nation's Fund for Nurses', as a permanent memorial to the nurses of the country. The Fund was divided into two parts, a benevolent fund to assist nurses whose health had been broken in the war, and an endowment fund for the College of Nursing. The Endowment Fund was to provide a building for the College headquarters in London and to enable the College to establish courses and scholarships for nurses' postgraduate training. The opponents of the College, led by Mrs Bedford Fenwick, denounced the fund as 'demoralising patronage by wealthy, leisured women'. In her opinion the College had no right to seek charity which would deprive nurses of their economic and professional independence.

## The Nurses' Registration Act 1919

In March 1919, the Central Committee was given the opportunity to introduce its Registration Bill in the House of Commons. The Council of the College decided to support the Bill in the interests of the profession. The Bill was passed without a division and went to the committee stage. The College drafted four amendments, the crucial one dealing with the number of seats on the provisional Nursing Council allotted to the nurses' societies and to the College. In the Bill, 11 places were assigned to the Societies affiliated to the Central Committee, and four to the College. The College considered this unacceptable, given the large membership of the College and the impossibility of ascertaining how many nurses the Central Committee actually represented. The second amendment aimed at securing a majority of nurses on the General Nursing Council (GNC). As the Bill stood, nurses would be in a permanent minority on the Council. The College asked that two thirds of the GNC should be elected by the nurses on the state register.

The Central Committee's Bill was still in debate, in July 1919, when the government announced that it would not support the Bill, nor would it support the College of Nursing Bill, which had been introduced in the House of Lords. The College had withdrawn its support from the Central Committee's Bill after the substance of the Bill had been altered by numerous amendments. Dr Addison, the Minister of Health, committed the government to the introduction of a Bill for the state registration of nurses at the earliest possible date, if the two Bills were withdrawn. Accordingly, the government's Bill became *The Nurses' Registration Act* on 23 December 1919. It followed the lines of the Bill promoted by the College in that it was merely a skeleton of legislation and left all the details to be decided by the GNC which it set up. The Bill also adopted the principle for which the College had fought, that a substantial majority of the General Nursing Council should be elected by the nurses on the General Register.

The establishment of the statutory body, the General Nursing Council, altered the role of the College. Two of the main objectives of the College, the introduction of a uniform standard of training and the registration of trained nurses, became the responsibility of the GNC. The founders of the College had given it 25 objectives in the Memorandum of Association, as Miss Swift had often said she did not believe one should stereotype one's ideas. The removal of the first two priorities from its objectives left the College free to develop in whatever direction the Council decided was in the interests of the profession. It decided to concentrate on an educational programme and the promotion of the professional status of nursing.

Since 1916, a considerable degree of cooperation had been achieved between the College and the nurse training schools on a voluntary basis. The involvement of matrons and managers of teaching hospitals in the policy making process of the College prepared the ground for the future role of the College as the chief voice of hospital based nursing. This role became of increasing importance as the standard of training set by the GNC for the registration of existing nurses, that is nurses who had trained before 1919, fell below the standard of the best training schools. The Council of the College believed that it was necessary to accept a lower standard at this stage as a division between the prestigious training schools and the other hospitals would have been disastrous for the future of the new GNC and for professional solidarity.

The Council of the College decided that the best way of ensuring that the GNC pursued a policy of raising the standard of the State qualification to the level of the best training schools, was to make an organised use of the votes of the 20,000 College members who would have a vote in the election of the first GNC, if their names were on the General Register by the time of the first election. Through the voting power of its members, the College acquired the influence on the GNC which reflected its position as the largest association of nurses.

By the summer of 1918 the offices in Vere Street had become too small for the rapidly increasing work of the College and larger accommodation was sought in the vicinity. In the spring of 1919, the College moved to 7 Henrietta Street. These premises gave the College additional office space and a committee room for meetings, but it did not allow for the development of educational facilities. The founders still hoped they would be able to find a permanent home for the College which would become the headquarters of the nursing profession and where they could provide postgraduate courses.

In June 1920, the town house of the Member of Parliament and former Prime Minister, Herbert Asquith, came up for auction. The College Council decided that the position of the house, on the south west corner of Cavendish Square, with its large garden and stable/

garage exit on to Henrietta Street, was an ideal site for the head-quarters of the College. They realised they could not raise the money in time for the auction but approached Lady Cowdray and asked her if she would purchase the property on behalf of the College. Since 1918, when she became involved in raising the Endowment Fund for the College, Lady Cowdray had become a generous benefactor to the College. Through her work for the Royal Free Hospital and the South London Hospital, she had long been aware of the need for improved educational facilities and opportunities for nurses and had expressed her desire to see the educational development of the pro-fession placed on a firmer foundation after the war.

Lady Cowdray agreed to purchase 20 Cavendish Square on behalf of the College and she declared her intention of refurbishing the 18th century town house as a professional club for women. The Council of the College intended to build a new headquarters for the College on the site of the stables and outbuildings of the property, with a façade on to Henrietta Street. When the property was transferred to the Council in October 1920, Lord and Lady Cowdray announced that they would undertake to build and equip the new building.

The Cowdray Club, 20 Cavendish Square, was opened in June 1922 and on the same day, Lady Cowdray laid the foundation stone of the new headquarters building. Lady Cowdray had a wide outlook on life and she believed that the narrow limits of institutional life were deadening to nurses, so she decided that the club would be more beneficial to nurses if the membership were open to women of other professions. It was resolved that the membership should be 55 per cent nurses, 35 per cent professional women and 10 per cent women without professional qualifications, who had to pay a higher subscription. The Council of the College was responsible for the club, which was to be self-supporting, and Miss Swift was appointed to the management committee.

The new headquarters building was opened on 31 May 1926, by Queen Mary. Her Majesty was received by Lady Cowdray and the President of the College, Dame Sarah Swift. Miss Swift had been appointed to the Order of the British Empire as a Dame Grand Cross in 1919. A guard of honour of nurses, representing all branches of the profession, and a distinguished reception committee, which included the Archbishop of Canterbury, the Minister of Health, Neville Chamberlain, the Mayor of Marylebone, and the architect of the building, Sir Edwin Cooper, greeted the Queen. Lady Cowdray asked Queen Mary to accept the deeds of the building and Her

*Fig 15. Opening of the College of Nursing Headquarters building, 1926. Queen Mary hands the deeds to Dame Sarah Swift. Lady Cowdray stands to the left of the Queen*

Majesty then presented the deeds to Dame Sarah, who accepted them on behalf of the nursing profession.

In a short speech, Dame Sarah thanked the Queen for her interest in the welfare of nurses and paid tribute to the generosity of Lady Cowdray, assuring her that she had the gratitude of the 25,000 members of the College. She believed that through the educational facilities offered by the new building the profession would be able to provide a better service to the community. The new building provided offices, class-rooms, a laboratory, a library, and a dining-room which communicated with the Cowdray Club. On the following two days, receptions were held to allow the members of the College to view the new headquarters. The receptions were organised by Lady Cowdray and both she and Dame Sarah acted as hostesses.

## The College as an Educational Force

After the war, the national Red Cross Societies in Europe took the decision to turn their attention to peacetime health problems and in 1919, the League of Red Cross Societies was formed to carry on this peacetime work. The Nursing Department of the League decided that the most urgent task was public health nursing and the lack of training available in many countries in this branch of nursing. The League decided to start a course in London which could be attended by nurses from different countries, who would then return home and undertake pioneer work in public health nursing.

Dame Sarah, as Matron-in-Chief of the BRCS, was closely involved in the organisation of the course. Through Sir Cooper Perry, Honorary Secretary of the College and Vice-Chancellor of the University of London, she arranged for the international students to attend lectures at King's College for Women and to reside in one of the University's hostels. The students also attended classes at the College of Nursing. The first course started in September 1920 and was attended by 19 nurses from 18 countries. The course was full-time and lasted nine months, the students receiving scholarships from the League and from the national Red Cross Societies.

The success of the first course led to its establishment as an annual event. Dame Sarah held a welcoming party each year at the College of Nursing for the students on their arrival and generally acted as 'mother' during their stay. In 1921, the course was transferred from King's College to Bedford College for Women and in 1924, a permanent home for the students was purchased. This home, at 15 Manchester Square, became an international nurses' hostel for foreign nurses working or studying in London. Dame Sarah represented the BRCS on the committee which ran the hostel. In response to repeated requests, a second international course was started in 1924 for nurse administrators and heads of nurse training schools. Like the public health course, this course was run jointly with the College of Nursing and Bedford College for Women.

The College of Nursing also played a significant role in the development of public health nursing in Britain. In 1921, the Council of the College appointed a Public Health Advisory Committee and in 1923 a Public Health Section of the College was established. In 1925, the Ministry of Health accepted the College's recommendation that the basic qualification for health visitors should be three years general hospital training and recognised the College as the first full-time training centre for health visitors. The first course was started in 1925/26 as a six months' full time course for trained nurses. The theoretical instruction was given in conjunction with the university courses at Bedford College, and some of the lectures were shared with the international students taking the League of Red Cross Societies' course.

The development of the educational programme of the College was slow until 1926, when the class-rooms and facilities of the new building became available. At this time an Education Officer was appointed and, in the autumn of 1926, the College offered courses in public health nursing, hospital administration, food values and sick room cookery, and lectures on economics, applied anatomy and physiology, communicable diseases, maternity and child welfare, sanitary law and social administration, the history of nursing, teaching methods and public speaking.

Dame Sarah never retired from her work for the College, she continued her committee work up to 1934, when she was 80. She was a member of the College Council from 1916 until her death in 1937, she was twice elected President of the College, 1925–1926 and 1926–1927, and appointed a Vice-President in 1928. She succeeded Dame Sidney Browne as one of the Honorary Treasurers of the College in 1927, an office which she held until her death. Her particular contribution to committee work was in the area of finance, salaries and pensions.

Her work for the Red Cross involved Dame Sarah in many of the developments which were taking place in nursing in the 1920s and 1930s. She represented the Red Cross on committees for district nursing, maternity and child welfare, and the care of cripples. In 1928 she attended an International Nursing Conference in Paris, organised by the League of Red Cross Societies and in October 1930, she was one of the representatives of the BRCS at the XIVth International Red Cross Conference. During the British Empire Red Cross Conference, held in London in May 1930, Dame Sarah held a reception at the College of Nursing, on behalf of the Council of the College, for the delegates. In 1929, she was awarded the International Florence Nightingale Medal. The medal had been instituted in 1912, in memory of Miss Nightingale's work, by the International Red Cross Committee and was awarded to women who had made a distinguished contribution to international nursing.

In May 1935, she retired from the post of Matron-in-Chief of the BRCS although she remained a member of the Council of the Society and on several of the committees. The Council held a special meeting to mark her retirement and the Duke of York, later George VI, presented her with an illuminated scroll. This recorded the appreciation of the Council and the Executive Committee of the Society for her years of service, both during the war and since, as Chairman of the Nursing Advisory Committee and as the representative of the Society in the work of many allied organisations.

Dame Sarah also made a significant contribution to the establishment of a trained prison nursing service. Up to 1918 no trained nurses were employed in prisons and the duty of attending sick

*Fig 16. Matron-in-Chief, British Red Cross Society at memorial service, Ypres, 1929*

prisoners was carried out by the prison wardens. In response to pressure from the nursing profession, two trained nurses were employed in the women's prison at Holloway in 1918, for a trial period, and the following year five were appointed at Holloway, again on a temporary basis. A voluntary nursing board was set up to promote the establishment of a permanent nursing service and Dame Sarah was asked to be a member of the Board. The Board was responsible for the introduction of trained nurses in six of the country's prisons over the following years and in 1928, the Prison

Nursing Service was inaugurated. In 1930, she was elected the Chairman of the Prisons Advisory Nursing Board.

Her last public appearance was at the coronation of King George VI, which she attended in the cerise velvet gown of a Dame of the Order of the British Empire. She died a few weeks later at her London home in Marylebone, after a short illness, on 27 June 1937. Queen Mary wrote to the Council of the College of Nursing expressing her sympathy on the death of their distinguished foundress and she wrote to the BRCS on the loss they had sustained at the death of Dame Sarah. The funeral was held at St Mark's Church, Marylebone, followed by a cremation service at Golder's Green. A memorial service was held at Guy's Hospital chapel on 1 July.

## Conclusion

Miss Swift's career as a nurse extended over 60 years. She said that when she took up nursing she was following her instinct. She had received a good education and her family were able to provide her with a comfortable income, but like many educated women of her background she chose to work. Her administrative abilities were perfected during her 19 years at Guy's Hospital as Assistant Matron, Lady Superintendent of the private nurses, and Matron. Her achievements in improving the efficiency of the nursing department were recognised by the hospital managers and established her reputation as a successful administrator. After she retired from Guy's, she became involved in several committees for the welfare of nurses which further developed her financial acumen and strengthened her links with hospital governors. As soon as the first world war started, Miss Swift volunteered her services and, within four months, was appointed Matron-in-Chief by the Joint War Committee of the British Red Cross Society and the St John Ambulance Association. Thus at the age of 60, she became responsible for one of the largest bodies of trained nurses and later added to this the responsibility of inspecting the 1500 auxiliary hospitals administered by the Red Cross. On top of this workload she took on the organisation of the nursing profession.

The success of Miss Swift's scheme for the organisation of the nursing profession, owed a lot to her personality. The circumstances of the nursing world in 1916 had produced conditions which were favourable for the establishment of the College of Nursing, but it took someone with the reputation of Miss Swift and the skill of a diplomat to succeed. Her winning move was to enlist the support of

Arthur Stanley, Treasurer of St Thomas' Hospital and Chairman of the British Red Cross Society. Despite the extreme pressure under which all hospital authorities were working during the war and the enormous undertaking of his work for the Red Cross, he gave Miss Swift and her scheme for the College of Nursing his immediate support. They shared a flexible approach to nursing politics, they were both prepared to negotiate with all parties, and this won the College the support of reasonable people.

Up to 1916 Miss Swift had remained outside nursing politics. She had a strong commitment to the advancement of the profession but the highly political approach adopted by the activists of the state registration movement was probably too extreme for someone who avoided publicity and confrontation as much as Miss Swift. Yet she entered the arena of nursing politics and took on the hostility and prejudice of the leaders of the state registration movement, in the interests of the profession. The success of the College of Nursing in gaining the support of influential matrons, like Alicia Lloyd Still, Rachel Cox-Davies and Ellen Musson, all prominent in the registration movement, is a mark of Miss Swift's reputation for integrity.

The success of the College was due to the foresight of Miss Swift and the other founders who gave it a constitution which was adaptable and allowed it to change its priorities as circumstances demanded. Miss Swift was proud of the work of the College, in a message to nurses in training, in 1927, as President, she wrote

> To the influence and work of the College of Nursing during the last eleven years the profession and the nation alike owe a deep debt of gratitude, for by these means the profession has been placed on a better educational, professional and economic basis and has brought the influence of the nurses to bear on all questions relating to the interests of women, political and social
>
> *Nursing Times*, 19 March 1927, p. 310

This work was recognised in 1928 and the College was granted a Royal Charter. However, it was not until two years after Miss Swift's death that it was granted permission to use the prefix 'Royal', and became the Royal College of Nursing.

Miss Swift said that she was happiest when she was organising and she spent more than 50 years of her life working, in a managerial role, to improve the standard of nursing and the lives of nurses. She had a genuine love of humanity and her work for the profession of nursing was always with a view to improving its service to the sick and poor of society. Friends spoke of her gentle dignity, quiet voice and modesty, she would neither speak of herself nor have herself spoken of. She left instructions that on her death nothing was to be written about her. The many honours she received she accepted as a tribute to her profession. On her death, Sir Cooper Perry was asked by the Secretary of the College of Nursing to write an appreciation of Dame Sarah. He wrote that although he knew her 'as a faithful friend' for over 30 years, he never felt that he had penetrated the core of her nature.

## Sources

### Greater London Record Office
Records of Guy's Hospital
H9/GY/A25/3–5 House Committee Minutes 1900–1905
H9/GY/A94/2–4 Annual Reports 1898–1909
H9/GY/C4/1–3 Matron's Journals 1896–1911
H9/GY/C5/3 Matron's Report Books 1899–1904
H9/GY/C16 Nursing certificates and prizes
H9/GY/C20/1 A Nursing Guide, 1911
H9/GY/48 Papers relating to the opening of the nurses' home, 7 July 1902

### Guy's Hospital Library
Guy's Hospital Gazette 1894–1909, 1914–1917

### British Red Cross Society Archives
J/WC/1/1/1–3 Joint War Committee Minutes, Oct 1914–Jan 1920
Personnel Records, Swift, Sarah

### Royal College of Nursing Archives
*Nursing Record/British Journal of Nursing*, 1890–1917
*Nursing Times*, 1906–1937
*Nursing Mirror*, 1920–1921
*The Hospital*, 1916–1918
RCN *Annual Reports* 1917–1920
RCN 1 College of Nursing, Ltd, 1916–1928
RCN 4 Papers relating to State Registration
RCN28 Papers relating to the history of the College

# 8

# Ellen Musson
## *A Wise Chairman*

(1867–1960)

*Matron of the General Hospital, Birmingham, 1909–1923;
Principal Matron, Territorial Force Nursing Service
1915–1918; Founder Member of the Royal College of Nursing,
Council Member 1916–1939, Hon. Treasurer 1938–1950,
Vice-President 1950–1960; Chairman of the General Nursing
Council 1926–1944; Hon. Treasurer of the International
Council of Nurses 1925–1947; President of the National
Council of Nurses 1945–1946; RRC, DBE, LL.D.*

ELLEN MARY MUSSON was born on 11 August 1867, and grew up in Clitheroe, Lancashire. Her father, William Edward Musson, was a surgeon, trained at St Thomas' Hospital. Ellen received a good education, spending some time in France and Germany and working as a governess before deciding at the age of 27 to train as a nurse. She started her training on 1 February 1895 at St Bartholomew's Hospital, London.

The matron of St Bartholomew's in 1895 was Isla Stewart, a pioneer in nurse education. Miss Stewart (see chapter 3) had improved the nurse training at St Bartholomew's so that the school was in the forefront of nurse education in the 1890s. The training scheme consisted of three years' practical work and lectures, followed by examinations and a final certificate. The practical work was divided up between the different wards, to provide experience in all types of hospital nursing, and the lectures were given by members of the medical staff and the matron. In accordance with the regulations of the time, Miss Musson served a three months' trial before she was accepted as a probationer. During her training she received good reports from all the sisters of the wards where she worked, 'kind and attentive, obedient, punctual, accurate, efficient, intelligent, pleasant'. She took her final examination in May 1898 and, gaining the highest number of marks, was awarded the Gold Medal for the year.

The probationers, on completion of their three year training, had to work a further year as a staff nurse. After six months as a staff nurse, Miss Musson was appointed Night Superintendent, a post she held for a further ten months, before being promoted to Sister of Luke Ward, a male medical ward. After three and a half years as a sister, she became Assistant Matron, in July 1903. As Assistant Matron, Miss Musson shared the responsibility with Miss Stewart for a nursing staff of 235 and it told on her health. In the spring of 1906, she took leave of absence and went abroad for a rest. When she returned to London in September, she successfully applied for the post of Matron of the Swansea General and Eye Hospital, leaving St Bartholomew's in December. She worked at Swansea for two years, a hospital of 130 beds and a nursing staff of 28. She next applied for the matronship of the General Hospital, Birmingham, a hospital of 346 beds. She was appointed out of a field of five candidates and took up her new position on 1 March 1909.

## Matron of The General Hospital, Birmingham, 1909–1923

The General Hospital, Birmingham, founded in 1765, was rebuilt at the end of the nineteenth century, on its present site nearer the centre of the city. The new building, opened in 1897, was a fine example of Victorian architecture. The accommodation provided was the best available at the time, the nurses' home had separate bedrooms for all the nurses and sisters, with three sitting-rooms and a reference library. An extension to the home was opened in June 1909, providing 43 bedrooms for the night nurses, and a classroom in the basement for instruction in sick room cookery.

One of the first changes Miss Musson made on her appointment was to improve the working conditions of the nurses. She reduced their hours from 10 and a half daily, seven days a week, and requested an increase of 13 nurses. The extra staff was granted over the next two years, bringing the total to 127, and allowing her to give the night nurses one night off a month.

The hospital's training school for nurses had been started in 1884 and had an established reputation, receiving over 600 applications a year for 15 vacancies. Candidates had to be between 21 and 35, well educated and produce a certificate of health. The probationers' contract was for four years' service, consisting of three years training

*Fig 17. The General Hospital, Birmingham, 1900*

and one year as a staff nurse. Probationers paying a fee of £21 were accepted for three years training. First year lectures were given by the matron on nursing theory, and classes in nursing practice were given by four of the Ward Sisters, which included making poultices, preparing leeches, and administering hot air and vapour baths. In the second year lectures on anatomy, physiology and bacteriology were given by members of the medical staff, lectures on obstetric and gynaecological nursing, given by the Assistant Obstetric Officer, and, from 1914, lectures on the nursing of ear, throat and eye cases by members of the medical staff. In the third year, lectures on medical and surgical nursing were given by an Assistant Physician and an Assistant Surgeon.

Miss Musson made minor alterations to the training school rules, including allowing the nurses to receive their certificates when they had successfully passed their final examination, instead of when they had completed their four years' service. She introduced the practice of staff nurses wearing a dark blue belt to distinguish them from the staff probationers. In 1914, she started tutorial classes for the third year nurses, which were taken by the Home Sister after each lecture to ensure that the lectures had been understood.

Between 1909 and 1914 the number of patients being treated in the hospital increased from 5,511 to 5,908. A new ward of ten beds was opened in 1913 to ease the pressure and the nursing staff was

*Fig 18. Ellen Musson, Matron of the General Hospital, Birmingham, with her staff.*

increased by four. In the same year, she requested an increase in the salaries of all the nursing staff which was granted, her own salary being increased from £150 to £170 per annum. In September 1913, she went under doctor's orders to Buxton spa for a rest, taking over three months' leave of absence.

## The First World War

Ellen Musson joined the Territorial Force Nursing Service (TFNS) when it was established in 1908. The TFNS was the nursing wing of the Territorial Army, it consisted of civilian nurses who would provide a reserve of trained nurses for the army, in the event of war. Under the organisation of the TFNS, the country was divided into six regions. Birmingham was in the Southern Region and Miss Musson was appointed one of the two matrons attached to the First Southern General Hospital. There were five General Hospitals in the Southern Region, based at Birmingham, Bristol, Oxford, Exeter and Portsmouth. Each required a nursing staff of 121 and Miss Musson, like other matrons in the service, encouraged her nurses to join.

In 1913, she had a week's training at a military hospital, which was considered necessary to familiarise civilian matrons with the routine of a military hospital. Later that year she was appointed the Principal Matron of the First Southern General Hospital, giving her responsibility for all the domestic and nursing administration of the hospital in the event of war. This hospital, like the other Territorial Force hospitals, had 520 beds at the beginning of the war but within months was increased to 3000 beds and finished the war with over 6000 beds, spread over several buildings. Once the war began, the amount of work involved in running a hospital of this size necessitated the appointment of a deputy matron to take over Miss Musson's work at the Birmingham General. The War Office paid for the replacement and as a further mark of their appreciation she was awarded a Royal Red Cross, First Class, at the beginning of 1916.

The General Hospital, Birmingham, was also taking in wounded soldiers. Like other civilian hospitals, it had allocated a certain number of beds for military and naval use and, as early as October 1914, had received its first wounded soldiers, in this case Belgian. By the end of the year it had 100 beds assigned to military use and later in the war the figure rose to 125. Members of the medical staff and 75 of the nursing staff of the hospital served in naval and military hospitals, at home and abroad. Their absence meant that the hospital was reduced to a minimum and admissions were confined to emergency cases.

At the end of 1918, the nurses in the army were demobilised and began returning to their civilian posts. A serious shortage of probationers was experienced by all hospitals in the aftermath of the war and the nursing staff of the Birmingham General remained 20 below the established number throughout 1919. Miss Musson considered the situation critical and reported to the Hospital House Committee

> Every hospital is suffering in the same way. The position is a serious one and requires careful consideration. There is no doubt that unless conditions are improved, it will soon be found impossible to carry on the work of the hospital. What is required is better remuneration for the trained nurses, shorter hours for all ranks, longer holidays, and better teaching for nurses in training.
>
> House Committee Minutes, 2/5/1919

Miss Musson's warning did not go unheeded. The Lord Mayor of Birmingham, who was one of the governors of the General Hospital, called a conference, in June 1919, of representatives of the hospitals and public health authorities in the city, to discuss the pay and conditions of nurses. The members of the conference agreed to act together regarding any increase in wages or shortening of hours, and appointed a committee to consider the question. The committee did not make any report until 1921, when it recommended that nurses' hours should be reduced to 56 a week and that the salaries of trained nurses should be improved to make the profession more attractive. It considered that the salaries of nurses in training were adequate.

In the meantime, the General Hospital lowered the entry age for probationers from 21 to 20, and increased the salaries of all the nursing staff. Miss Musson's salary had been increased to £200 in 1918 and was now raised to £350 (October 1919). The Assistant Matron's salary rose from £120 to £150 per annum, Departmental Sisters' salaries from £70 to £90 for the sister of the X-Ray Department, from £85 to £100 for the Home Sister, and from £70 to £85 for Ward Sisters. Probationers received £18 in their first year, £22 in their second year and in their third year when they became staff nurses, £28. In the fourth year they were paid £40, and in their fifth year £50.

The number of patients being treated in the hospital annually had exceeded the pre-war figures by 1919, and in 1920 was 6,930. The number of out-patients in the same year was 42,376, a figure well below the pre-war figure. It was not until 1920 that all departments of the hospital reopened for the first time since the beginning of the war, including a new Venereal Disease Department which opened in 1917. The shortage of nurses created a problem by increasing the work load of an already reduced staff. Miss Musson was given permission to close a ward when illness among the staff necessitated such action. The hospital was mainly dealing with acute cases, convalescent patients were transferred to other institutions as soon as practicable. The surgical wards alternated, week by week, to receive accident cases and spread the workload. During busy periods, emergency beds had to be arranged quickly to meet the demand and the four theatres worked to capacity.

By 1922, Miss Musson and the medical staff were reporting problems with the building and the equipment. It was 25 years since the hospital had been built and the number of beds had risen from 346 to 372. Advances in medical and surgical knowledge made it difficult to provide adequate treatment for patients and training for students. Like most voluntary hospitals, the Birmingham General was short of funds and a deficit of £13,885 in 1921 caused the closure of 50 beds. The nursing staff helped to raise funds by holding a series of 'Entertainment Teas'. The first was attended by Princess Beatrice who visited the wards and took tea with Miss Musson, while the nurses provided a musical programme in one of the closed down wards.

In December 1922, Miss Musson gave notice of her intention to retire. Her resignation was accepted with regret by the Board of Governors. They passed a resolution recording their appreciation of her work for the hospital and the prestige she had earned for the nursing school 'by her exceptional abilities and wide knowledge of administrative and nursing questions'.

The reputation of the training school had grown under Miss Musson's matronship. The syllabus of training had been developed over the years to keep abreast of advances in medical and nursing practice and in 1920, a sister tutor was appointed to oversee the class work of the probationers. The new General Nursing Council syllabus was adopted in 1922 and in speaking about it, Miss Musson said that the subjects did not present any difficulty, the problem was finding time to study each subject sufficiently. Apart from lowering the minimum entry age to 19 in 1922, the other conditions of admission to the school remained the same as they had been in 1909 when Miss Musson arrived. She had developed post-certificate training for nurses in radiography and the treatment of venereal diseases, and an important school of massage was run in association with the Royal Orthopaedic Hospital.

Although she had improved the nurses' working conditions and salaries, Miss Musson was far from satisfied with the position in 1923. The nurses' average week was still in excess of 56 hours. In her final report to the governors, she pointed out that the shortage of suitable applicants for training was still a matter of concern

> The need for shorter hours and better conditions in the profession generally is a very urgent one if the right type of probationer is to be attracted and without a good type of nurse, it is impossible to maintain a high state of efficiency in the hospital.
>
> House Committee Minutes, January 1923

Ellen Musson retired in February 1923, at the age of 55. Her active nursing career had spanned 28 years, half of which had been at the Birmingham General Hospital. She was to spend another 21 years working to improve the status of nursing through her involvement with the College of Nursing and the General Nursing Council. As if to complete one phase of her life, while continuing another, she saw one of her longtime dreams come true when a nurses' club was established in Birmingham in 1923. With the help of the local branch of the College of Nursing and Mrs Cadbury, the Lady Mayoress of the City in 1920, she had raised £22,000 towards the club. It was situated at 166 Hagley Road, Edgbaston; a lovely, old house which provided 15 bedrooms, a dining room, sitting rooms, a committee room, a lecture hall, a well-stocked conservatory and extensive gardens. Membership, which was limited to 1000, was open to all trained nurses and probationers, members of the College or not, and to professional women and students.

## Professional Development

Miss Musson had taken an interest in the development of the profession of nursing since her training and was strongly influenced by Isla Stewart, the matron of St Bartolomew's, with whom she trained and worked for over eleven years. Miss Stewart was primarily an educationalist, believing in the need for a higher standard of education and training for nurses, but she was also committed to the professional status of nursing through state registration. When Miss Stewart died in 1910, Miss Musson wrote an appreciation in the nurses' League News in which she described Miss Stewart's influence in nursing as more far-reaching than that of any other woman, except Florence Nightingale, during the first half century of modern nursing.

Miss Musson shared Miss Stewart's opinions on the importance of the education of nurses and the need for nurses to have professional independence. She was a member of the executive committee of the League of St Bartholomew's Nurses, the first nurses' league in Britain founded by Miss Stewart, and continued to support the league after she left St Bartholomew's. She appreciated the value of nurses' leagues in providing nurses with a basic professional association for their mutual benefit. Later, when she was appointed matron of the General Hospital, Birmingham, she became the president of that hospital's league and honorary editor of its journal.

She was a member of the Matrons' Council, the professional association for matrons founded by Isla Stewart, which met quarterly to discuss nursing theory and practice. At the winter meeting in 1910, Miss Musson read a paper on 'Hospital Kitchens', based on her experience of the good design of the kitchens at the General Hospital, Birmingham. She referred to the fact that few matrons were without difficulties in the kitchen department, difficulties usually connected with the construction of the kitchen, the cook, or the committee. She regarded hospital catering as an important part of a matron's responsibilities and was particularly concerned about the monotony of hospital food, pointing out that it was the nursing staff that suffered where this was a problem, as few patients stayed in hospital more than three weeks and, for some inexplicable reason, the medical staff were always provided with a higher scale of food than the nursing staff. She attributed the monotony to economy in kitchen salaries which made it impossible to attract a 'high-class cook', and due to the limited number of staff, a regular routine was the only way to cope with the amount of work.

> . . . it is very false economy to supply food which is not appetising, and although there are still some people who seem to think that coarse, rough food is the proper thing for a nurse, and all the more ennobling if carelessly served, this is not usually the view of hospital managers, who rely on the Matron to warn them if the narrow line which divides economy from stinginess is in danger of being crossed.
>
> *British Journal of Nursing*, 5 February 1910, p. 109

Later that year, she spoke at a conference organised by the National Food Reform Association, on 'The Feeding of Nurses in Hospitals', developing her ideas on the important role of diet in maintaining health. As long as nurses were required to carry out heavy physical tasks and work long hours they would suffer from fatigue and this, combined with a poor diet, would undermine their health. She returned to this topic at the Annual Nursing and Midwifery Conference in London, in 1913, where she spoke on 'Hospital Catering'. She proposed the establishment of a course in hospital catering, a theoretical training with instruction in the chemistry and economy of foods, which might be given in a technical school. She believed that a general improvement in nurses' diet would not be achieved until the old idea that rough food was part of the self-abnegation of a nurses' life had been displaced.

In June 1913, Miss Musson read a paper at the nursing conference in Dublin, organised by the National Council of Trained Nurses of Great Britain and Ireland. Her subject was 'Post-graduate Training for Trained Nurses' and she drew attention to the need for nurses working alone, such as district nurses, nurses in private practice and nurses working in small hospitals, to keep up to date with advances in medical and surgical knowledge. She suggested that a six week course, every six to eight years, would keep these nurses in touch, and could be given in teaching hospitals where the most modern methods were accessible and where the medical staff were teachers. She realised that the biggest problem would be finance, combined with the limited means of nurses, the difficulty they would have in taking time off to do the course, and the indifference of the majority of nurses. These drawbacks made it far from certain that sufficient nurses would be forthcoming to provide adequate funds for a worthwhile course. She concluded that nurses' education, like that of any other profession, needed adequate funding and endowments and until this was realised there would be little improvement in the provision of postgraduate training for nurses.

## State Registration

Miss Musson was a member of the various societies working for state registration of nurses and took an active part in the campaign. In the summer of 1910, she organised a meeting of the Matron's Council at the General Hospital, Birmingham, and took the opportunity to invite the matrons of the hospitals in the surrounding area to an open meeting to discuss state registration. Mrs Bedford Fenwick attended the meeting and spoke of the many advantages which state registration would bring, not least the guarantee that all nurses would receive an adequate training. She believed that not until there was a statutory, minimum standard of training would all hospitals provide adequate training for their probationers.

When the war started, Miss Musson's work as a Principal Matron in the TFNS brought her into contact with hundreds of nurses. She was shocked by the low standard of many of the so-called trained nurses. At the annual meeting of the Society for the State Registration of Trained Nurses, in June 1915, the members were all agreed that the war had demonstrated the absolute necessity of state registration and Miss Musson, a Vice President and member of the executive committee, proposed the resolution, 'That as State Registration of trained nurses is a non-party question, of national importance to our sick and wounded sailors and soldiers, the present moment is opportune for a non-party government to deal with it'. She pointed out that had such a system been in force before the war, a record of nurses' qualifications would have been available and an enormous amount of time saved. As it was the matrons of training schools were almost worn out answering inquiries about nurses' qualifications. If nurses lacked ability it was more the fault of their training than of themselves and she looked forward to state registration as a means of improving the profession. The resolution was carried.

## The College of Nursing

At the beginning of 1916, the supporters of the campaign for state registration were shocked by the move to establish a College of

Nursing. They were suspicious of the motives of the promoters of the College scheme who had previously opposed state registration. The National Council of Trained Nurses organised a meeting in London, in February, to discuss the scheme and all the speakers were against it, including Mrs Fenwick and Miss Musson. The latter moved a resolution reaffirming the priority of state registration and urging the government to take action. She said that the one point on which they agreed with the promoters of the College was in their reference to 'the present unsatisfactory condition of affairs'. They all realised that at the end of the war the situation would be even more unsatisfactory when the question of the VAD workers would have to be faced. These women would have four years' nursing experience in a war hospital but would be less trained than an ordinary pro-bationer of one year's experience.

The main objection to the proposed College of Nursing was that it would divert attention away from state registration, which was the priority for the profession. Miss Musson said that she could not understand why the promoters of the College had not consulted the representative nurses' societies which existed. Disorganised as the profession was, they did have a number of associations who were in a position to give advice. Also, she objected to the proposed composition of the College Council, which seemed to represent only London hospitals. Miss Musson's resolution was passed unani-mously and it was agreed to forward it to the representatives of the organisations supporting the College, and to every Member of Parliament.

During February and March 1916, three meetings were held between the promoters of the College and the representatives of the nurses' societies, in an attempt to reconcile their differences. At the second meeting, Miss Musson said they could not support the proposed College of Nursing unless the promoters made state regis-tration the first priority, and she objected to the presence of hospital governors on the first Council of the College, because this Council would be responsible for drawing up the constitution of the College. She joined Mrs Fenwick in calling for a conference to discuss a joint Bill for state registration, with the support of matrons who had formerly opposed state registration, particularly the matrons of Guy's and St Thomas' Hospitals, the government would be more likely to grant time in the House of Commons for an agreed Bill.

At the third meeting, Arthur Stanley, Chairman of the British Red Cross Society and the main spokesman for the College, said that the College was for nurses and would be governed by nurses. He was impressed by the level of support for state registration among nurses and pledged that the College would proceed with a Bill as soon as possible. As the meeting progressed, fundamental principles were agreed between the two sides and some of the representatives of nurses' societies began to accept that the psychological moment had arrived for the campaign to enter a new phase.

Ellen Musson was torn between loyalty to her colleagues in the state registration campaign, with whom she had worked for so long, and the desire to join this new and possibly powerful body, to gain its support for registration, and to prevent further fragmentation within the profession. Miss Cox-Davies, matron of the Royal Free Hospital, London, was in the same predicament. She had been active in the various societies campaigning for state registration but, like Miss Musson, she felt that the College offered a promise of unity within the profession. She telephoned Miss Musson in Birmingham and asked her to meet the express train from London. They discussed their problem walking up and down the platform at Birmingham New Street, until the next express to London drew in and Miss Cox-Davies returned to London. Between them they had decided to accept the offer of seats on the first Council of the College of Nursing. They would work within the College to bring others to their way of thinking, and if they could not, they would resign.

In March 1916, Miss Musson informed the governors of the Birmingham General, that she had been offered a seat on the Council of the College of Nursing and they approved her acceptance. As a member of the first council, she was appointed to the Examination Committee and the Registration Committee. The Registration Committee was to confer with the representatives of the various nurses' societies on the subject of state registration and, if possible, to draw up a joint Bill. Miss Musson believed that a joint Bill, supported by the College and the Central Committee, which represented the various nurses' societies in favour of state registration, was possible. For two years she worked to achieve this, attending meetings, negotiating, and speaking at conferences.

That summer, 1916, at a conference organised by the National Union of Trained Nurses and where the audience was mainly opposed to the College of Nursing, Miss Musson gave a paper on 'The Political Position in the Nursing World'. She spoke of the reasons which influenced her to support the College and hence to join the former opponents of state registration. Before the war, the strongest opposition to state registration had come from the matrons of the large London training schools, but the conditions arising out of the war had caused these same matrons to realise that registration was necessary. Through the initiative of the promoters of the College of Nursing, they were now prepared to support an organisation which advocated state registration and with this unity, she believed, they could reach an agreed Bill which would be given time in the House of Commons as a war measure.

Negotiations between the two parties progressed slowly and by 1918 Miss Musson realised, that although the differences between them were negligible, the fundamental trust necessary for agreement was absent. The older nurses' societies, which had been founded by Mrs Fenwick and which were still under her influence, would never trust the College. In the autumn of 1918, the Central Committee revised and relaunched its Bill, and in December the College went ahead with a separate Bill for registration.

At an open meeting to promote the College's Bill, in January 1919, Miss Musson was one of the main speakers. She addressed the audience of 500 as a fellow nurse

> You know that the State Registration of trained nurses has been for many years a subject of the greatest interest to me. I consider it of such vital importance, not only to the nursing profession but also to the general public, that I would do anything I possibly could to get this put into a Bill. My chief reason for joining the College of Nursing, Ltd., was that it appeared to me likely to hasten this reform. After many years of somewhat disheartening work the Bill brought forward by the Central Committee seemed no nearer becoming an Act . . .
>
> I do not intend to say one word against the societies supporting the Central Committee's Bill. I have belonged to three of them. Though, to my sincere regret, I am at present at variance with them, it must be conceded that all the attempts at organising the nursing profession before 1915 were made by those societies, and to them belongs the honour of having broken up the rough ground.
>
> *The Hospital*, 1 February 1919, p. 383–393

Miss Musson addressed the public challenge which had been made by Mrs Fenwick, that the societies were more representative of nurses than the College of Nursing. The societies referred to were, the Royal British Nurses' Association, the Matrons' Council of Great Britain and Ireland, the Society for State Registration of Nurses, the National Union of Trained Nurses, the Irish Nurses' Association, the Scottish Nurses' Association, and the Fever Nurses' Association. She pointed out that only the first of these societies elected its governing body by ballot and, after 32 years, it had a total membership of approximately 4000. All the other societies elected their executive by a show of hands at a general meeting. She considered the College, which now had a membership of nearly 12,000 and a Council elected by postal ballot, was the most representative and the most democratic body of nurses with which she had been connected.

Miss Musson considered the claim, made in a leaflet published by the Central Committee, that the College Bill was an Employers' Bill while the Central Committee's Bill was a Workers' Bill. It was alleged that the College proposed to give control of the General Nursing Council to the governors of hospitals, poor law guardians and matrons. She explained why she considered the system proposed by the College Bill would elect a Council that was more representative of general-trained nurses than the system proposed by the Central Committee's Bill. Miss Musson appealed to nurses to wake up, to think for themselves, and to exercise their vote on all matters concerning their profession. She stressed the need for unity in the profession and the relatively minor differences between the two Bills.

In April 1919, Miss Musson, her friend Miss Cox-Davies, Matron of the Royal Free Hospital, London, and Miss Lloyd Still, Matron of St Thomas' Hospital, proposed the formation of a 'really representative association of hospital matrons'. They wrote to the matrons of 50 of the leading hospitals in London and the provinces asking for their support and the response led to the formation of a provisional committee of which Miss Musson was a member. On 8 May a meeting was held at St Thomas' and the 89 matrons present agreed to form the Association of Hospital Matrons.

The stated objects of the Association were to maintain the honour and further the interests of the nursing profession, with particular reference to legislative proposals which affected the interests of the profession. The real cause behind the formation of the Association was the progress of the Central Committee's Bill for state registration in the House of Commons. This Bill allocated a specific number of seats on the proposed General Nursing Council to representatives of the Matrons' Council, the organisation founded by Isla Stewart in 1894.

The provisional committee of the new Association drafted a petition which was distributed throughout the provinces for the signatures of matrons and was then sent to all Members of Parliament. It stated

> In the interests of our profession and for the safe-guarding of the public, we desire to have adequate representation on the General Nursing Council to be set up under the Bill for State Registration of Nurses. Under the Bill at present before the House such representation is provided for by the Matrons' Council of Great Britain and Ireland – a body which is in no sense representative of the heads of the nursing profession as is proved

by the fact that none of the undersigned are in any way connected with it.

By July 1919, the Association of Hospital Matrons had a membership of 193 and applications were still being received daily. By this time the two private Bills for state registration were dead but the Government had promised the introduction of its own Bill. The Government Bill became the *Nurses' Registration Act* 1919, and introduced the state registration of nurses from 1922.

In the spring of 1919, as one of the nominated members of the first Council of the College, Miss Musson retired, and in the election which followed, she was elected as a representative of provincial hospitals. She was reelected at every election over the next 20 years. Between 1916 and 1923, she travelled up from Birmingham for the Council and committee meetings, then after her retirement from the General Hospital, she moved to Pevensey Bay, Sussex. At this point she took on even more committee work, and also represented the College on various outside committees, including the Ministry of Labour Demobilisation Committee and the Consultative Committee on Medical and Allied Services.

Like many of her nursing contemporaries, Miss Musson was aware of the need for public health nurses. In 1920, she was the College of Nursing delegate at the congress of the Royal Sanitary Institute and, later that year, when the College appointed a public health committee she was nominated a member. Two years later a Public Health Section was established within the College to deal with the growing number of members who worked in this field and their problems. Miss Musson was a member of the executive committee of the section and this committee played an important role in drawing-up the conditions of service and minimum salaries for public health nurses.

One of the questions which had to be decided was the type of training required for public health nursing. Miss Musson advocated that public health nurses should be general trained nurses with an additional qualification. The length of this additional training was much discussed, it was feared that too long a training would reduce the number of candidates, leaving the field open to the untrained. The Public Health Section of the College decided that a 12 months' course was the minimum that could adequately deal with the social and economic problems confronting the public health nurse. However, the College eventually supported a six months' course as the salaries paid to nurses made it impossible for them to afford a longer training and, in 1925, the Ministry of Health accepted that a nurse's general training was the most suitable basic training for health visitors.

In January 1924, the College, the Association of Hospital Matrons and the Poor Law Matrons' Association, held a dinner in honour of the first women Members of Parliament. Miss Musson proposed the toast to the guests

> The Nursing Associations represented here tonight include women of every class of society, every religious denomination, and of every political party, women who are united by a love of their common work and by a desire to build up the profession of nursing to a high state of proficiency.
>
> I can assure our guests that in anything they can do to promote better housing conditions, better supplies of pure milk and other foods, better facilities for healthy recreation and other measures of social reform, they can count on the backing of every trained nurse on the Parliamentary Register. We believe that there are no social reforms likely to come before parliament in which nurses are not interested, and few in which our knowledge might not be of service, for we need no imagination to picture the homes of the poor, we go into them and see with our own eyes, and in the wards and out-patients' departments of our hospitals, as well as in the crowded city slums, and in the insanitary country dwellings we learn only too well the conditions under which some people live.
>
> *Nursing Times*, 19 January 1924, p. 62

A large part of Miss Musson's work for the College in the 1920s was to improve the economic position of nurses. She had always been concerned about the low level of nurses' salaries and its effect on their health and the status of the profession. She was a member of the Salaries Committee of the College of Nursing from its foundation and this committee published a report in 1919 with the first recommended salary scales for nurses. The report was based on details of nurses' salaries and conditions throughout the country collected by the committee. The recommended scales remained higher than actual salary levels but had the effect of raising the minimum levels paid in the 1920s.

At the Annual Conference of the College in June 1920, one of the sessions was devoted to the problem of the shortage of probationers and Miss Musson, as one of the speakers, outlined some of the changes which she thought were necessary to make the profession more attractive to new recruits. Among these were, lowering the entry age, improving the conditions of training and work, and raising the level of pay. She also stated that the economic position of nurses would remain unsatisfactory until they had a national pension scheme. In 1923, the College began negotiations with King Edward's Hospital Fund for London about establishing a superannuation scheme for nurses working in hospitals. A committee was appointed to draft a scheme and Miss Musson, as Chairman of the College's Salaries Committee, and Miss Rundle, the Secretary, represented the College. The draft scheme was presented to the British Hospitals Association, which represented hospital governors and managers throughout the country, and after four years of slow negotiations, the Federated Superannuation Scheme for Nurses and Hospital Officers (FSSN) was inaugurated in 1928. The registered offices of the scheme were at the College headquarters and Miss Musson was one of the signatories of the Articles of Association. After the establishment of the FSSN, Miss Musson continued to serve on the executive committee and the council of the scheme.

## Chairman of the General Nursing Council

The first General Nursing Council for England and Wales (GNC), nominated by the Minister of Health in April 1920, went out of office at the end of 1922, and was succeeded by the first elected Council. The elected Council consisted of 16 members, representing general hospitals, poor law hospitals, public health nursing, private nurses, general nurses, male nurses, mental nurses, sick children's nurses and fever nurses, and nine members appointed by the Minister. Miss Musson was elected as one of the two representatives of provincial general hospitals, receiving the second highest number of votes of all the candidates. On her election she decided to resign from the matronship of the General Hospital, Birmingham, believing that she could not perform the duties of a matron and give her best to the Council.

When the new Council took office, Miss Musson was appointed to the Registration Committee, the Disciplinary and Penal Cases Committee and the Uniform Committee. In February 1924, she was elected Chairman of the Registration Committee, the most important committee of the Council at the time. In 1926 she was elected the Chairman of the Council, the first elected member of the Council to become the chairman – the two previous chairmen, Mr Priestley (1920–1921) and Sir Wilmot Herringham (1922–1925), had both been nominated members of the Council. The Council was elected every five years and Miss Musson was reelected in 1927, 1932 and 1937. She was also reelected Chairman on each occasion, maintaining the office for 18 years, until she stood down in 1943.

The work of the GNC in the inter-war years was never routine or easy. Although the first, nominated Council had dealt with the two most contentious issues facing the profession, the conditions for the registration of nurses and the rules for the election of the Council, there remained the syllabuses of training and of examinations to be drawn up, and the conditions for the approval of training schools. On each of these points the Council was in dispute with the Ministry of Health for many years. All the rules made by the Council were subject to the approval of the Minister of Health and both Houses of Parliament and these authorities were not reluctant to exercise their veto. This was demonstrated as early as 1923, when the rules drawn up by the Council for the registration of 'existing nurses' were significantly altered by the House of Commons. The amendment widened the definition of 'existing nurses' to include a level of experienced, but untrained, nurses that the majority of the profession considered unwise.

The incident illustrated the delicate balance which the Council had to maintain between the standards which the GNC wished to impose on the profession, and the extent to which the Minister and Parliament were prepared to allow the profession to introduce restrictive practices. On the standard of education required for entry to the profession and on the standard of training itself, the Council was again at odds with the Ministry. It drafted a syllabus of training, in 1922, which it intended to be compulsory for all training schools. However, the Minister insisted that the syllabus should be advisory, and that its adoption should not be made a condition for the approval of training schools. If the syllabus was compulsory it would have to be limited to such requirements as the Ministry considered practical to impose on training schools at the time. The syllabus was based on the one in use at the Nightingale Training School, at St Thomas' Hospital, and the Ministry considered that it demanded too high a standard of general education from probationers and was impractical for poor law nurse training schools.

The following year the Council submitted an examination syllabus to the Minister. It listed subjects on which candidates might be examined and, like the training syllabus, divided the training into first year work, which would be followed by the Preliminary Examination, and second and third year work, followed by the Final Examination. The Minister approved the examination syllabus and the first compulsory examinations were held in 1924.

By 1926 the Council had drafted a scheme for the inspection of training schools but once again ran into opposition from the Ministry. The staff of the Ministry of Health were already responsible for the inspection of Poor Law Institutions and were not prepared to hand over this duty to the GNC. No progress was made on the subject for several years and in the meantime, members of the Council who had the time started to inspect the training schools themselves, among them Miss Musson. In 1931, Miss Musson asked the Minister for another meeting to discuss the issue and pointed out that the scheme could not start until the Ministry sanctioned the appointment of inspectors and their expenses. She and the other members of the Council who were not in active work visited about four or five schools a month but they could not continue to do this indefinitely. In 1936, after waiting ten years for a decision from the Minister, the Council decided to finance a limited scheme out of its own investments. It was some years later before the Council and the Ministry agreed to cooperate over the inspection of, what was then, Public Assistance Hospitals.

In the 1930s the GNC became involved in the growing debate over the shortage of candidates coming into the profession. Miss Musson had been aware of the problem since the end of the war when she had, on more than one occasion, advised the governors of the General Hospital, Birmingham, to increase the nurses' salaries. She had also expressed her views on the subject at the Annual Conference of the College in 1920 and in 1927. This latter conference was held in Birmingham, and Miss Musson presided at the session at which the Minister of Health, Neville Chamberlain, was the guest speaker. In introducing Mr Chamberlain, Miss Musson referred to his connections with Birmingham and her own acquaintance with him through their work in Birmingham. She welcomed his appointment as Minister of Health, as she considered that he was uniquely qualified for the job, and she hoped that he would establish a nursing department at the Ministry, as nurses considered this had now become a necessity.

Mr Chamberlain spoke on 'The place of education in the provision of a proper nursing service'. He considered one of the major factors contributing to the shortfall in probationers was the 'fatal gap' between the age at which a girl left school, at 17 or 18, and the age at which she was eligible to become a probationer, 20 or 21. He suggested that the College of Nursing might usefully consider how to utilise that time in such a way as would not interfere with the girl's subsequent career as a nurse. He thought that some local authorities might be persuaded to provide central preliminary training schools as part of their technical education. The 'fatal gap' was regarded by many within the profession as one of the causes of the declining numbers of probationers. The medical journal, *The Lancet* appointed a commission, in December 1930, to inquire into the reasons for the shortage of candidates entering the nursing profession, and it concluded that the 'gap' was one of the contributory factors. Miss Musson was involved in preparing the evidence submitted by the College of Nursing to the Lancet Commission, and she also gave oral evidence. Among the recommendations made by the College to make the profession more attractive, were higher salaries and better working conditions, and a relaxation of the petty rules and regulations which were imposed in most training schools.

The Lancet Commission recommended that the Preliminary Examination of the GNC, taken at the end of a probationer's first year of training, should be split into two parts and that the first part could be taken two years before entry to nurse training, in recognised centres such as secondary schools. The College of Nursing, the Headmistresses' Association and the National Council of Women were in favour of this split, but when the GNC discussed the issue in 1933, it voted against the proposal. Miss Musson was against it, she considered that a broad general education was preferable for entrants to the profession and she was not in favour of a nurse taking a part of her professional training, however elementary, before she entered her training school. 'Splitting the Prelim' became one of the issues in the next election of the GNC, in 1937, and the new Council voted in favour of the split. The new arrangement was passed and came into practice in 1939.

A second issue raised by the Lancet Commission's report, and which caused the profession much soul-searching in the 1930s, was the question of assistant nurses. These formed a major part of the nursing workforce, particularly in the institutions for the chronic sick. As far as the profession was concerned, these were untrained men and women and it resisted the use of the term 'assistant nurse', preferring to use the terms orderlies or auxiliaries. The Lancet Commission and the College of Nursing were in agreement that the standard of education required for entry to the profession could not be lowered without having a detrimental effect on the standard of nursing. However, by 1936 many in the profession felt that it would be preferable to recognise a 'second grade of nurse' rather than to continue ignoring the situation, which meant that much of the nursing care in the country was provided by unregistered nurses.

The College of Nursing held several meetings to consider the subject and, by 1937, had voted in favour of setting up a Roll of Assistant Nurses. The College wrote to the GNC on the subject and Miss Musson replied that the Council had no power to act in the matter. Under the terms of the *Nurses' Registration Act* 1919, the Council could not recognise general nurses with less than three years' training. Miss

Musson advised the College to consider the matter carefully before proceeding.

At the end of 1937 the Government appointed an Inter-departmental Committee on Nursing Services to look at the arrangements for the recruitment, training and registration of nurses. Miss Musson was one of the four nurse members of the committee, which consisted of 20 members, under the chairmanship of the Earl of Athlone. The work of the Committee was overtaken by the outbreak of the second world war but it did publish an interim report in December, 1938. Among the many reforms recommended in nurses' conditions of work and training, the committee recommended that the 'Assistant Nurse' should become a recognised grade. The legislation necessary to empower the General Nursing Council to set up a Roll of Assistant Nurses was passed in 1943.

In 1938, as the international situation became more serious, the Government appointed an Emergency Committee to coordinate nursing manpower for civil defence purposes. The committee was composed of 20 members, of which five were trained nurses, Miss Musson, as Chairman of the GNC, a representative of the College of Nursing, and the three Matrons-in-Chief of the army, navy and airforce nursing services. Miss Musson, who was 71 that year, appointed Miss Cox-Davies to deputise for her. The inadequate representation of nurses on the committee was immediately criticised by the College of Nursing and the nursing press, and indeed the committee proved to be inefficient and was replaced by an Advisory Nursing Board, at the beginning of 1940. The new Board consisted of 14 members, including representatives of all the main nursing organisations. The GNC appointed Miss D. M. Smith, the Vice-Chairman, as its representative.

During the war, the work of the General Nursing Council was carried on by Miss Musson, Miss Smith, the Vice-Chairman, and the chairmen of the standing committees. Miss Musson had intended to retire from the Council at the next election but, due to the war, the election was postponed and she agreed to stay on as Chairman. In January 1944, at the age of 76, she retired from the office of Chairman and served as Vice-Chairman until the end of the year.

## Treasurer of the International Council of Nurses

When Mrs Fenwick founded the International Council of Nurses in 1899, Miss Musson was a staff nurse at St Bartholomew's Hospital. She was involved in the movement from the start, through Isla

Stewart, but her work prevented her from attending the first two international congresses held in Buffalo, U.S.A. (1901), and in Berlin (1904). At the time of the third congress, held in London in 1909, she had just taken up her appointment as Matron of the General Hospital, Birmingham, and was able to attend. She welcomed the opportunity to meet the distinguished international delegates and particularly remembered Annie Goodrich, President of the American Nurses' Federation at the time, and Sister Agnes Karll, President of the German Nurses' Association.

Illness prevented Miss Musson from attending the next congress, in Cologne in 1912, and then the first world war and its aftermath intervened so that it was 13 years before the next international congress took place. This was held in Helsinki, in 1925, and Miss Musson was selected as the representative of the College of Nursing. She was not part of the official British delegation, as the College did not affiliate to the National Council of Nurses of Great Britain and Ireland until after the Helsinki congress, but the President of the Finnish Nurses' Association had invited the College of Nursing to send an 'observer'. Miss Musson remembered the Congress in Helsinki as a unique experience,

> I only had two days in which to get my tickets and make my preparations after which I had an unforgettable journey by sea to Gothenberg, thence by the Gotha Canal to Stockholm, and after a two nights' stay there, by sea to Abo in Finland . . . all berths on board had been sold! I spent the night in a deck chair from which I was able to appreciate the glow of the setting sun and the brilliance of the rising sun, which both in turn had the effect of turning the sea into mother of pearl. It was one of the most beautiful sights I ever remember. As our ship put into one of the islands at 3 a.m., the sun was already high in the sky and a band was playing in our honour . . .
>
> *International Nursing Review*, July 1959, p. 11

The hospitality of the Finnish nurses and authorities provided an ideal setting for the reunion of old friends after the war, and for the many delegates attending their first congress it was an inspiring occasion. At the final meeting of the Grand Council, Miss Musson was elected Honorary Treasurer of the ICN. She was very surprised to learn of her new appointment as she had never been asked and was not aware that she had been nominated. After the congress, the new Board of Directors met for discussions at Halila, near the Russian border. Miss Musson attended the Board meetings in her new role as treasurer, a post she was to hold until 1947.

The congress in Helsinki took several important decisions, one of which was to establish a permanent headquarters for the ICN in Geneva with a salaried staff, and a second, to introduce the payment of 'per capita' dues by the national associations. The congress also decided to address the problem of the widely varying standards of training for nurses in different countries and Miss Musson was asked to visit schools of nursing in several European countries to collect information. She was shocked by the conditions in many of the countries and impressed by the pioneer work being done by nurses in difficult circumstances. She spoke of this experience at the College of Nursing Annual Conference in 1927, at a session devoted to international cooperation. After describing the work of the ICN, she said that through this international organisation, nurses could influence the health and wellbeing of every country, by improving the training of nurses they were promoting better health in the world.

When Miss Musson presented her first report as Treasurer to the Board of Directors, in Geneva in 1927, she pointed out that the implementation of the decisions taken in Helsinki involved expenditure for which no allowance had been made. The Council was dependent on private donations to meet its expenses. She recommended that the finances be placed on a more secure basis by raising the 'per capita' dues, from five cents to eight cents. She successfully carried this resolution at the next meeting of the Grand Council, held at the international congress in Montreal, in 1929. By 1931, Miss Musson was able to report a credit balance for the first time and, throughout the rest of her term as Treasurer, the finances of the Council remained healthy. She was also responsible for the appointment of an accountant and the introduction of a new system of book-keeping.

In 1934, the Florence Nightingale International Foundation was inaugurated. This was the International Council of Nurses' Memorial to Florence Nightingale and was established to provide funds for postgraduate training for nurses. Miss Musson was a member of the provisional committee which drafted the constitution of the foundation and served on the Committee of Management until 1938.

There were two more congresses held before the outbreak of the second world war, the first in 1933, hosted jointly in Paris and Brussels, and the second in 1937, in London. At the congress in London, it was agreed to move the headquarters of the ICN from Geneva to London but in 1939, on the outbreak of war, they were transferred to the United States. During the war, the international activities of the Council were suspended and the membership dues were frozen in each country.

The first meeting of the Board of Directors after the war was held in London, at the Royal College of Nursing, in September 1946, at

which the President, Effie Taylor, outlined plans for the reorganisation of the ICN. Miss Musson told the meeting that she did not
wish to continue as Treasurer after the congress the following year,
in Atlantic City. At that congress, the largest in the history of the
ICN, she was granted honorary membership in recognition of her
services as Treasurer over 22 years. Dame Ellen attended her last
international congress in 1949, at the age of 81, when she travelled
to Stockholm for the 50th anniversary conference of the ICN.

The National Council of Nurses of Great Britain and Northern
Ireland reassembled, after six years suspension, in June 1945. The
president, Mrs Fenwick, indicated that she wished to resign, having
held the office since the foundation of the Council in 1908. Miss
Musson was elected as her successor and held the office for just 18
months, resigning in November 1946, as she considered that it was
time for the younger generation to take over. She, like Mrs Fenwick,
was elected an Honorary President of the Council. One of the last
roles she carried out for the profession was to represent the National
Council of Nurses on the Council of the British Empire Nurses War
Memorial Fund, established in 1946 to commemorate those nurses
who lost their lives in the war.

In 1953, the Royal College of Nursing opened an Education Department in Birmingham. This was a development of the work which
Miss Musson and the local College branch had undertaken, in 1922,
when they raised over £22,000 for the establishment of the nurses'
residential club in the city. The money had also been used to set up
a scholarship fund and a benevolent fund for nurses and, in 1950,
the trustees decided to use the fund for the wider benefit of the
community. This was made possible by the generosity of Mr and
Mrs Cadbury who presented the deeds of 162 Hagley Road, the
house adjoining the Garden Club, to the College. They also undertook to pay half the cost of the alterations and equipment of the
Birmingham Education Centre. It was decided that the Centre would
provide specialised courses, in all branches of nursing, for trained
nurses. The Centre relied on financial support from the Birmingham
Regional Hospital Board and the board of governors of the United
Birmingham Hospitals, teaching assistance from the university
departments, hospitals, public health departments and local industries and, initially, a supply of students from the area.

Miss Musson died on 7 November 1960, in Eastbourne, at the age
of 93. Her life had stretched from the days of Florence Nightingale's
nursing reforms to those of the National Health Service and her
contribution to the development of nursing in those years was
immeasurable. After 28 years as a nurse and matron, she spent

*Fig 19. Dame Ellen Musson, President of the National Council of Nurses of Great Britain, 1945*

another 24 years working to improve the conditions of nurses and the status of nursing. This work was channelled through her role in the three professional organisations, the Royal College of Nursing, the General Nursing Council and the International Council of Nurses. During her life she received many tributes for her work, including a CBE in 1928 and Dame Commander of the British Empire in 1939. In the same year, she was awarded the International Florence Nightingale Medal, a medal awarded by the International Red Cross

Society every two years for outstanding service to the nursing profession.

## Conclusion

The decisive influence in Miss Musson's career was her training at St Bartholomew's Hospital while Isla Stewart was matron. Her years at St Bartholomew's coincided with the formation of the first nurses' professional organisations, and Miss Musson found herself at the heart of the movement for professional independence. Starting as a member of the executive committee of the nurses' league at St Bartholomew's, she went on to become the first nurse chairman of the General Nursing Council.

Up to 1916, Miss Musson was an active member of the campaign for the state registration of nurses, led by Mrs Fenwick and, until her death in 1910, Miss Stewart. During these years, Miss Musson attended meetings and conferences, gave talks and recruited nurses for the cause. Then, in 1916, she chose to leave the 'official' party for state registration and to support the College of Nursing. This defection, as it appeared to her former colleagues, was an important turning point for Miss Musson and the profession. Her decision influenced many nurses and contributed to the success of the College of Nursing, which gave nurses in Britain a representative organisation for the first time.

Her work for the College of Nursing spanned 44 years, from 1916 when she was the sixth name on the membership roll, to 1950 when she was appointed a Vice-President. During those years, as a Council member she was able to achieve many reforms in the social and economic conditions of nurses, particularly the establishment of their first superannuation scheme. She also contributed to the development of the Education Department of the College, and was a regular lecturer on hospital administration and ethics.

Her role in the General Nursing Council was probably even more significant for the development of the profession than her work for the College of Nursing. As the first nurse chairman, she had a lot to prove about the readiness of nurses for professional self-government. She had an aptitude for legal matters which contributed to her success as chairman and was described by a contemporary as having a clear brain, worthy of a first class barrister. This was recognised by the conferment of an Honorary LL.D. by the University of Leeds, in 1932. She also possessed financial ability which she demonstrated during her years as treasurer of the ICN and in her work on the Salaries and Superannuation Committee of the College of Nursing.

Miss Musson's outstanding characteristic was her integrity, a quality which made her popular on committees. Despite the very real divisions within the profession, Miss Musson was accepted by all parties as a fair negotiator. This was illustrated by her election as the first nurse chairman of the General Nursing Council, and subsequent reelection over 18 years, and by her appointment as treasurer of the International Council of Nurses. In both these offices, Miss Musson represented a bridge between the College of Nursing and its opponents.

The year before she died, she was asked to contribute an article for the 60th jubilee of the International Council of Nurses. She wrote

> As I think back over my years with the ICN I am apt to forget the problems of finance and the discussions there have been over the raising of dues or the balancing of budgets; but memories of my dear friends – those courageous leaders in nursing – will always remain with me.
> *International Nursing Review*, July 1959, p. 13

## Sources

**St Bartholomew's Hospital Archives**
MO3/1/3 Register of Probationers 1894–1898.
MO53/1 Preliminary Training School Register 1877–1900.

**General Hospital, Birmingham, Archives**
House Committee Minutes 1906–1913.
*Annual Reports* 1909–1923.

**Royal College of Nursing Archives**
Association of Hospital Matrons, Minute Book.
*British Journal of Nursing* 1906–1939.
*Nursing Times* 1910–1958, 1960.
*International Nursing Review*, Jubilee Issue 1899–1959,
    ICN Vol 6. 3 (RCN/C78/13).

# Index